ONE ILLNESS AWAY

ONE ILLNESS AWAY

WHY PEOPLE BECOME POOR AND
HOW THEY ESCAPE POVERTY

ANIRUDH KRISHNA

OXFORD
UNIVERSITY PRESS

OXFORD

UNIVERSITY PRESS

Great Clarendon Street, Oxford ox2 6DP

Oxford University Press is a department of the University of Oxford.
It furthers the University's objective of excellence in research, scholarship,
and education by publishing worldwide in

Oxford New York

Auckland Cape Town Dar es Salaam Hong Kong Karachi
Kuala Lumpur Madrid Melbourne Mexico City Nairobi
New Delhi Shanghai Taipei Toronto

With offices in

Argentina Austria Brazil Chile Czech Republic France Greece
Guatemala Hungary Italy Japan Poland Portugal Singapore
South Korea Switzerland Thailand Turkey Ukraine Vietnam

Oxford is a registered trade mark of Oxford University Press
in the UK and in certain other countries

Published in the United States
by Oxford University Press Inc., New York

British Library Cataloguing in Publication Data
Data available

Library of Congress Cataloging in Publication Data
Data available

Typeset by SPI Publisher Services, Pondicherry, India
Printed in Great Britain
on acid-free paper by
Clays Ltd., St Ives Plc

ISBN 978–0–19–958451–2

1 3 5 7 9 10 8 6 4 2

To Vidya

CONTENTS

List of Figures   viii

List of Tables   ix

Preface   xi

1. Refilling the Pool of Poverty   I

2. Poverty Flows   26

3. The Rising–Falling Tide   48

4. Reasons for Descent: The Health Poverty Trap   69

5. Reasons for Escape: Diversification and Agriculture   96

6. Connecting Capability with Opportunity: Investing in
   Information   122

7. A Two-pronged Strategy: Protection and Opportunity   144

Appendix. Measuring Poverty: Testing *Stages-of-Progress*   164

Notes   178

References   195

Index   221

LIST OF FIGURES

1.1 The Simple View   10

1.2 Accounting for Simultaneity   15

1.3 Poverty Dynamics in Practice   21

5.1 Relationship Between Household Events and Change in Status   110

LIST OF TABLES

2.1 Stages of Progress (Western Kenya) — 38

2.2 Initial Stages of Progress (Before the Poverty Cut-Off) — 40

3.1 Escape and Descent — 54

3.2 Variations across Communities in the Same
Province and Region — 55

3.3 A Common Finding — 57

3.4 Escape and Descent over Two Time Periods in Uganda — 64

3.5 Percentage of Households Who Fell into Poverty in
Different Livelihood Zones of Kenya — 65

4.1 Principal Reasons for Descent into Poverty — 79

5.1 Principal Reasons for Escaping Poverty — 100

5.2 Variations Across Space and Time (an Example from Uganda) — 112

5.3 Kenya: Average Land Cultivated by Poor Households (in Acres) — 117

6.1 Software Engineers in Bangalore: Parents' Education Levels
(Percent of Respondents) — 128

6.2 Highest Positions Achieved in 20 Karnataka villages (1996–2006) — 132

6.3 Percentages Reporting Different Career Aspirations — 136

A1 *Stages-of-Progress* and Asset Ownership (36 Communities
in Uganda) — 170

A2 Stages (as Recalled) v. Assets Possessed Seven Years Ago
(61 Communities of Rajasthan, India) — 171

A3 Impoverishment and Reduced Land Holdings — 173

PREFACE

Few who define or investigate poverty have experienced it directly in their lives. They project onto poverty an image born in their imaginations, based on what they have seen and read, what they have heard and hypothesized. I am guilty similarly of viewing from the outside a world some of whose inner workings I describe in this book. I feel immensely grateful to my parents and to fate for my never having lived in poverty.

I am more grateful yet to the thousands of poor and near-poor people in different countries who spoke generously about their lives and about the changes that they have experienced. I could hardly have interviewed so many people without the help of many colleagues and research collaborators. I am thankful as well to these individuals, and am particularly in debt to many among them—including Patti Kristjanson, Kiranpal Singh, Milissa Markiewicz, Daniel Lumonya, Mahesh Kapila, Wilson Nindo, Mahendra Porwal, Judith Kuan, Nelson Mango, Sharad Pathak, Maren Radeny, Leslie Boney, and Virpal Singh—who helped in different ways to develop the methodology and the tools of analysis that we implemented together. The collective voice—'we'—that I so often use in this book shows that I could not have done this work without your partnership and advice.

In each of the different regions that we studied across five countries and four continents, a team of research assistants was recruited and trained. These young men and women, too numerous to name individually, hail from communities such as the ones that we studied together. I remember these people respectfully and with warm feelings, and I am still in touch with many among them, especially those who have access to email.

Nearly ten years have elapsed since I commenced the fact-finding exercises that resulted in the production of this book. Many things that seemed difficult to accomplish at that time now appear simple, even ordinary.

A crucial hump that needed to be crossed at the beginning required developing a reliable methodology, one that could be utilized to investigate poverty flows in multiple settings with the active involvement of the people involved. Tracking the flows of people into and out of poverty is beset with a number of methodological difficulties. Pinpointing the reasons responsible for these movements has proved to be especially difficult in the past. Because no pre-existing methodology could help accomplish these tasks satisfactorily, I had to invest a great amount of time and effort in developing a new set of methods. I relate for the first time in this book the process that resulted in developing, incrementally and not without initial mis-steps, this recall-based and community-centered methodology that is very helpful for investigating poverty flows.

Initiated nearly a decade ago, this new and unconventional methodology, named *Stages-of-Progress*, has found growing acceptance among scholars and practitioners. It has been adopted by academics, NGOs, and government agencies in diverse countries. Research organizations associated with the United Nations have adapted *Stages-of-Progress* for their research and policy evaluation exercises. A recent multi-country study undertaken by the World Bank employs a methodology that is heavily influenced by *Stages-of-Progress*. I am gratified that this influential organization elected to use so much of my previous work, helping mainstream a methodology that I initiated and reinforcing some important results.

The countries and regions that I selected to study followed from a combination of personal preference, the interests of colleagues, and the availability of research funds. I wanted to carry out this work across a cross-section of countries where poverty is widespread and longstanding. I elected to start in Rajasthan, a state of India where I have worked on many occasions in the past. One makes a number of mistakes while developing a new methodology, including some that can appear foolish in hindsight. I felt, rightly as it turned out, that people in Rajasthan would be more forgiving of my mistakes, not dismissing the entire effort on account of the early bumbling steps, and allowing me an opportunity to learn from my errors.

Once this initial study was completed, the bugs removed, and the results publicized, a follow-up study was undertaken over the next year in the adjoining Indian state of Gujarat. A number of safeguards and validation procedures were incorporated that helped triangulate the information collected and cross-check it against other data sources. Patti Kristjanson helpfully stepped in at this time with an offer of collaboration for a study in Kenya, which we undertook in 2003 with the help of an initial small grant from USAID. A third study in India was undertaken one year later in the southern state of Andhra Pradesh. Milissa Markiewicz and Daniel Lumonya helped to organize and obtain funding for the next round of study, undertaken in two regions of Uganda. Later, Patti Kristjanson came through once again, engaging with the Food and Agriculture Organization of the United Nations and their strong regional partnerships in Peru. My students at Duke University, getting together with Leslie Boney and Milissa Markiewicz, helped set up yet another study in this sequence. Undertaken in North Carolina, USA, this study helped compare and contrast the natures of poverty flows within high-income and low-income countries.

It was revealing and valuable to hear people speak in great detail about significant events in their lives. A necessarily small selection of these accounts is reproduced in this book. Some people's names have been changed to preserve anonymity. Others, heroes or heroines in their own chronicles of bravery and grit, are presented as exemplars of what hundreds of individuals are doing all the time, overcoming poverty and moving ahead in spite of the odds.

What I learned from studying this vast number of human experiences is summarized tersely in the following equation:

Poverty = Frequent downward tugs + Restricted upward mobility

Events beyond their individual control tend to push people downward on an everyday basis. People remain poor or they fall into poverty because they cannot individually cope with these negative occurrences. Positive influences also exist that can help individuals and households neutralize the downward tugs they experience, but these positive forces are often weak in comparison. Hardly anyone we met has risen all the way up from acute poverty to great prosperity. Upward movements, while plentiful in number, were mostly quite small in magnitude. Occasional rags-to-riches success stories give reason to believe that much more can (and should) be achieved—but simply liberalizing or otherwise 'fixing' the national economy is hardly enough for this purpose.

Micro-level interventions are necessary in addition to macro-level economic cures. Context-specific micro poverty traps must first be identified and then removed. Simultaneously, individuals' prospects for upward mobility have to be substantially improved. Behind the aggregate numbers, diverse individuals exist and struggle daily. They aspire for their sons and daughters to rise above their own lowly status, becoming doctors, lawyers, musicians, television personalities, government officials, sports stars, and so on. It is these aspirations and these struggles that we should be looking at more closely. Adding up the numbers below some externally mandated poverty line, such as dollar-a-day, is only partly useful. It tends to homogenize and fix in place what is essentially diverse and ever-changing.

After more than 25 years of working for and with poor people, first as a practitioner employed by the Indian government between 1982 and 1996, and later as scholar, researcher, and policy advocate, I have come to see poverty not as it is sometimes purported to be—an undifferentiated mass living beneath some theoretical or statistical line—but as it is in practice: A diverse group of individuals with different aspirations, varying capabilities, and separate needs, moving simultaneously in opposite directions. This book reports upon the decade-long journey of discovery that has led to these realizations.

I am deeply grateful to the organizations that provided financial support for various parts of this research enterprise. I especially admire those who placed faith at an early stage in a new, and as yet unproven, methodology of poverty research. Sources at Duke University supported the first research project in Rajasthan. Subsequent projects were supported by the Ford Foundation, USAID, the International Livestock Research Institute, the Food and Agriculture Organization of the United Nations, the Cross-Sectoral Research Program at Duke University supported by the Glaxo Smithkline Foundation, Makerere University, and MDC Inc. Duke University generously let me take time off from teaching duties in order to spend several weeks, often months at a time, living and working in different countries.

Several colleagues at Duke provided helpful advice, including Marc Bellemare, Pablo Beramendi, David Brady, Charles Clotfelter, Philip Cook, Ted Fiske, Christina Gibson-Davis, Kristin Goss, Ruth Grant, Jay Hamilton, Bruce Jentleson, Karen Kemp, Robert Keohane, Judith Kelley, Bruce Kuniholm, Helen Ladd, Francis Lethem, Stan Paskoff, Karen Remmer, Orin Starn, Alessandro Tarozzi, Jerry Van Sant, and Jacob Vigdor. Graduate and undergraduate research assistants, some of whom are also co-authors of journal articles, helped develop several important ideas. Especially notable are the contributions of Vijay Brihmadesam, Aurélie Brunie, Liz Clasen, Chad Hazlett, Amanda Glover, Adam Hosmer-Henner, Jesse Lecy, and Nicolas Perez.

Receiving the Olof Palme Visiting Professorship from the Swedish Research Council for academic year 2007–8 provided me with the undisturbed space of time required for writing the first draft of this book. As scholar-in-residence at the Department of Government in Uppsala University, Sweden, I received further helpful comments from faculties in the disciplines of development studies, economics, government, history, and sociology.

A manuscript workshop was held in Uppsala with the help of the Olof Palme fellowship and additional assistance from the Department of Government. Over three days, from May 8–10, 2008, a distinguished group of international scholars and practitioners discussed a complete first draft of this book. I am fortunate to have received detailed comments and criticism at this workshop from Arne Bigsten, Li Bennich-Bjorkman, Hans Blomkvist, David Hulme, Imran Matin, Ruth Meinzen-Dick, Öle Therkildsen, Tapio Salonen, Emil Uddhammar, and Sten Widmalm. Silje Dahl and Emma Karlsson did a splendid job of organizing this memorable event.

Several other individuals have provided helpful comments, advice, and encouragement over the years, including Donald Attwood, Subroto Bagchi, Chris Barrett, Bob Baulch, Harry Blair, Michael Carter, Robert Chambers, Stefan Dercon, Milton Esman, Alan Fowler, John Harriss, Sam Hickey, Aditi Iyer, Ravi Kanbur, Aradhna Krishna, Michael Lipton, Charles Lwanga-Ntale, James Manor, Patricia McManus, Mick Moore, Caroline Moser, Sushma Narain, Philip Oldenburg, Elinor Ostrom, Agnes Quisumbing, Indira Rajaraman, Nilakantha Rath, Sanjay Reddy, Bo Rothstein, David Rueda, Arunava Sen, Geeta Sen, Abusaleh Shariff, Yasmin Saikia, T. N. Srinivasan, M. S. Sriram, K. Sivaramakrishnan, Judith Tendler, Susan Wadley, Norman Uphoff, Martin Valdivia, and anonymous referees of several journal articles. I thank all of these individuals, while clearly accepting sole responsibility for all remaining errors and omissions. I also thank the anonymous referees of the book manuscript, originally submitted to Oxford University Press in November 2008.

Conversations with my parents, Indu and Anand Krishna, both practical and down-to-earth people, helped hone many among these ideas, toning down the most abstract ones and sharpening others that seemed more worthy of implementation. My daughter, Aditi, and several of her friends, all recent college graduates, provided an additional set of critical comments. Students in my seminar classes at Duke University and others at the University of North Carolina in Chapel Hill also weighed in with useful reactions and new ideas, for which I remain grateful. People, such as these, willing and eager to pitch in for making positive changes, are what the world needs in ever larger numbers.

Different parts of the research leading to this book were presented, starting in 2003, at conferences and workshops organized at the Chronic Poverty Research Center at the University of Manchester; Duke University; the University of Wisconsin, Madison; Syracuse University; Stanford University; the Johns Hopkins University's School of Advanced International Studies; the University of California, Berkeley; the World Bank; on National Public Radio; before government groups in India, Kenya, Uganda, and Peru; at the Expert Group on Development Issues organized by the Swedish International Development Agency in Stockholm; at the Brookings Institution in Washington, DC; at USAID; the Brooks World Poverty Institute; and as the inaugural Krishna Raj Memorial Lecture on Contemporary Issues in Health and Social Sciences, named after a venerable former editor of India's most influential social sciences journal, the *Economic and Political Weekly*.

During academic year 2007–8, while I was on sabbatical leave, living and writing in Uppsala, Sweden, I had the opportunity to present different parts of the book manuscript and related arguments at the International Conference on Taking Action for the World's Poor and Hungry People, organized in Beijing by the Chinese government and the International Food Policy Research Institute; at the International Conference on Information and Communication Technologies and Development (ICTD 2007), organized by Microsoft Research and the Indian government in Bangalore, India; and at workshops and seminars at Oxford University; University College, London; the Juan March Institute, Madrid; the Institute of Social Studies at the Hague; the Quality of Governance Institute, Gothenburg University, Sweden; the Danish Institute for International Studies, Copenhagen; and at the universities of Oslo, Lund, Växjö, and Uppsala. Subsequently, I have presented these arguments at Yale University; at the University of North Carolina in Chapel Hill and in Greensboro; at BRAC headquarters in Dhaka, Bangladesh; at an international conference on poverty and employment organized by the Government of India and UNDP; before senior officials of the governments of India, Kenya, Uganda, and Peru; at Indiana University; and at Cornell University. Questions and suggestions received on each of these occasions helped refine the formulations presented in this book.

My editors at Oxford University Press, first Sarah Caro then Georgia Pinteau, and their colleagues guided me ably through the production process. I owe each of them a debt of gratitude.

I dedicate this book to my wife, Vidya Krishna, a long-suffering companion, true friend, and severe critic, who endured, with few but strident complaints, my frequent and prolonged absences from home. During the years that it took to complete this work, our children, Aditi and Abhay, after completing high school and college, took up jobs. I hope they will find vocations as fulfilling as the one that drove me to this research enterprise.

Durham, North Carolina   Anirudh Krishna

CHAPTER 1

Refilling the Pool of Poverty

On September 9, 2007, the day I started writing this book, two articles appeared side by side on BBC Online's South Asia home page. The first article, headlined 'Indian growth tops expectations,' depicted an economy growing at 9 percent per annum, with steady increases in agricultural production and strong manu-facturing and services. 'Every sector is growing rapidly,' one analyst stated cheerfully. The prospects for Indians looked bright, or so it seemed until one came across the second headline on the same page: 'Cholera-hit Indians face hunger,' it announced bleakly. 'When the BBC team visited the affected districts we found people with no food surviving on leaves. They had seen no rice since last year. We were offered leaves to eat. Drinking water comes from waterfalls and drains.'

Contrasts like these between growing wealth and acute deprivation are hardly uncommon in the developing world. Glittering skyscrapers rise next to rickety shacks, expensive restaurants look out upon ragged street children, big-ticket tennis and golf tournaments are hosted in places where most people never get to hold a tennis racket or golf club.

What does the future hold for those left behind? Does one merely need to wait: Economic growth will overcome poverty? Or is something more active and purposeful required? Many inquiries into these issues start by looking at national examples and asking: Which countries have reduced poverty most successfully? What can be learned from studying these experiences? This book considers these issues instead from the viewpoints of individuals and households.

Over six years between 2001 and 2007, I worked with teams of investigators in different parts of four developing countries—India, Kenya, Uganda, and

Peru—and some parts of North Carolina, USA. We went into a total of nearly 400 diverse communities, rural and urban, large and small, and we retraced the pathways over time of more than 35,000 households. Many people have risen out of poverty in each region and community. We identified such people, and we heard their life stories. In each location, we also found many others who have fallen *into* poverty. They were not poor 10 or 15 years in the past, but by the time we met them they had become desperately poor.

Kadijja Nantoga is one such person. She was 45 years old when I met her, in 2004, in a village of central Uganda. Ten years previously, in 1994, Kadijja and her husband held full-time jobs in a coffee-processing plant. They owned the house in which they lived as well as a plot of land on which they planted cassava and beans. Their daughter and son attended a private school.

Kadijja's saga of misfortunes began in 1996. First, her husband died as a result of a road accident. Ten other people riding in the same *matatu* (minibus) were also killed or fatally wounded. Overnight, the family lost one of its primary earners. No monetary compensation was paid out. Kadijja had to spend a great deal of money for her husband's funeral ceremony. 'But we could still manage,' she told me, 'because I had my job, and we owned some land, some cows, and a few goats.'

Five years after her husband's death, however, Kadijja was laid off from work. Disease devastated the local coffee crop, and the processing factory was shut down. With her job gone, Kadijja lost her steady income. Worse, her expenses shot up at the same time. Her 10-year-old son was stricken by an illness that was never clearly diagnosed, even though she spent large amounts of money and consulted different healers and doctors. Kadijja sold her cows and goats and ultimately her land in order to pay for these medical treatments, but they did not help save her son's life. Two years after he had fallen ill, he died.

She lives with her daughter now in the house that she still owns. They have no productive assets and no steady income. Odd jobs come by occasionally. Kadijja is called upon to cook for weddings. When people from her village go away for a while, she tends their animals and crops. She does not earn very much from doing any of these things. Her daughter no longer goes to school. They get by precariously from one day to the next, working for wages whenever some opportunity arises but are often forced to look for handouts.

Kadijja has fallen into dire poverty. Indications are that she will continue to remain poor. While it is unfortunate and depressing, her case is hardly peculiar

REFILLING THE POOL OF POVERTY 3

or rare. In every community we met people like Kadijja. They have fallen into poverty, becoming the new poor.

Large numbers of descents into poverty have occurred in low-income countries; large numbers have also occurred in countries with higher incomes and faster rates of growth. Higher wealth in the United States has not reduced descents into poverty. In fact, 'the chance that families will see their income plummet has risen. The chance that they will experience long-term movements up the income ladder has not increased.'[1] Astonishingly high rates of economic growth in China 'have produced not only the new rich but also the new poor.'[2] In parallel with growth, China has witnessed an 'increase in the number of people who fell into poverty.'[3] In India, as well, the problem of poverty creation has worsened, as we will see presently.

Strangely, this side of the poverty equation—the creation of poverty—receives relatively little attention in policy discussions. The efforts of national governments, donor agencies, NGOs, and others are mainly directed toward moving people *out* of poverty. The problem of falling into poverty is hardly ever discussed.

It seems almost as if we have taken it for granted that all poor people are born poor—which they are not! A large proportion of currently poor people were not born to poverty; they have become poor within their lifetimes. In the 398 communities that we studied, as many as 3,784 households (11 percent of the total) were not poor in the past. Like Kadijja, they have suffered descents into poverty. Simultaneously, other households escaped poverty.

Two parallel and opposite trends have operated everywhere. Some individuals have moved upward and out of poverty; their neighbors have concurrently become poor. Communities, even quite small ones, have not moved up or moved down all together. Within every community, poverty escapes and descents have occurred in parallel.

Large-scale events and national conditions do not help explain these simultaneous and opposite individual experiences. Colonialism, international economic relations, bad macroeconomic policies, failed states, catastrophic events, and the like, have been variously put forward to account for differences in aggregate poverty among countries. Such country-level knowledge is important to acquire, but it does not help account for ground-level facts. Why do some households in one country or region or community move out of poverty, while other households in the *same* country, region, and community—operating under the same policies, social norms, and national economic and political conditions—fall into chronic poverty?

Other factors are at work, which need to be understood with the help of examinations conducted closer to the levels where poverty is actually experienced. The granularity of the analysis, the level at which poverty is studied, greatly influences what one can learn about its sources and solutions.

At root, poverty is nothing more than the sum of poor people in a country or region. It increases when people fall into poverty, and it declines when more people move out than have moved in. In order to provide more effective assistance we need to ask: *Why* have some (but not other) poor households succeeded in escaping poverty? What have they done individually or collectively, or what was done for them by outsiders, that distinguishes them from other, less successful, poor people? We also need to learn more about the reasons for descent: *Why* did another lot of households fall into poverty over the same period?

Few answers have been available for any of these questions. The reasons responsible for escape and descent in each particular context have not been clearly identified. Having studied poverty mostly at the country level, we are able to say more about the nature of policies that can help national economies grow, but we known relatively little about why neighboring households can have vastly different experiences. These gaps in knowledge need to be filled urgently. Factors associated with escape and with descent in each particular context need to be clearly identified. Only then can the available resources be put to better use.

This book provides one of the first large-scale examinations of making and un-making poverty and of policies and programs that can be more effective. It will take you on an illustrative journey, filled with facts, analyses, and the life stories of people who fell into abject poverty and others who managed to escape their seemingly predetermined fates. No single factor or set of factors helps explain these diverse trajectories. By comparing the experiences of hundreds of households in different regions, we were able to identify micro-level reasons for escape and descent.

We found that escape and descent are not symmetric in terms of reasons. One set of reasons is associated with escapes from poverty, while a different set of reasons is associated with descents. In each context studied, this basic asymmetry was obvious. The inflows and the outflows affecting the pool of poverty are separately responsive to different reasons. Further, reasons associated with escapes or descents vary considerably across and within countries. What helps to accelerate escapes or prevent descents in one state or region of a country can have little or no impact in other regions and states.

Understanding these facts results in changing fundamentally our conception of poverty and our ideas about what needs to be done. 'Lifting' people out of the pool of poverty will not be enough to reduce the level in this pool. Unless descents into poverty are simultaneously addressed, the pool of poverty will continue to grow. Two sets of poverty policies are required in parallel: one set of policies to help augment and accelerate escapes from poverty, and another set to help prevent descents. Both sets of poverty policies need to be sensitive to differences across contexts. Smaller streams of influence need to be identified and addressed. Considering the aggregate of reasons operating across an entire country (or worse, across a large group of countries) will not be helpful. Grand causes and large-scale events are not all that matter.

Reducing poverty more effectively in the future will require attending carefully to the minutiae of everyday lives. Context-specific poverty knowledge is necessary for developing more effective policy designs. Such context-specific knowledge about reasons for escape and descent is provided for the first time on a large scale in this book.

Preventing Future Poverty

Study teams composed of between 12 and 16 individuals were selected and trained separately in each of the eight regions that were studied. These teams were led by scholars or NGO officials, and they were staffed by young men and women whose homes are in these study areas. We retraced the poverty pathways of all 35,567 households who lived within the 398 communities examined, finding out who had moved out of poverty, who had fallen into poverty, and who else had remained poor or non-poor. For a sub-set of nearly 10,000 households, we also put together detailed event histories, drawing upon extensive interviews. I led or co-led these teams in five of eight regions studied, and I trained and worked for several weeks with the other three teams.

Different types of communities were selected for these studies, including smaller and remotely located rural communities, larger villages situated close to major highways, small and middle-sized towns, and also capital city neighborhoods. The modal community is a rural village or middle-income urban neighborhood in a developing country. In addition, there are some North Carolina communities.

We did not impose upon such a diverse collection of people any standardized definition of poverty. We let them define the material standards associated with being poor (or not) in their specific contexts. Our methodology, discussed in the next chapter, enabled measurement and comparison to be made accurately, reliably and reasonably quickly, while working with understandings of poverty that are theirs and not of our making.

I learned that the experts' definitions of poverty are hardly the only relevant ones. People in these communities have their own robust understandings of poverty that are *shared* across communities within the same region. These shared understandings and common metrics helped construct a scale of measurement that has appeal and relevance to people in a wider region. This new realization was an important and useful one, but even more basic changes in my worldview were to follow.

I learned that poverty is not composed of any static group of people. One-sixth of all humanity is poor at the present time, but it is not the same one-sixth from one year to the next. The inherited stock of poverty is being reduced constantly. At the same time, future poverty is being created. Thus, it is not just the existing poor about whom we—concerned citizens of the world, scholars, practitioners, and policy makers—should be making plans. Equally, and I believe even more, we should be worrying about those who will be poor in the future—if they are not assisted now.

A great deal can be done to halt, or at least, considerably slow down, the creation of future poverty. Relatively few people get plunged into poverty precipitously. Most descents are played out over extended periods of time. Chains of events, rather than any single calamitous event, are involved. Breaking this chain at any of its links can help reduce the incidence of poverty in the future. There are many opportunities for preventing or reversing descents before people become chronically poor.

An example will help illustrate how people fall into poverty incrementally, pushed along by successive everyday events. In Gujarat, an economically fast-growing part of India, I met Chandibai, a woman of about 50 years. Fifteen years previously, her husband, Gokalji, had owned a general-purpose shop in the village square. They also owned a house and some agricultural land, which they leased out for a share of the crop.

In 1989, Gokalji developed an illness that confined him to bed, sometimes at home but quite often in a hospital ward. Doctors and nurses, testing facilities and pharmacists, steadily exacted a heavy cost. Assets were sold. Debts were incurred. Nearly all of their agricultural land had to be mortgaged. Three years later, Gokalji died. Following his death, the shop in the village square was taken away by Gokalji's brothers. As is the custom in this region, the widow inherited only the house in which they had lived along with a small remaining piece of agricultural land.

Two years after her husband died, Chandibai arranged for her oldest daughter's wedding ceremony. In a manner befitting a middle-class bride, an elaborate ceremony was organized. More debt was incurred in order to pay for these expenses. By 2002, Chandibai's outstanding debt had mounted to 45,000 Indian rupees (or roughly US$1,000). In her village, one earns this amount by working for almost two years at the official minimum wage. Eight percent of the outstanding amount was added on as interest every month. Unless she repaid her loan rapidly, the amount she owed would double every year.

Faced with these circumstances, Chandibai cut her losses as best as she could. She sold the land that she had left, and she settled her debt. She still has the house—home sales are not easily transacted in Indian villages—but Chandibai is left with very little else of value. She labors on construction projects, on other people's fields, and in their homes, usually earning less than the official minimum wage. She has no credit remaining at the local grocery shop, so she eats poorly or not at all when there is no money. It was a sad sight to see: Two faded sepia photographs of Chandibai's and Gokalji's wedding ceremony, everyone smiling and clearly well fed, hanging above a broken-down string cot upon which the forlorn woman sat, with little hope that things would get any better.

Far from being a foregone conclusion, Chandibai's descent into chronic poverty could have been prevented. *If* cheaper and more effective health care had been available, *if* laws related to inheritance by women had been truly enforced, *if* credit had been available on easier terms, *if* dowries and ostentatious weddings were not the dominant norm—then the chain of events leading to chronic poverty could have been broken. Ten years have passed, but none of these 'ifs' has been resolved. Dozens of others fall into poverty on account of similar chains of events.

In Chandibai's community, avoiding poverty seems to be a matter of circumstance and luck. Only those who never suffer serious illness or lose a family wage-earner can expect to avoid the pull of poverty. Moreover, versions of her story were repeated in every region that we studied. Even quite well-to-do people have become persistently poor, driven down by chains of negative events against which safeguards can and should be put in place.

Why don't policy makers better attend to these widespread, persistent, and traumatic factors in poverty creation? In large part, this neglect has been due to a paucity of persuasive information. The main sources of poverty data, including government statistics offices and international agencies, have so far concentrated on measuring national stocks of poverty. Because poverty flows have not been separately investigated, especially within developing countries, information related to descents and escapes has been hard to come by.[4] This situation has changed considerably in recent years. A growing mass of studies, reviewed later, has helped close these knowledge gaps in some part. These studies have shown that descents into poverty are a common occurrence. Despite this accumulating evidence, however, policy priorities have not changed by very much.

In general, policy makers have been predisposed to assume that descents into poverty are temporary affairs, small dips from which people will generally recover within relatively short periods of time. Previous studies of poverty flows did not provide the additional evidence that could help dispel these misguided assumptions. While they calculated the numbers of people who fell into poverty, these studies did not go further to investigate the depth and the duration of descents. Were descents suffered only by those who lived marginally above the poverty line, or have people higher up also been exposed to the same kinds of risks? How many among those who fell into poverty were able to bounce back relatively quickly; how many others have become persistently poor? Answers to these critically important questions were not available in the past, so it was possible to underestimate the gravity of the problem of descents.

This book introduces some new evidence which helps establish that descents into poverty are neither transitory nor marginal events. We found that relatively few among those who fell into poverty in the past were able to bounce back in later years. Further, it was not only the near-poor who were vulnerable to a fall into poverty. Many households who were comfortably off in the past also fell into poverty and became persistently poor. Descents into poverty, resulting in long-term experiences of poverty, were common everywhere we went, in remote communities, located amid jungles and deserts, but also in bustling small towns and capital cities.

It is no longer possible to assume that descents into poverty are of marginal significance or quickly reversed. In order to stem the growth of future poverty, preventive measures must be put into place urgently.

Macro–Micro Links

Different ways of investigating poverty will be helpful for these purposes. The instruments and methods that were used in the past have helped serve a particular image of poverty. New instruments and new methods are required in order to understand how micro poverty traps can be better addressed.

In the past, instruments akin to telescopes have been used to investigate national stocks of poverty. Scanning large numbers of countries, analysts have drawn conclusions about the nature of policies that could help accelerate national economic growth rates. Such telescopic inquiries consistently revealed that as countries' economies grew their stocks of poverty tended to diminish. Reliance was placed, therefore, upon growth, a broad stream of influence, for moving people out of poverty.

The image of poverty that prevailed as a result of these views is represented graphically in Figure 1.1 below. For simplicity's sake, only two states of the world are shown: Below, there is a pool of poverty; above, there is a city on the hill. An elevator transports people upward, from the pool to the city. Travel in the opposite direction is not visualized or foreseen.

This image of poverty reduction is both incomplete and simplistic. It is incomplete because it does not pay heed to the possibility of movements *into* poverty. And it is simplistic because it ignores the fact that macro (aggregate or country-level) achievements, such as a nation's economic growth rate, are not always or immediately translated into micro (or individual-level) results.

A long chain of influences links from macro to micro. Influences originating at different levels—national, regional, and community—merge to produce what is experienced by particular households. National growth rates and national policies make very important impacts. Regional events can matter as well. Poverty can become smaller within some regions of a country while simultaneously increasing in other regions.[5] Within the same region, communities

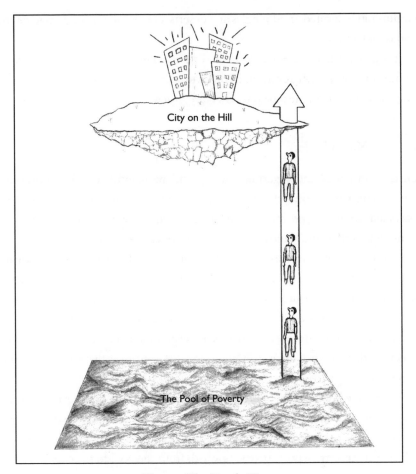

City on the Hill

The Pool of Poverty

Fig. 1.1   The Simple View.

can fare differently from each other.[6] Significant differences also can arise among households of the same community, as we will see below.

What happens on average in a country or region does not, therefore, reflect the reality that is experienced on the ground. As Martin Ravallion states, 'People are often hurting behind the averages. It will be of little consolation to those suffering to be told that poverty is falling on average.'[7]

Going beyond the averages requires beginning with facts and practices on the ground. Carefully tracing the macro–micro links is critically important for this purpose. 'The consequences of macro policies cannot be traced without a more accurate picture of how people respond and adapt to those policies.'[8]

Why does economic growth translate into a movement upward for one group of households and a movement downward for other, neighboring households? Taking a telescopic view—comparing macro-level trends across different countries—does not help to answer this question. Microscopic inquiries, tracing events on the ground, are required in order to ascertain who gains, who loses, and how.

The seed of this realization was planted in the summer of 2001 in a village of the state of Rajasthan, India. For 13 years, between 1982 and 1995, I had managed development programs in Rajasthan on behalf of the Indian government. I organized rural communities across the state for integrated watershed development; implemented programs of tree plantation in areas populated by poor indigenous people; managed many other rural development initiatives; and supervised the municipal administration in Rajasthan's capital city. Despite my rich and varied experience in this region, my conception of poverty reduction remained rooted in an image of uplift. It had not yet occurred to me that, in practice, efforts to lift up poor people are counteracted by a host of other influences. A variety of macro–micro links operate concurrently, not all of which are beneficial for the individuals concerned.

On this occasion, I was speaking with a group of young people, many of whom I have known for a number of years. Based on what I had read in books and articles, I presented the view that rapid economic growth in India would help remove poverty in the near future.

My village interlocutors were not visibly impressed. 'Show us the mechanisms,' they demanded. 'When will India's high rate of growth remove poverty from *this* village? There are many poor people here. How will *their* poverty be removed? Will they all get jobs? Will their agricultural fields begin to yield more? Will something else happen to make their earnings greater and their expenses fewer than before?'

I found it difficult to provide good answers for any of these questions. Relatively little is known about the micro–macro links, so one cannot say precisely how aggregate countrywide effects get transmitted to particular communities or individuals. The telescopic view has helped ascertain that, in general, aggregate poverty falls alongside economic growth. In the absence of complementary microscopic views, we cannot say how deep or how widespread these effects will be in any particular case.

In an effort to find out more about which households have actually benefited in the past and what nature of micro–macro links have helped in their cases, I started conducting some original inquiries. Together with my young village interlocutors, who have helped me undertake other research projects in the past, I went into 12 separate villages of Rajasthan, identifying the households who have escaped from poverty, and speaking with them about significant events in their lives.[9]

Investigating what has actually happened at the household level helped bring to light some important distinctions. Some households in each community had, in fact, escaped poverty, but other households had concurrently become poor. Macro or countrywide explanations could not help us come to grips with these facts. If national and regional effects were all that mattered—and if uplifting were all that occurred—then such instances should be rare. In fact, simultaneity was a regular feature. In every one of these 12 communities, one set of households moved out of poverty while other households experienced descents over the same period of time. Without viewing these experiences individually, at the micro level, one cannot begin to construct a plausible explanation.

Consider, for example, the following pair of experiences. Heera and Shantilal live across the road from one another in one of the 12 villages investigated initially in Rajasthan. Both were born at about the same time. Both went to school for seven years. Heera experienced a descent into poverty. Shantilal moved out of poverty. National and state policies were the same for both individuals, but the micro events they experienced were considerably different ones.

Twenty years ago, Heera and his family were among the more prosperous households within this village. 'We owned land,' Heera told me. 'We also owned many heads of cattle. But things changed for the worse, and today we are among the poorest people in our village, the recipients of community handouts on religious holidays.' Heera recounted the following sequence of events.

> My father fell ill about 18 years ago. We must have spent close to 25,000 rupees on his treatment, but to no avail. When my father died, we performed the customary death feast, spending another 10,000 rupees. We sold our cattle, and we also had to take out some loans. We worked harder in order to repay these debts. Then, about ten years ago, my wife fell seriously ill, and she has still not recovered. We borrowed more money to pay for her medical treatments. More than 20,000 rupees were spent for this purpose. It became hard to keep up with our debts. Somehow we could make do for another two or three years. Then the rains failed for three years in a row, and that was the end of the road for us. We sold our land. Now, my sons and I work as casual labor, earning whatever we can from one day to the next.

Heera narrated his story calmly and openly. Being poor is not something to be ashamed of in these communities; anyone can fall into poverty, and many do. Other households in this village also fell from comparative wealth to relative poverty within the space of a single generation. Concurrently, another group of households moved upward and out of poverty.

Shantilal's household is one among many who have escaped poverty. When he was a young boy, they faced very difficult circumstances. They possessed no land of their own. His mother and father worked on other people's farms and in their homes. They had no other sources of income. On days when no offer of paid work was made to the parents, the family survived by borrowing grains from the local merchant. A high rate of interest was levied from the borrowing family, which was also required to pledge a portion of its future earnings to the lender.

An older relative visited them one day and persuaded Shantilal's father to go with him to Ahmedabad, an industrial city, located about 250 kilometers away from their village. 'You are not doing very much around here that helps your family. Why don't you come with me and try your luck in the city?' This relative worked for a cotton textile mill, and he helped Shantilal's father find a position in the same processing unit. Unloading raw cotton from farmers' carts was seasonal work, grueling and poorly paid to boot, but it provided the family with additional income for four months of every year. Shantilal's parents used a part of this amount to pay for their children's education. They also bought a small herd of goats and built some additions to the family home.

In time, Shantilal also traveled to Ahmedabad in search of a job. Because he was lettered, more than his father and others, he was made responsible for overseeing their work and keeping the daily accounts. Shantilal also has a seasonal job. He is hired by the cotton mill for a few months following the harvest, and he spends the rest of his time in his village. This family has overcome poverty, but they have not yet become prosperous. There is still no refrigerator or television in their home, but there is no need any more to make do with less food. Shantilal's three children, two sons and a daughter, attend the village school. He has plans to pay for their college educations.

Referring to the rate of economic growth in India or in the state of Rajasthan does not help explain why Heera fell into poverty at the same time when Shantilal escaped poverty. Events closer to the ground better tell apart these experiences. One family started rising out of poverty when a visiting uncle helped provide the father with the connections necessary for landing a paying job. The other family concurrently fell into poverty, pushed along by frequent illnesses.

Ordinary Events

No momentous or large-scale events formed part of these households' event histories. Ordinary events, occurring routinely and unremarkably at the household level, resulted in producing different trajectories. Ordinary events have also made the critical difference in each of the other contexts examined.

The poverty traps that ensnare individuals and households are different from other kinds of poverty traps that affect entire countries. For instance, geography—countries' locations on the globe and the nature of terrain—has been advanced as an explanation for why some countries have more poverty than others. Similarly, climate, natural disasters, and mineral resources, particularly petroleum, have been put forward as reasons for widespread poverty in some countries.[10] Such monumental or large-scale factors can help explain differences in aggregate poverty among countries, but they shed little light on why some individuals were able to escape poverty while others in their neighborhoods remained or became poor.

Ordinary events, occurring below the radar screens of policy makers, are more productive by way of explanation. Ordinary events, such as frequent ill-health episodes, crop diseases, expensive marriage and funeral ceremonies, lack of affordable credit, and the like, were very frequently experienced by those who became impoverished. These types of ordinary events were not as often experienced by the households who stayed out or moved out of poverty.

Ordinary events take place regularly. Their effects build upon and reinforce one another. Monumental events—like earthquakes or palace coups—have bigger immediate effects when and where they occur, but ordinary events occur everywhere and all the time, eating away at people's livelihoods.

Investigations have revealed how ordinary micro-level events tend to have large cumulative impacts. For example, a study in Bangladesh found that 'household- and individual-level factors have been much more important in the explanations for upward and downward movements than other, village- and district-level, factors.'[11] A study undertaken in southern India showed similarly that, compared to regional or national events, household- and individual-level factors accounted for the larger part of the variance in people's incomes.[12]

Examinations conducted within other regions of the world have also concluded that micro-level and ordinary events have large cumulative impacts.[13] Over time, ordinary events tend to outweigh the effects of larger scale and momentous ones.

Compared to momentous events, such as bad rulers or catastrophes, ordinary events are also more easily controlled. That suggests it is within our means to mount more effective responses against descents into poverty.

In order to do so more effectively, our collective imaginations will need to be informed by a more true-to-life picture of poverty flows, such as the one depicted in Figure 1.2. An elevator takes people upward just as it did earlier in Figure 1.1,

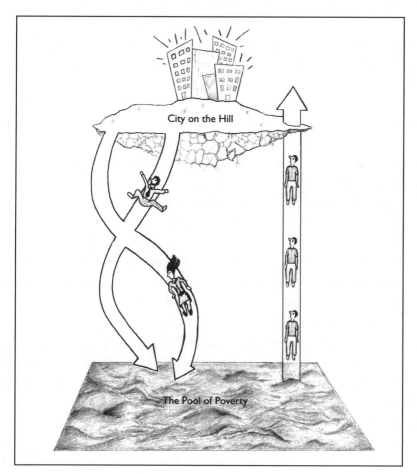

Fig. 1.2 Accounting for Simultaneity.

but now there are also drains that lead downward—into poverty. The level of water in the pool of poverty gets lowered on account of the elevator. The level rises when more people get pulled down through the drains.

Different mechanisms are associated, respectively, with the elevator and the drain. This asymmetry has important consequences for policy design. Because reasons for descent and reasons for escape are separate from each other, two sets of micro policies are required in parallel.

The Balance of Events

Discrete events rather than any particular household characteristics influence households' economic trajectories over time. Two types of everyday events can be distinguished. Negative events (such as illnesses and high health care costs) tend to have a depressing effect, pushing households downward. Positive events (such as higher crop yields) tend to place households upon an ascending trajectory.

While the events that affect households can be distinguished between positive and negative ones, households themselves are not so easily sorted between types of events. Over the longer term, nearly all households experience both positive and negative events. The balance of events is what matters most. Households who experience more negative and fewer positive events tend to suffer a reversal of fortune. Other households, who experience the opposite balance of events, are the ones who climb up the economic ladder.

Influencing households' balance of events is the critical task of public policy. Exclusively supporting upward mobility is of relatively little value. In situations where the downside risks are large, escapes from poverty can become precarious affairs. Households who live in fear of impending descents are deterred from making investments. Thus, in addition to helping avert needless descents into poverty, better preventive policies will also help improve the prospects for escape. Faster and more enduring progress against poverty will be promoted when a mix of policies is in place that reduces the frequency of negative events while simultaneously augmenting positive events.

Detailed micro-level inquiries will help ascertain what needs to be done within each particular context. It is not enough for this purpose to examine how well some particular intervention of a government or donor agency has worked. Knowledge about what works that *we* have implemented is certainly important to acquire, but knowledge about what works that *they* have done must also be acknowledged, acquired, and learned from,[14] for it is certainly hubris on the part of policy makers, government agencies, scholars, or philanthropists to imagine that people escape from poverty only because of what we do. Lots of people escape poverty without our learning anything about it—and many others slide into poverty because of lack of any assistance.

Structures at different levels along the micro–macro chain influence these events; human agency matters in addition.[15] What households do or fail to do, what they experience and what they can safely avoid, quite often makes the difference between those who escape poverty and those who fall in.

Until we know better what households and individuals do by themselves to cope with poverty, our assistance packages, often shots in the dark, can end up displacing rather than reinforcing these efforts. Taking the microscopic view and finding out more about micro events and household strategies is, therefore, of fundamental importance. Depending upon the nature of positive and negative reasons that have relevance, separate types of policy supports will be required in different parts of each country.

One critical element of preventive policy is required almost everywhere. Thousands of households in every region studied have succumbed to poverty on account of a combination of ill-health, lack of access to qualified medical attention, and high health care costs. Thousands of other people continue to live only one illness away from poverty. Large numbers of people have fallen into poverty on account of health-related events in the low–average income economies of rural Rajasthan and Western Kenya as well as in the higher income economy of North Carolina.

Health care needs to be provided more affordably, effectively, and reliably, including to people who are the least able to cope with the expenses involved. The specific nature of the most serious and costly ailments varies across and within different countries. In general, success in reducing poverty creation is to a considerable extent dependent upon providing more effective healthcare services.

Reducing the incidence of diseases is important for this purpose. However, merely regarding these widespread incidents as 'health shocks' and attributing them to physical pathologies, including killer diseases such as HIV-AIDS, is to ignore the basic fact that fast-rising health care expenses, as much as ill-health itself, are to blame for the resulting descents into poverty. Markets can help boost individual initiatives, but markets can also enfeeble and impoverish people by intensifying the impacts made by negative events. A rapid commercialization of medical services—mostly unregulated by governments and unfettered by social norms—has helped multiply the large and growing risks of falling into poverty. Expanding health insurance coverage is critically important, but regulating the market for health care is also necessary. Later in this book we will examine these aspects in greater detail.

Improving health care services is not, however, the only response that is required for controlling descents into poverty. Some other reasons for descent also matter considerably, but their effects vary both across and within countries.

Social and customary expenses, especially expenditures associated with marriages and funerals, have contributed in some regions to large numbers of descents into poverty. In other places, this type of drain on households' resources has either never been very significant or it has been rendered less important by collective efforts of different kinds. Other context-specific reasons for descent include crop diseases, irrigation failures, pest infestations, commodity price crashes, land erosion, and high-interest debt.

People who moved upward were assisted by another set of micro events. Their crop yields grew; new crops became known; a son or a daughter found a paying position (usually within the urban informal sector); a new business was developed; and so on.

It is important to learn how they were able to arrive at these pathways and why others in similar situations were not. Putting it down to luck or hard work or inner strength hardly serves as an adequate explanation, particularly since nearly everyone who is poor has no recourse except to work hard.

I found in my first study, conducted in Rajasthan in 2001 and 2002, that laziness is not particularly a trait of those who are poor. The analysis showed that hardly anyone had become poor or remained poor on account of alcoholism, drug use, or idleness.[16] Alcohol use, while common in some communities, was not particularly widespread among those who were poor. Evidence collected in other regions and countries supported the same conclusion. Among all eight regions studied, slothfulness, drunkenness, and other such factors were associated with less than 5 percent of all recorded descents.[17] A subsequent World Bank study has helped extend this important result, finding that in other regions as well very few people have fallen into poverty on account of factors such as these.[18]

By and large, people do not become poor or remain poor for reasons of their own making. The events that have contributed to the largest numbers of descents have occurred for reasons beyond most individuals' control.

Reducing the growth of future poverty will require dealing more forcefully with these context-specific events. Rather than fully centralized or entirely decentralized policies and programs, a polycentric response will be more effective, as discussed later in this book.

Raising the Bar

Preventing future poverty is an essential requirement. Simultaneously, a second set of policies is needed for supporting more escapes from poverty. Attention needs to be paid not just to the numbers of escapes but also to the *quality* of individual escapes.

A binary view considering only two possible states—above and below the poverty line—has unfortunately informed poverty policies of the past. Because reducing the aggregate *numbers* in poverty was the over-riding concern, the quality of individual escapes was not separately evaluated. A marginal escape above the US$1 poverty line—from, say, 99 cents to US$1.01—was counted as one success in the war against poverty. A more substantial escape, from, say, 79 cents to US$2.50, was totted up similarly.

Because of the manner in which success was evaluated and the form in which statistics were compiled, relatively little was learned in relation to the following kinds of questions: How many individuals who escaped poverty in the past ended up just above the poverty line? How many others were able to climb all the way up to the city on the hill? What factors helped enable higher-quality escapes? What impediments have held up the rest?

In our investigations using the *Stages-of-Progress* methodology (discussed in the next chapter), we examined these questions carefully. The answers we obtained have a dampening effect on the enthusiasm that ought to be generated by evidence of large numbers moving up.

Many people have succeeded in moving out of poverty, but only a tiny number were able to rise high. Most of those who escaped poverty have found positions such as maid, gardener, chauffeur, pushcart vendor, security guard, rickshaw puller, mason's assistant, and the like. Hardly anyone became a software engineer, university professor, business magnate, or airline pilot. Not all individuals have the capacity to perform well in such high-paying positions, but those who have the capacity and the will to progress should not be denied the opportunity—just because they happened to be poor at a previous time.

Letting a farmhand's son or daughter remain a farmhand, even though she or he is potentially the next Marie Curie, Tiger Woods, or Bill Gates, is perhaps the greatest living tragedy that poor people in many countries witness time after time. Opportunities for self-advancement need to become more widely available, especially to children and young adults from less-well-off families.

More people need to be supported to rise, not just above the poverty line, but as high as each one is individually capable. This is not simply a question of distributing benefits subsequent to economic growth. It relates more critically to how an individual becomes associated in the first instance with the processes whereby wealth is produced. What position does he or she occupy in this machinery? People who remain in the position of unskilled laborers and marginal farmers are unlikely to command a growing share of the national dividend. Some poor people will unfortunately remain in these positions. For them, it is important to provide better wages and social services and more social protection, helping especially to prevent further impoverishment. For the rest—the more talented and hardworking ones—preservation and protection are hardly enough.

Over and over, in interviews with poor mothers and fathers, I was brought back to one essential fact: One's own poverty is easier to bear with fortitude if future opportunities for one's children are bright. People are deeply concerned about their children's future. Many are investing more than they can afford to spend on sending their children to schools.

Data from around the developing world bears witness to an explosive rise in literacy, most noticeably among rural residents and younger age groups. Very few among these belt-tightening investments have yielded any rich dividend. I inquired within a diverse group of developing-country communities about what residents, including former residents, have achieved in the past and what current residents, especially younger ones, aspire to achieve in the future. Separately, I also looked to see which young people, from what social and educational backgrounds, have been newly recruited as software professionals in Bangalore, India. There are many happy parts to the story that I learned, but the sad part is that none among these new recruits was born poor.

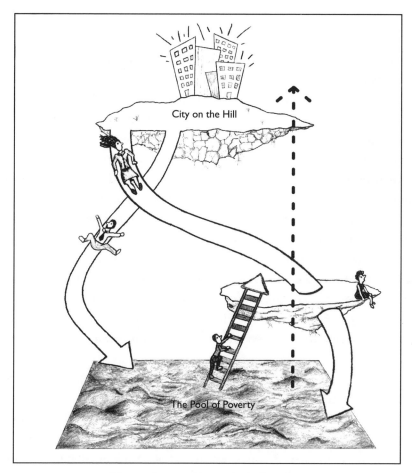

Fig. 1.3 Poverty Dynamics in Practice.

The image of poverty that we saw in Figure 1.2 still does not capture the full variety of human experiences. Poverty and prosperity are not the only possible states of well-being. Many intermediate positions also exist. One such position is shown for illustrative purposes in Figure 1.3.

As seen earlier in Figures 1.1 and 1.2, there is an elevator (the dotted arrow) that connects from the pool of poverty to the city on the hill, but now there is also a ladder, which leads only to the intermediate position, not going all the way up to the city on the hill. The lucky few who gained access to the fast elevator have joined the ranks of the globally connected. The rest, the bulk of those who escaped poverty, have instead used the slow ladder to wend their ways up. Such people do not suffer hunger any more, and they may never need to pull their children out of school. But they do not own a credit card, travel abroad, drive a car or even a motorized two-wheeler, access the internet, or possess more than one or two pairs of shoes.

Shantilal, whose example of escape from poverty we read about previously, has only just risen to such an intermediate position. Most others who escaped poverty have also not gone further beyond. For the majority of those who moved out of poverty, the city on the hill remains still a distant dream.

Globally, the real picture of poverty most resembles Figure 1.3. Many are climbing out of stark poverty, but very few are going beyond a second cutoff. World Bank figures show that in the 24 years between 1981 and 2005 the aggregate number of people living in acute poverty (below US$1.25/day) fell by *500 million*. The World Bank also reports aggregate figures related to a second poverty line, calculated at the higher rate of US$2 per day. Over the same 24-year period, the aggregate number of people living between US$1.25 and US$2 *increased by 600 million*.[19] The large reduction in the numbers of the acutely poor appears to have been entirely absorbed within the ranks of the near-poor.

What needs to be done in order to significantly improve the prospects for upward mobility among talented individuals born in poorer households? As a preliminary step, we need to acquire a new set of monitoring tools that can better distinguish between marginal and substantial improvements. Simultaneously, our criteria of success in poverty reduction need to be rethought. Raising a mass of people out of poverty is certainly a praiseworthy achievement—but it is hardly enough. Imagine if someone like Einstein had been born into poverty. Would it be a sufficient achievement to raise him to day laborer?

Capacity and not merely poverty should be regarded as an individual's defining feature, as Nobel laureate Amartya Sen has frequently advised. Purposive action needs to be taken along a broad front in order to nurture individuals' capacities and provide them with better opportunities for personal growth. Better education and more effective health care are essential. Better infrastructure, transportation, and communication links also count for a lot.

One other factor also matters critically, but it has not been given enough attention in the past. In the regions and communities where poor people typically live, there is a great shortage of career-related *information*. Many people simply remain unaware of the pathways and career opportunities that can potentially become available to them. Institutions providing reliable career-related information—such as counseling centers, employment exchanges, college guides, or vocational centers—simply do not exist within (or even close to) the communities in which poor people, especially rural ones, live. Word-of-mouth information sets the limit to what many people can aspire to become. They derive their examples and their aspirations from the kinds of people whom they come across on a regular basis.[20] The absence of better role-models and mentors keeps thousands of bright-eyed young people trapped within low-productivity, low-compensation situations. Even those who have innate ability and a will to rise higher are unable to achieve very much.

Faster economic growth will help open up several new opportunities for self-advancement. Who will benefit from these opportunities is, however, an open question, needing more and better answers derived from careful micro-level investigations. Concerns have been expressed that inequality has started rising fast in China and India and some other countries.[21] We urgently need to learn more about how institutions can be built and linkages fostered that will enable more people to benefit from growing aggregate opportunity.

Individuals' talents will be better rewarded when more people have a real opportunity to rise high. Paralleling these micro-level advances, the gross national product will also grow faster when a country's talent pool is more productively employed. Macro–micro linkages can be made more productive in both directions. The real question is where to begin.

Conclusion: A Two-Pronged Strategy

Policy makers tend to take aerial views, but it is in the realm of the ordinary, on account of commonplace events, that cracks appear, which, growing deeper, become micro poverty traps. Everyday experiences, operating below the radar screens of policy makers, take a constant toll upon ordinary people's lives.

Large numbers of people have fallen into poverty within every region studied. Along with those who lived marginally above the poverty line, others who were comfortable, or even well-off previously, have become the poor of today. In most cases these changes did not come about suddenly, brought on by natural calamity, political disorder, or economic collapse. Chains of ordinary events occurring at the micro level pushed people into poverty. Bit by bit, families dropped, until they could no longer recover.

Action at multiple levels is required in order to reduce poverty faster and more enduringly. The macro poverty traps that hold an entire country's progress in check should be tackled in ways indicated by economist Paul Collier and others.[22] In addition, micro poverty traps need to be dealt with urgently. In each region studied, under the same umbrella of national and regional structures, one group of households escaped poverty, while another group of households simultaneously fell into poverty. Micro events, more than national economic trends, help explain these ubiquitous divergent trends.

The balance of ordinary events matters critically for each family. Nudging this balance in the right direction will require mounting two sets of micro policies. Preventive policies that better guard against future descents are required in addition to curative ones that accelerate and augment the quality of escapes. Improvements in health care have a very important role to play by way of forestalling the creation of future poverty. If we are able to prevent descents more effectively, soon there will be fewer people left to assist. Future poverty will diminish. Fewer public resources will be required down the line.

Simultaneously, widening and deepening the channels that raise people higher will help level the economic playing field. Attention needs to be given not only to the aggregate number of poverty escapes in a country but also to the nature and quality of individual escapes. For most of those who rose out of poverty in the past, progress came to an end soon after poverty was surmounted but before prosperity could be properly achieved.

Assistance is required to enable poor individuals to go further, as far beyond the poverty line as they are individually capable. A number of related interventions are required for this purpose. Information provision is critical among them. While hardly sufficient by itself to guarantee upward mobility, information is a necessary resource which, because it is frequently missing, imposes a low glass ceiling upon poorer individuals' achievements and aspirations. Widening opportunity and raising upward mobility will require investing in information institutions.

The layout of the rest of this book is as follows. In Chapter 2, I explain how I arrived at the results presented in this book. The *Stages-of-Progress* methodology is presented, which relies upon carefully compiling and analytically comparing a large number of individual life stories. Told in the hubbub of community meetings or in the quiet of people's homes, these stories were coded according to some intuitively simple yet analytically rigorous schemes.

In Chapter 3, I present the data about making and un-making poverty. No matter which region of the world is studied, and no matter which measure of poverty is employed, the same result is obtained: rising tides and falling tides tend to flow concurrently. Context-specific micro reasons associated with each type of poverty flow are examined in Chapters 4 and 5, with the first of these chapters looking at descents and micro poverty traps, and the second one examining why, despite there being such traps, some households were still able to escape poverty.

Chapter 6 looks at limits to upward mobility. Why do so many ascending households not ascend recognizably higher? Chapter 7 ends the book with a discussion of what should be done.

Two messages are central. Waiting until someone has fallen into poverty is hardly the only time when assistance can or should be provided. Preventive assistance must become the norm. In parallel, efforts must be made to substantially augment the prospects for upward mobility. By addressing descents directly and effectively, and at the same time, by promoting more and better pathways for escape, we will be able to make faster progress against poverty than we have at any time in the past.

CHAPTER 2

Poverty Flows

Conventionally, poverty has been measured as a stock variable. Surveys carried out by national governments and international agencies estimate the total number of people who are poor in a country at particular moments in time. We can deduce the *net* change in the stock of poverty between successive measurements, but we can say nothing from these data about how many people actually escaped poverty and how many others fell into poverty.

An example taken from India's national poverty statistics will help make clear how this knowledge gap arises. A total of 32 percent of all Indians were found to be poor in 1994, according to government sources, while 8 percent fewer Indians, 24 percent in all, were estimated to be poor in 2004.[1] The stock of poverty in India fell by 8 percent overall, but how many people actually rose out of poverty over this ten-year period? We cannot tell simply by looking at these figures. Any 8-percent reduction in the stock of poverty can come about in a number of different ways. For instance:

Possibility A: 8 percent of the population escaped poverty, and no one fell into poverty over this period; *or*

Possibility B: 16 percent of the population escaped poverty, while 8 percent concurrently fell into poverty; *or*

Possibility C: 24 percent escaped poverty, and 16 percent fell into poverty.

All three of these flow configurations (as well as many others) can result in producing an equivalent 8-percent reduction in the stock of poverty. But these different possibilities are hardly similar in nature, and it is critically important to distinguish among them.

Because we lack knowledge about the underlying flows, we cannot make out what actually occurred, and we are forced to make assumptions about what might have been the case. The ordinary assumption that one implicitly makes is similar in nature to Possibility *A*: If poverty went down by 8 percent in the aggregate, it *must* have been because 8 percent of the poor were raised out of poverty—and no one fell into poverty over the same period. Our minds pass over without even considering that people can actually experience descents.

Multiple flow possibilities can lead to the same observed change in the stock of poverty. However, treating identically every 8-percent reduction is a mistake. Are Possibilities *B* and *C* truly identical with Possibility *A*? A rate of descents of the order of 16 percent over ten years is hardly fanciful. As evidence advanced in the next chapter will show, even higher rates of descents have been recorded in specific instances. Should national planners be equally content with Possibility *C* as with Possibility *A*, noting only the 8-percent net reduction and dismissing the underlying flows? More to the point, should the same sorts of policy interventions be mounted to deal with Possibility *C* as with Possibility *A*?

Critically, escapes and descents are not responsive to the same reasons, as we will see in the chapters that follow. People move out of poverty on account of one set of reasons. They fall into poverty on account of a different set of reasons. Because separate reasons are associated with each poverty flow, two separate sets of policies need to be implemented in parallel. One set of policy responses is required to promote more escapes. Simultaneously, a second set of policies is required to block descents into poverty. The faster the pace of descents in some region, the more urgently will policies of the second set be required, but where descents are fewer in number resources can be concentrated, instead, on promoting more escapes from poverty. Different combinations of poverty policies are required, therefore, depending upon the relative rates of escape and descent.

The policy mix appropriate to any particular country's situation cannot be determined simply by looking at the stock of poverty. If Possibility *C* reflects the true underlying conditions, then much more needs to be done for reducing descents, but if Possibility *A* better reflects these underlying flows, then accelerating escapes must be given higher priority in anti-poverty plans.

Information about poverty flows—about the respective rates of (and reasons for) escape and descent—is essential for identifying what needs to be done.

Because the flow aspect of poverty has not been given nearly as much attention as has been given to measuring and explaining its stock, we have remained ignorant about the reasons that underlie the changes observed.

Much more attention needs to be paid to poverty flows in the future. Conventional methods of measuring poverty are insufficient and need to be supplemented. Methods that directly probe poverty flows need to be developed and put to use.

Starting in 2001, I developed one such methodology for the studies that I conducted. The *Stages-of-Progress* methodology is a useful diagnostic tool for identifying context-specific threats and opportunities at the grassroots level with the participation of the people concerned. It helps identify, relatively quickly, reliably, and cost-effectively, the natures of the micro reasons that are associated with escaping poverty and becoming poor in each particular context. This methodology and the findings resulting from its application have been reported in a series of peer-reviewed journal articles and seminars beginning in 2003.[2] Several other individuals and organizations have subsequently adapted this methodology for use in their own research and programming efforts, as discussed later.

Developing a Methodology

What led me to believe in the need for developing a different methodology? Why could some existing methodology not be used instead?

When I started this body of research, I looked at a number of existing methods and measures, and I learned a great deal. Given the vast amount of work that has gone into studying poverty no new methodology can be entirely unique. The *Stages-of-Progress* methodology borrows insights from several pre-existing methods, including panel data studies, participatory poverty assessments, and ethnographic examinations.[3] Individually, however, none among these existing methods seemed particularly well suited for dealing with the questions that concerned me the most.[4]

Two *why* questions were central to my investigations: Why—for what reasons—do some (but not other) poor people escape from poverty? Why do some non-poor people simultaneously fall into poverty? These questions are particularly important for policy purposes. Knowing the reasons for escape and descent helps design more effective interventions.

In principle, these questions are simple to address. Here is what needs to be done: Poverty status needs to be ascertained for the same group of individuals or households at two points in time. Some households will be found to have moved out of poverty over the intervening period. Other households will be found to have remained persistently poor. Yet others will have fallen into poverty, and a fourth sub-group, those who have remained non-poor, will also be identified. Comparing experiences among households belonging to these different sub-groups can help uncover answers to the two *why* questions. Events and characteristics that are common among households who have escaped poverty—and not common among households who continued to remain poor—will provide important clues about what helps promote escapes from poverty. Similarly, features and events commonly experienced by households who fell into poverty—and commonly not experienced by those who remained non-poor—will be identified as micro-level reasons for descent.

While logically it seems simple, in practice a number of difficulties arise in tracking households or individuals over time. No censuses of poor people are available for developing countries. Information is not at hand about who is poor today and who was poor earlier.[5] No pre-existing data were available for the communities that I studied. As a result, the identification exercise had to be undertaken afresh. Identifying who is poor at the present time is hard enough; multiple understandings and competing definitions tend to complicate this task. Identifying who was poor in the past is harder yet.

Most previous studies of poverty flows, particularly those that have relied upon constructing panel data, have, therefore, tended to take a prospective view. Investigators conduct an initial survey at the start of the study period. They return several years later, conducting follow-up surveys among the same groups of households. Data related to the numbers of escapes and descents can be generated using this method. If household interviews are also conducted and event histories are constructed, then the reasons associated with escapes and descents can also be identified.

Typically, however, households' event histories have not been compiled in panel data studies. As a result, such studies have had very little to say in regard to the two *why* questions. 'We are swamped with facts about people's incomes and about the number and composition of people who inhabit the lower tail [of the income distribution], but we don't know very much about the processes that generate these results.'[6] Thus, one can tell which households escaped from (or fell into) poverty over the period considered, but one can say relatively little about the factors responsible.

What we get usually from panel studies are consumption (or income or assets) data at two points in time, with additional information being provided in some cases about village or regional conditions prevailing at the starting and ending points. Analysts can use such data to compare some characteristics of households who fell into poverty with those of others who successfully avoided descents, for instance, initial education levels and landholdings can be compared. Analysts can also examine other data related, for example, to village or regional features, to national policies in force, and to the occurrence of large-scale events, such as famines and wars.

However, without being informed about micro-level processes and events, they are unable to deduce why some landholding or educated households fell into poverty while others did not, or why the effects of the same village or regional characteristics, of national policies or macro events, were distributed so unevenly across different households. Because virtually 'no attention is focused on the events which lead people into and out of poverty, it [has proved] very difficult [using these methods] to trace the processes whereby people may suddenly or gradually escape poverty.'[7]

Further, relatively short intervals of time have been usually considered by panel studies. No more than three- to five-year-intervals have been examined in most cases. However, household strategies are typically made in terms of generational time horizons. For instance, people invest in the education of their children so that when these children come of age they are better able to escape poverty. Farmers make improvements incrementally upon their agricultural fields, leveling the land and digging irrigation canals, so that they can reap a bigger harvest in years to come. Thus, in order to understand better what households do by themselves, one needs to examine households' experiences over relatively long periods of time. The investigators who conducted one of the earliest prospective studies advise that 'even nine years [the length of time considered by them] is too short a period to analyze issues that pertain to household mobility.'[8] Periods ranging from 15 to 25 years are better suited for this purpose.

> If we wish to take a longer, inter-generational or dynastic, perspective, then panels of 20 years or more are needed by definition. However, a majority of developing countries do not have panel data at all ... Quantitative panel-based

analysis on poverty dynamics, therefore, is largely an analysis of fairly short-run fluctuations in well-being and poverty.[9]

A new set of panel studies, commenced relatively recently, have been designed to examine changes over longer periods of time. By conducting detailed household interviews and compiling event histories, these studies will also generate more knowledge about micro-level reasons for escapes and descents.[10]

Investigating trends over longer periods of time, 20 years or more, presents, however, an interesting conundrum. A prospective study that is initiated today will produce results only after this long period has elapsed. Because of the extended period of study and the need for repeat visits to the communities concerned, a prospective study of this kind can quickly become a high-cost enterprise, involving a very long wait, during which time important underlying conditions can change.

A carefully designed retrospective can help uncover reasons for escape and descent more expeditiously and at much lower cost. If we can learn reliably about the forces that need to be augmented and other influences that need to be blocked, policy interventions can be made more immediately and effectively— without having to wait for 15 or 20 years.

Thus, retrospective studies are potentially useful for examining the two *why* questions. It is important, however, to recognize the risks and the limits that are involved. Recall can be biased, incomplete, or selective. Not everything can be recollected equally well. Retrospective inquiries are more usefully employed to study the things that are more easily and accurately remembered. A number of safeguards and validation procedures need to be built in. Carelessly implementing a retrospective method can result in imposing a series of costs.

In the 12 communities that I studied initially in Rajasthan, India, I started to experiment tentatively with a retrospective design. I asked people about their situations at the current time. Separately, I asked them to recall how things had been in the past. In order to facilitate these comparisons and to act as a guide to memory, a common yardstick was developed in consultation with the people interviewed. Before-and-after comparisons were not made in terms of some vague assessments of better or worse. More precise comparisons were carried out using a clear and commonly agreed scale of poverty measurement, as detailed below.

A number of precautions were developed progressively. Because recall can be tricky, especially about smaller details, poverty was evaluated in relation to larger more easily remembered distinctions. The scale that is used for assessing poverty has only 14 or 15 intervals rather than the continuous gradation common to income- or consumption-based measures, and it relies upon assets or capabilities that because they are lumpy can be more easily distinguished and more clearly recalled.

Each item of information was recorded only after it had been carefully triangulated after consulting multiple independent sources. Community groups served as one source of information. Multiple household members were interviewed separately in the privacy of their homes. These different information sources supplemented one another and served to cross-check the information obtained from each source. People filled in the details that other people had forgotten to mention.

For the sake of verification, data obtained from these oral inquiries were tallied against recorded data wherever it was available. The Appendix at the end of this book reports upon the results of these validation exercises. It also discusses in more detail other safeguards and cross-checks that were progressively incorporated within *Stages-of-Progress*.

Regions and Sites Investigated

The first *Stages-of-Progress* study was undertaken in 2002 within a group of rural communities in Rajasthan, India. I had thought that my prior familiarity with the region and its people would help me uncover relatively quickly a useful working methodology. But it took more than six months of field research, including an initial four months experiencing a series of failures, before a potentially workable method began to take shape. I experimented with a number of different approaches at the start. None of these initial efforts was very productive in terms of providing answers to the two *why* questions.[11] Gradually, after suffering reversals and frustrations, I came around to experimenting with what would later become *Stages-of-Progress*.

A basic insight that I gained while floundering initially in Rajasthan was that people in these villages had their own functional understandings of poverty. Creditors would not press too hard for repayment upon people who (in the villagers' estimation) had fallen upon hard times. Food and other forms of community assistance were provided on special occasions to people identified by their neighbors as poor. Poverty, where it existed, was commonly recognized, even though hardly anyone assessed it in a manner known to me at that time. I started asking people in these villages to speak about the indicators that they explicitly or implicitly used in order to assess whether some household was poor. Once they knew that no material benefits were involved in these investigations—I made clear that I was not putting together any list of 'beneficiaries'—they began to share these identifications with me.

I learned that people thought by their peers to be poor in these contexts typically lacked a core set of material capabilities.[12] Participatory studies undertaken in the past have shown how local understandings of poverty are most often expressed in terms of assets and capabilities. It made sense, therefore, to construct a scale of ascending material well-being through identifying successively acquired assets and material capabilities.

I began to develop a means for constructing such a locally relevant scale that would help me identify in community meetings—with common consent—who was poor at the time of the study and who else had experienced poverty in the past. These initial formulations, implemented in the first Rajasthan study, were successively improved upon in additional studies, undertaken with research partners and community groups in other parts of India, and later in Kenya, Uganda, Peru, and North Carolina, USA.

Separate studies were conducted in three diverse states of India: Rajasthan, Gujarat, and Andhra Pradesh.[13] While Rajasthan has been regarded as an economically backward state, Gujarat is regarded as a poster child of economic and industrial growth in India. Andhra Pradesh, the third Indian state, falls somewhere in between, neither growing as fast as Gujarat over the past two decades nor sharing with Rajasthan the status of a *bimaru* (sickly) or socially backward state.[14] Within each state we selected three quite diverse districts. For example, in Gujarat, we selected Panchmahals, an economically backward district, and we also selected Vadodara, which has experienced rapid economic growth and forms part of the state's 'golden corridor' of industrial development.

Within each district, a mixed bag of communities was selected for study. Small communities were selected together with larger ones; communities located closer to market towns and major roads were selected along with others that are more remotely situated; and communities with mixed caste or ethnic compositions were selected along with others where a single ethnic group is more dominant. These studies were implemented in collaboration with a group of NGOs: Chitra and Seva Mandir in Rajasthan; SEWA and Sarathi in Gujarat; and Disha in Andhra Pradesh.

Later in 2002, a Kenya study was commenced in collaboration with Patti Kristjanson, Nelson Mango, and Maren Radeny of the Nairobi-based International Livestock Research Institute. We worked initially in a diverse though small group of communities in the western part of this country, later conducting a second study within a larger and nationally representative sample of 71 urban and rural communities.[15]

Compared to Kenya, which was relatively stable in the two or three decades preceding our study, its neighboring country, Uganda, had emerged from a brutal and lengthy civil war. After peace was restored, Uganda's economic performance outstripped that of its neighbor to the east. In the 1990s, Uganda's economy grew at an average rate of nearly 7 percent per annum, while Kenya's economy grew at a much slower annual rate of 1.6 percent. Poverty continues to be a problem in both countries. At the end of the 1990s, 42 percent of the population of Kenya and 55 percent of the population of Uganda had incomes below these countries' national poverty lines.

A study in 36 communities of Uganda was undertaken in collaboration with Daniel Lumonya, Agatha Kafuko, and Firminus Mugumya of Makerere University. Three quite diverse districts were selected in each of the Central and Western Regions.[16] Communities were selected, as in the studies conducted in India, with the intent of examining a wide range of variation. Different patterns of rural settlements commonly found in these areas are represented within the mix of communities selected.

In Peru, the next country studied, 49 percent of the national population had incomes below the national poverty line in the late 1990s. Working in collaboration with Hector Cisneros and Judith Kuan of CONDESAN-CIP, a diverse group of 40 communities was selected in Cajamarca and Puno, two of the poorest regions within this country. Within each region we selected 20 communities that vary in terms of altitude, economic activity, market access, population size, and also, especially in the Puno region, in terms of ethnic group and language.[17]

In North Carolina, my students at Duke University worked in partnership with a group of community organizers, who were identified and financially supported by MDC, a well-known and well-regarded non-profit agency of this region. We conducted investigations within four geographically and economically diverse counties,[18] selecting communities that are diverse in racial and occupational terms. Compared to the other studies, the North Carolina study is smaller in size; it is substantially more expensive to work in the United States, even within its less developed regions.

Each study was self-contained. Each was preceded by a pilot study, which helped adapt the methodology to the new terrain.

Training for a period of two weeks or longer was built in at the start of every new study. Following three days of classroom discussions and simulations, the study teams would go out to conduct a practical exercise, first in one set of communities, and following feedback and discussions, in a second set of communities. Every study team worked in the language of the region investigated.

In each case, we shared our initial results with members of the communities that we studied. We also presented the final results to policy makers, NGOs, scholars, and interested citizens. Feedback and criticisms obtained from each of these groups helped refine the results and improve our methods.

The *Stages-Of-Progress* Methodology

As practiced today, this methodology has seven successive steps that are implemented in sequence each time any study is conducted. These steps are not very different from those described in the first few publications that came out of the *Stages-of-Progress* research work. They are described briefly below. A fuller description of the methodology and a training manual are available at the author's web site (www.pubpol.duke.edu/krishna). Techniques to deal with different sources of risks have been developed and incorporated. The Appendix presents this discussion, and it also provides the results of diverse tests carried out to ensure reliability.

Step 1. Assembling a Representative Community Group
In each community that we studied—consisting of villages in rural areas and neighborhoods in urban areas—a representative community group was assembled at the start, including males and females, higher status and lower status members, and older as well as younger individuals. Advance notice had to be given in some instances to the community and its leaders.

Seasonality is an important consideration, especially for people in rural and agrarian communities. We conducted these investigations during the lean period of the seasonal work cycle, so that community members could more easily spare the time required to participate in these discussions. In some instances, specifically in north India where women let men do all the talking in mixed groups, a parallel meeting was convened for the women of the community. Information obtained from these women's meetings served as a useful cross-check upon the information obtained from the men's meetings.

Step 2. Presenting our Objectives

We introduced ourselves as researchers, making it clear at the start that we did not represent any government agency or NGO, so there would be no benefits or losses from speaking freely and frankly with us. We were neither implementing any development project nor selecting beneficiaries. We mentioned these facts in order to remove any incentives people might have for misrepresenting their own poverty status or that of anyone else within their community.

Step 3. Describing 'Poverty' Collectively through Identifying the Stages of Progress

This step was the most important one in this study. It builds upon a realization that I had gained while studying the initial group of Rajasthan villages, namely, that people's understandings of poverty are most often expressed in terms of successively acquired capabilities.

Community groups were asked to delineate the sequence in which assets and capabilities were typically acquired as households made their ways out of extreme poverty.[19] 'What does a household in your community typically and usually do,' we asked the assembled community members, emphasizing 'typically' and 'usually,' 'when it climbs out gradually from a state of acute poverty? Which asset or capability is acquired first?' 'Food'—or rather, the capability to acquire food on an ongoing basis—was the answer given invariably in every community that we studied. What follows immediately after? 'Sending children to primary school,' we were told invariably in villages of Rajasthan. As more money flows in incrementally, what does the typical household do in the third stage, in the fourth stage, and so on?

I had thought initially that there would be considerable differences in the stages of progress reported in different villages in Rajasthan, and indeed some differences were recorded in terms of the higher-level stages. At the lowest stages, however, when households are still desperately poor or just about coming out of dire poverty, there were *virtually no differences* in the sequences narrated in different villages of this region. The first four stages, in particular—having food on a regular basis, sending children to primary school, possessing clothes to wear outside the house, and repaying debt in regular installments—were common not just to different villages of Rajasthan; they were also commonly reported by the men's and women's groups that we organized and consulted separately. There was common agreement in both sets of groups assembled in all 36 villages studied that households usually progress out of poverty through pathways that go successively through these four consecutive stages. It was community members and not researchers who defined these stages of progress. The similarity in stages is more remarkable for this reason.

'After crossing which stage is a household no longer considered poor?' we asked the assembled community members, after drawing up this progression of stages. This cut-off was drawn by all village groups after Stage 4, indicating a common social construction of poverty existed among communities of this region.

Two years after completing these exercises in Rajasthan, I returned to some of the same communities. Working with differently composed community groups, since attendance was voluntary on both occasions, I conducted afresh this exercise of identifying successive stages and the cut-off line. The stages of progress generated by these later groups were identical with the ones generated earlier. The same poverty cut-offs were identified. This repeat exercise served as one important test of validity, and it helped reinforced my faith in *Stages-of-Progress*. These results were robust ones, reflecting something that people in these communities had experienced and therefore believed.

What these Rajasthani villagers recounted as their stages of progress made a powerful statement about what constitutes poverty in their understanding: You are poor when you cannot afford to send your children to school (even when such a school charges no tuition fee). You are poor when your creditors no longer press you for payment, because they know you cannot repay. You are poor if when it rains you get drenched *inside* your house. And if you are not capable of obtaining food regularly then, of course, you are the poorest of the poor, unlikely to survive for very long without external assistance.

The process of identifying successive stages of progress worked equally well in each of the other regions studied. People participated enthusiastically, and everywhere, including in North Carolina; they had little hesitation in constructing commonly agreed-upon stages of progress. There were hardly any

Table 2.1 Stages of Progress (Western Kenya)

1. Food
2. Clothing
3. Repairs to house (primarily thatched roof)
4. Primary education for children
5. Purchase chickens
6. Purchase a sheep or goat
- -
> *Poverty Cut-off*: Beyond this line, households are no longer considered poor

7. Purchasing local cattle
8. Improvements to housing, furniture
9. Secondary education for children
10. Buy or lease land
- -
> *Prosperity Cut-off*: Beyond this line, households are considered relatively well-off

11. Purchasing dairy cattle
12. Buying land/plots
13. Constructing permanent houses
14. Investing in a business

disagreements about the successive stages, particularly about the initial ones that lie below the poverty cut-off.

Table 2.1 reproduces the successive stages of progress that were reported *in common* by all 20 rural communities studied in Western Kenya. Notice how the poverty cut-off is drawn after Stage 6. Possessing chickens or sheep and goats is not enough. In addition, some cattle must be acquired in order to cross over the line.

Housing is not such an immediate need in rural settings, perhaps because few people are entirely homeless in these contexts. In urban areas, however, housing appears prominently and at an early stage. In Kenya's capital city, Nairobi, the first few stages below the poverty cut-off were commonly reported as follows: food, clothing, renting a small house, primary education for children, and investing in a small business. Somewhat different livelihood requirements between rural villages and cities lead to somewhat different social constructions of poverty. Yet, similarities also exist.

Notice how 'prosperity' is not simply the obverse of poverty. Additional progress needs to be made—another four stages need to be covered beyond the poverty cut-off in Table 2.1—before a household is considered to be prosperous or rich. Between poor and rich there is an intermediate category, consisting of those who are neither poor nor rich. Large numbers of households inhabit this intermediate zone, including many who have escaped poverty in the recent past.

Table 2.2 reproduces the sequence of stages reported in all of the other regions studied. The dotted line corresponds to the poverty cut-off in each case. Households advancing past this threshold are no longer considered poor, either by themselves or by others in their community and region.

The constitution of poverty as locally understood—in terms of sequentially acquired assets and capabilities—was nearly identically defined within each particular socio-cultural context. The same initial stages of progress were identified, with very few differences arising from one community to the next. Higher-level stages, those located far above the poverty cut-off, varied in some respects. But stages below the poverty cut-off and just above were virtually identically identified within each region.

Across regions as well, there are considerable similarities, with understandable differences arising in the case of North Carolina, USA. Two poverty lines, a lower one and a higher one, were separately defined in the case of North Carolina. The lower line signifies extreme poverty. Community members considered a household to be in extreme poverty if it was at or below Stage 4, that is, if it was unsuccessful in obtaining shelter, food, transportation, and clothing. Above 'extreme poverty,' was a middle category defined as 'poor.' Households continue to be considered 'poor' in these North Carolina communities until they cross past Stage 8, when they can repay the debts that they have accumulated in the past. In the next stage, Stage 9, they are able to purchase a home (often a mobile or starter home), and at this point, the household is said to be 'not poor' or 'doing alright.'

A commonly known and widely agreed-upon understanding of poverty exists in each case, and this everyday understanding of poverty is much more real for these residents than any definition that is proposed from the outside. These locally constructed understandings of poverty constitute the criteria within these communities for identifying who is poor. They also constitute a threshold or an objective that defines the goals and the strategies of poor people. What people do in order to deal with poverty depends on what they understand to be the defining features of this state.

For our purposes, the stages served as a commonly agreed metric, a yardstick or marker, for assessing households' material well-being. Based on these well-defined and clearly understood criteria, community groups could classify which households are poor at the present time and which households had been

Table 2.2 Initial Stages of Progress (Before the Poverty Cut-Off)

Stage	Peru (Cajamarca and Puno)	Western Kenya	Uganda (West and Central)	Andhra Pradesh, India	Gujarat, India	Rajasthan, India	North Carolina, USA
1	Food	Food	Food	Food	Food	Food	Basic Shelter
2	Clothing	Clothing	Clothing	House repairs	Clothing	Primary education	Food
3	House repairs	House repairs	Primary education	Debt payments	Primary education	Clothing	Transportation—gas money, cheap used car
4	Purchase small animals	Primary education	House repairs	Clothing	Debt payments	Debt payments	Clothing
5	Primary education	Small animals			House repair/roof		Telephone
6	Purchase small plot of land				Renting in a small tract of land for sharecropping		In-home entertainment, usually TV
7							Better car
8							Debt payments

Note: The dotted line corresponds to the poverty cut-off in each case. Households advancing past this threshold are no longer considered poor, either by themselves or by others in their communities.

poor in the past. The next few steps in the *Stages-of-Progress* methodology utilized these criteria for probing the *why* questions that initially motivated these investigations.

Step 4. Treating Households of Today as the Unit of Analysis, Inquiring about Households' Poverty Status at the Present Time and in The Past

Households in existence at the time of inquiry served as the units of analysis for these exercises. The basic idea was to ascertain how many of these households had been poor in the past but had since risen out of poverty. Conversely, how many others, who had not been poor previously, had fallen into poverty over the period examined?

Household composition has clearly not remained constant. Households headed by older villagers may have existed even 25 years ago, but presently younger households did not exist at that time. Such individuals lived in their parents' (or guardians') households; and in their cases we asked about poverty in relation to these parents' or guardians' households. Thus, by considering households of today as our units of analysis, we were conducting a comparison, particularly in the case of younger households, of inherited versus acquired status: Did a person who was born to poverty continue to remain poor at the end of the period examined, or did she manage to escape poverty? Is another person, who was part of a non-poor household ten years ago, still non-poor, or has he, regrettably, fallen into poverty? What significant processes and events were associated with each type of trajectory?

Before starting with these classification exercises, a large chart recording the stages of progress was put up for all to see. A complete list of all households in each community was also prepared and displayed. Consulting key informants in advance of the community meeting, we were able to put together such household lists within two to three hours. These lists were further verified in the course of community discussions.

In most rural communities, we considered two separate recall periods: 25 years and ten years. It helps to consider as long a period as is practically possible. Implementing a study with a longer time horizon was more feasible in rural areas, where people have lived together over multiple generations and can more easily recall and verify important events in each others' lives. In urban communities and in some others that are more fluid in terms of household composition, we worked with shorter time horizons, no more than eight or ten years in all.

In order to avoid confusion, the earlier periods were denoted by some significant and commonly remembered event. For instance, in India, we referred to the national emergency of 1975–7, which is clearly remembered particularly by older villagers. In Kenya, we referred similarly to the year of President Kenyatta's demise.

Referring to the shared understanding of poverty developed in the previous step and consulting the publicly displayed stages of progress, community groups identified each household's current status in terms of the specific stage where it was located at the present time. Each household's status was also identified for one or two earlier periods.

The Appendix discusses how recall even over the longer period of 25 years was made reliable by the nature of this methodology and how some other risks, related, for instance, to migration and elite capture, were mitigated. It also presents the results of verification exercises that compared these recall data with data actually recorded in the past. There is a close match between these two types of data, indicating that the precautions employed have helped generate more accurate and reliable information.

Step 5. Assigning Households to Particular Categories

After ascertaining their poverty status for the present time and for 25 years ago (or for eight years or ten years ago, as the case may be), each household was assigned to one of four separate categories:

Category A. Poor earlier and poor now   (*Remained poor*);
Category B. Poor earlier but not poor now   (*Escaped poverty*);
Category C. Not poor earlier but poor now   (*Became poor*); and
Category D. Not poor earlier and not poor now   (*Remained not poor*).

A residual category, E, was also defined. Households who could not be placed in Categories A–D because of lack of information were assigned to this residual category. In fact, very few households, less than half of 1 percent in all, were required to be placed within Category E.

Step 6. Compiling Event Histories: Inquiring About Reasons for Escape and Descent for a Random Sample of Households

The *why* questions—those which had concerned me the most and for addressing which this methodology had been developed initially—could be taken up for the first time at this point in the inquiry process. We selected a random sample of 30 percent of all households from each of the four categories A–D, and we inquired in detail—first from the assembled community groups and in the following step from members of the households concerned—about the sequence of events that were associated with each particular household's trajectory. Such event histories were compiled separately for each selected household.

Training was central for developing this ability to record households' event histories accurately and comprehensively. The research assistants were trained to re-construct events in the sequence that these had occurred. 'Did they sell their cattle first, or did the father fall ill first? What happened in the beginning that put this household on a downward path? What happened next? What did they do or what befell them that led over time to their particular trajectory? What else occurred that helped improve their situation?' Both sorts of events, positive as well as negative ones, were recorded in chronological order for each household selected for interviews.

A comparative perspective was adopted while inquiring about household-level processes and events. For example, it was not sufficient that someone suggested 'bad luck' or 'God's will' as a reason for falling into poverty. 'How did God's will manifest itself in this particular case?' members of the study team probed. 'What happened in this household that did not also happen in other households of this community?'

Event histories were put together for households who escaped poverty. Event histories were also compiled for households who did *not* escape, that is, the ones who continued to remain poor. Similarly, event histories were compiled for households who fell into poverty and separately for households who remained non-poor. Thus, for each category of households that experienced transition, a comparison (or control) category was available, consisting of households who did not undergo a similar transition.

Step 7. Following Up by Interviewing Household Members

More complete accounts for each selected household were obtained from interviews conducted in private with this household's members. The goal here was to delve in more detail into processes and events associated with this household's movement (or stability) and to cross-check the information that had been provided earlier by the community group.

At least two members of each household were interviewed separately in their homes. As a practice, women investigators interviewed female members of these households, while male investigators interviewed men. A comparative perspective was retained in these interviews, which elicited through gentle probing the sequence of events associated with this household. In some cases, these events were painful to recount. On others occasions, they served as a source of solace or catharsis for the individuals concerned. 'At least someone has come to ask about our situation,' a woman in Kitovu, Uganda said to one of us.

Multiple sources of information were consulted in this manner for eliciting the reasons associated with each household's experience. Information, particularly about events and processes, was triangulated before being recorded. Discrepancies, when found, brought forth repeat interviews. Community groups and the household were consulted repeatedly until their accounts agreed with each other. Such occasions were relatively rare, arising, for example, in fewer than 20 among more than 1,000 households selected for interviews in Rajasthan.

After completing these investigations in each community, we conducted some quick analyses, sharing the preliminary results with the community group. The conversations that followed were very interesting ones. As the results came to light, vigorous discussions broke out about important reasons and possible remedies.

It took a team of six to eight individuals three to four days on average to complete these inquiries within any one community, constituted on average of about 175 households in rural areas and smaller numbers in urban neighborhoods. An additional day was needed for coding these data and for filling out the forms that help transfer the collected data to computer-based formats. (All data entry formats are available at the author's web site: www.sanford.duke.edu/krishna.)

For ease of data entry and to facilitate more quantitative kinds of data analyses, the reasons—processes and events—that had been recorded for each household were coded using a code-sheet that had been developed earlier and finalized toward the end of the training period. Examining the raw, un-coded details of the recorded event histories helps place a qualitative lens upon this information, while statistical analysis using the coded data helps adds the complementary quantitative dimension. Combined qualitative-and-quantitative (or Q2) analyses can thus be undertaken, which are richer and more reliable than purely qualitative or entirely quantitative ones.[20]

Supplementary (though short) household questionnaires helped collect some additional information. We inquired about education levels and assets in nearly all regions. In specific regions, depending upon the particular interests of the investigators or the funding agency involved, we also inquired about some other aspects. We asked, for example, about people's livestock holdings, about the kinds of community development benefits that different households had received, and about the nature of different individuals' participation in diverse democratic activities.

This ability to be combined together with other instruments makes *Stages-of-Progress* more useful. The fact that time periods of different lengths can be considered makes it possible to investigate a wide variety of communities.

Conclusion: Identifying Reasons

The *Stages-of-Progress* methodology was developed in order to distinguish escapes from descents and to examine more closely the nature of micro-level reasons associated with each poverty flow. Other methods have also been utilized to assess the extents of both poverty flows. However, the nature of the method used does not result in changing one basic conclusion. As we will see in the next chapter, diverse inquiries utilizing an assortment of methods have commonly established the simultaneity of escapes and descents.

The asymmetric nature of these flows—arising because of the differences in micro reasons associated, respectively, with escapes and descents—needs to be probed in addition. This is where *Stages-of-Progress* plays an important role. With the help of participatory inquiries, *Stages* helps identify reliably, after triangulation and verification, the nature of micro reasons associated with different households' experiences over time. The length of time studied can be varied depending upon the nature of the community examined. Relatively long periods of time can be studied while working with rural communities. Shorter periods of time work better in urban communities. In each case, information is collected and compiled not only for households who escaped poverty or who fell into poverty, but also for those who remained poor or non-poor. Thus, comparisons can be made across categories of households.

Micro-level events, those affecting particular households, can be reliably investigated using *Stages-of-Progress*. Other methods are better suited for examining macro-level features of poverty and for undertaking cross-national comparisons. As discussed in the Appendix, combining different methods of investigation will help us learn jointly about micro-level reasons as well as higher-level structures and policy regimes.

At levels closer to the grassroots, *Stages-of-Progress* is useful, not only for research purposes but also in various practical ways. It can help us learn reliably and relatively cheaply about the nature of micro poverty traps that operate within particular contexts. More precisely targeted programs of assistance can be designed as a result of this knowledge.

Degrees of poverty can be distinguished: the poorest can be differentiated from those who are less poor. Further, those who have been persistently poor can be recognized apart from others who have fallen into poverty in the recent past. Development agencies interested to provide different forms of assistance to diverse sub-groups of poor people can utilize *Stages-of-Progress* for the purpose of identification.

Community groups can participate easily in the inquiry process. Given some training, they can also compile, code, and analyze these data. Thus, community-based poverty monitoring exercises can be undertaken using *Stages-of-Progress*. These exercises can also help provide an objective and transparent basis for evaluating alternative community investments and development projects. Once the reasons for escape and descent become known, investments can be selected that best address the most important reasons.

I am pleased that other scholars and several practitioners have selected *Stages-of-Progress* for their academic and practical projects.[21] Development support organizations have also found *Stages-of-Progress* useful.[22] Several adapted versions of this methodology have resulted. Their authors have graciously acknowledged having learned from *Stages-of-Progress*. The World Bank's Ladder of Life methodology also shares some core insights with *Stages-of-Progress* and has a similar sequence of steps, which is gratifying. No acknowledgment is given by these World Bank authors, but the direction of influence seems obvious: *Stages-of-Progress* was developed, made public, and shared with the World Bank team much before Ladder of Life was put together.[23]

To the best of my knowledge, *Stages* is the first retrospective methodology that has been employed on a large scale to track households' experiences over time. Many improvements have been made, and important safeguards have been incorporated, as this methodology was successively implemented in diverse locations. Some improvements that I am currently attempting to develop are discussed in the Appendix. Further refinements will be made in the future. Newer and better methodologies will also emerge as the task of investigating poverty flows gets mainstreamed.

CHAPTER 3

The Rising–Falling Tide

As scholars have developed new methods to examine poverty flows, new and encouraging results have come to light. The good news is that poverty is not an unchanging mass. Not all poor people in developing countries are mired in persistent poverty. The efforts that poor people make to cope with and overcome their unfortunate situations regularly produce large movements out of poverty.

Such hope-inspiring trends were visible in every region where I conducted such inquiries. In the very first community that I went into—the village of Khatikhera in Rajasthan, India—I found that a majority of formerly poor households had moved out of poverty. A total of 35 households had been poor a generation ago, but by 2002 as many as 19 of these 35 households no longer lived in conditions of poverty. They had no fear of being hungry in the immediate future, their children regularly attended schools, their houses did not leak during the rainy season, they had bought clothes which they could wear in public without feeling a sense of shame, and they were repaying their remaining debts in regular installments. In terms of their own reckoning and as judged by their neighbors, these households had succeeded in moving out of poverty.

Diverse pathways had been taken by these households. Bheru, son of Uda Raigar, set up a small grocery shop close to the bus station in a nearby large village. The profit that he made added to what his family had traditionally earned from flaying animal skins and manufacturing rough leather. Ram Singh, son of Man Singh, after attending school for eight years, was hired as a bus conductor by the government's transport agency. His regular monthly salary supplemented what his family earned by growing produce upon their small, unirrigated farm. Sitaram Purohit, assisted by a fellow villager who works in Mumbai, found part-time employment in a small cafeteria and sweet shop of this big city. Kishan Gujar sank a well on his family's farm, and he began to harvest two crops in most years instead of the single rain-fed crop that he had previously farmed. Varda, son of Chena Bhil, traveled to Ahmedabad, Gujarat, where he sold ice cream from a small cart that he pushes around from morning to night.[1]

Through these different means these households had managed to surmount the conditions of poverty in which they previously lived. None among them had become rich, to be sure, but all of them had experienced significant improvements.

Over the next several weeks, I was to hear similar accounts in every one of the 36 Rajasthan communities that I visited. Escapes from poverty were common and widespread. On average, 38 percent of all formerly poor households had escaped poverty within these communities. Many other people were traveling along similar pathways and it seemed likely that they would also escape poverty in the near future.

I was very glad to learn about these experiences, but at the same time I was perplexed. If many people had, in fact, moved out of poverty, then why did the aggregate poverty rate change so very slowly? I know the answer now, but at that time it still eluded me.

Were these communities of Rajasthan especially favored in some regard? The available statistics seemed to indicate otherwise. Compared to other states of India, Rajasthan has not been especially economically progressive, and I had deliberately selected a very diverse group of communities. However, large numbers of people had escaped poverty in every kind of community studied. I heard accounts of escape in large communities served by major roads as well as in smaller communities located deep in the interior. Community type did not seem to make any important difference to these results, nor was there anything extraordinary about the households who had escaped. None among them had received any windfall gains or sudden bequests, nor had any patronage benefits been given to them.

The answer to my puzzlement about the aggregate poverty rate was to be found elsewhere. I soon came to see what should have been obvious all along.

The good news about escapes formed only one part of the overall story. There was also, concurrently and consistently, a bad side to this news. In these communities, people had not only come out of poverty—large numbers of people had also fallen *into* poverty. Of the total of 6,376 households who inhabit these 36 rural communities, as many as 506 households (8 percent) had fallen into poverty within the past generation. Everywhere, there were the old poor and the newly impoverished. In all villages, both types of households lived side-by-side.

No caste group has remained immune from these parallel and opposite movements. The stock of poverty was higher, in general, among ritually lower castes, and it was especially high among people of the scheduled castes (former untouchables or present-day *Dalits*) and the scheduled tribes (India's aboriginal people). However, the relative rates of escape and descent were quite similar across caste groupings. Saddening experiences—as well as gladdening ones— were recounted in every caste-denominated village neighborhood.

It was disheartening, for instance, to hear the account narrated by Lakshman Singh. His family had started out quite well, inheriting the largest share of property bequeathed by Lakshman's grandfather, but a steady decline had commenced almost immediately. It had begun 15 years ago when his father died suddenly at a young age. Lakshman, who had then been just 18 years old, had been obliged to take charge of the household economy. Over the next seven years, a combination of illnesses, dowry expenses, and debts had aggravated this family's initial misfortune. Lakshman's son, Kalyan, who was about 12 years of age at the time of my visit, should have been attending school during the day, but since his parents could no longer afford to pay for a school uniform, textbooks, and other school supplies, Kalyan Singh stayed behind at home, helping his father farm the small piece of agricultural land that they still owned. Lakshman Singh was most worried, however, about his two young daughters: 'How are they to be married? We have no money left. Who will arrange for their dowries?' Lakshman was in poor health himself, made weak by a succession of illnesses, and I felt that if anything worse were to happen in the future, it would surely be the proverbial last straw, breaking this family's resolve and plunging them deeper into chronic poverty, with hardly any hope of finding a way out.

Sadly, this family's account was not an isolated one. I heard many other accounts of descents into poverty, many of which could very conceivably have been averted if some suitable support systems had been put in place earlier on.

This fact of widespread poverty creation came as a novel realization to me. I had all along thought that poverty could only be removed, implicitly assuming, along with many others, that all poor people *must* have been born poor. But my investigations showed that I was seriously mistaken. Members of nearly *one-third* of all currently poor households in these Rajasthan communities—31 percent to be exact—were not born into poverty: They had fallen into poverty within their lifetimes. Households who had previously lived reasonably comfortable lives were no longer able to send their children to school. Stocks of cattle had been sold by many of them in order to pay for mounting household expenses; debts had been run up at sky-high rates of interest; and outlays on food and clothing had been sharply cut back. I was beginning to see another—and very different—face of poverty.

Thinking that poverty creation might be more prevalent in Rajasthan, because this state had relatively low scores on many socio-economic indicators, my colleagues and I began our next set of investigations in Gujarat, an adjoining state of India, regarded by many as a poster child of industry-led economic growth. It seemed likely that a qualitatively different story would emerge from studying communities of Gujarat.

At first glance conditions certainly looked better in villages of this state. Many more cars and tractors were visible in the Gujarati countryside. I sensed that people in these villages were by and large more prosperous than those in Rajasthan.

But these surface impressions, gained in passing as one looked at village life through a car window or at roadside tea shops, were soon replaced by a very different set of facts. Poor people are plentiful in these Gujarat villages. Many have fallen into poverty within their lifetimes, and most of those who succumbed to poverty have remained poor for long periods of time. Conditions are such that many poor people have virtually no viable means available for escaping poverty. In a diverse group of ten communities of the Vadodara (formerly Baroda) district, part of the famed 'golden corridor' of industrial development in this state, the underlying dynamics were quite similar to those I had observed earlier in Rajasthan. A total of 165 households had escaped poverty in these Vadodara communities, but another 101 households had simultaneously fallen into poverty. Quite disparate trajectories were experienced by different households within each community.

Overall, in the 36 rural communities studied in four dissimilar districts of this more 'forward' state, only 560 households (9.5 percent of all households in these communities) had risen out of poverty over the 25-year period studied, but another 370 households (6.3 percent) had fallen into poverty. A higher economic growth rate has not helped to forestall descents into poverty, which have occurred alongside escapes within every Gujarati community studied.

Such parallel and opposite trends are hardly peculiar to these two Indian states. In other parts of India, as well as in the other countries and regions that I examined later, quite similar trends were in evidence. For instance, in the 20 communities of Western Kenya that I studied next, 18 percent of all households escaped poverty over the period 1977–2002—which is good news—but another 19 percent concurrently fell into poverty. Paradoxically, the stock of poverty in these communities *grew* by 1 percent, even as almost one-fifth of all households moved out of poverty.

Jane Okotti Ojola of Kalaka Village in Western Kenya informed me of the events that brought about her descent into poverty. Only about 25 years of age at the time that we met, Jane had been widowed two years earlier. Her husband died of a disease that was suspected to be some form of elephantiasis. He was ill for more than one year before he died. A great deal of money was spent on his treatment, for which the family arranged to take him to a hospital in Kisumu, the biggest city of this region. When he died, a lavish death feast was organized, involving the slaughter of two bulls and three goats, and the preparation of other delicacies. After paying for these medical and funeral expenses, Jane was left with no assets other than her shack and a donkey. She ekes out a bare living, selling drinking water from door to door. Jane has no children, so one might take some comfort from the fact that only one person was added to the pool of poverty. Her co-villager, Christina Opot, on the other hand, has four of her own children in addition to two orphans who were left in her care when her oldest daughter died, reportedly after suffering from HIV/AIDS. Christina's descent into poverty is more troublesome by comparison, because so many children's lives are also implicated.

Everywhere we looked—in India and Kenya, and later in Uganda, Peru, and North Carolina—a similar story emerged of poverty being created alongside poverty being overcome. The number of descents was smaller in some communities, for reasons that will be discussed in the next chapter, but not a single community moved up or moved down in unison. In every community, among nearly 400 studied, escapes and descents have occurred in parallel.

Rather than conceiving of poverty in terms of a pool with a rising tide—one that raises all households at the same time—I began to see how poverty is affected concurrently by a rising *and* a falling tide. One set of forces pushes people upward and out of the pool of poverty. Simultaneously, some other people are pushed downward and into this pool. The pool of poverty is regularly refreshed everywhere. Attending to poverty flows gives us a better idea of the magnitudes and the reasons involved.

In the rest of this chapter, we will explore the relative extents of both poverty flows. In the following chapters, we will look at the reasons associated with each flow, finding that the inflow and the outflow are separately responsive to different reasons.

The Natures of the Flows

Aggregate statistics continue to paint dismal pictures about large numbers living in poverty. However, analyzing the underlying trends reveals that there are also significant reasons for hope. In every one of nearly 400 communities studied in five separate countries, large numbers of formerly poor people have moved out of poverty. These positive achievements have been compromised everywhere, because another group of households concurrently fell into poverty.

Table 3.1 reproduces the extents of the two poverty flows that were observed in each region of study. Each row in Table 3.1 relates to a separate study, and each row illustrates how inflows and outflows have operated in parallel. The figures related to individual regions have been reported before in journal articles. Readers who are interested to learn more in respect of any specific region of study should look at the related journal article, mentioned in the second column of Table 3.1.[2]

Consider, for example, the row of Table 3.1 that reports the results from Andhra Pradesh, India: 14 percent of all households escaped poverty in the 36 rural communities studied here, which is remarkable and encouraging, but another 12 percent of all households fell into poverty over the same period. Overall, only a 2-percent net reduction in poverty resulted, but a total of 26 percent of households experienced a change in their poverty status.

Similarly large movements were also observed in other regions. A heartwarming rate of escapes from poverty was recorded in the 36 communities studied in Central and Western Uganda. A total of 24 percent of all households in these communities moved out of poverty over the 25-year period, 1980–2005.

Table 3.1 Escape and Descent (Percent of Total Households in Each Region)

Region	Study	Escaped Poverty	Became Poor	Change in Poverty
Rajasthan, India (35 communities, 6,376 households, 1975–2002)	Krishna (2004)	11%	8%	3%
Gujarat, India (36 communities, 5,817 households, 1976–2003)	Krishna, et al. (2005)	9%	6%	3%
Andhra Pradesh, India (36 communities, 5,536 households, 1976–2003)	Krishna (2006)	14%	12%	2%
Kenya (Western) (20 communities, 1,706 households, 1977–2002)	Krishna, et al. (2004)	18%	19%	Minus 1%
Uganda (Central and Western) (36 communities, 2,631 households, 1980–2005)	Krishna, et al. (2006b)	24%	15%	9%
Peru (Cajamarca and Puno) (40 communities, 3,817 households, 1979–2004)	Kristjanson, et al. (2007) and Krishna, et al. (2006a)	17%	8%	9%
North Carolina (four counties) (13 communities, 312 households; 1995–2005)	Krishna, et al. (2006)	23%	12%	11%

However, the drains into the pool of poverty have also flowed fast. Over the same period, an additional 15 percent of all households fell into poverty. Even in communities of North Carolina, where per capita income is an order of magnitude higher than in any of the other regions studied, large numbers of households, 12 percent in all, fell into poverty over the ten-year period of study.

Poverty is essentially dynamic in nature. Change constantly reconfigures the pool of the poor, which is simultaneously both ebbing and growing.

Disaggregating poverty, considering its two constituent flows, helps us to understand better what is actually happening in some region. It is otherwise impossible to understand why the stock of poverty fell by only 9 percent in the 40 communities studied in Peru, even though a total of 17 percent of households moved out of poverty—or why the stock of poverty grew in

Table 3.2 Variations across Communities in the Same Province and Region

Location	Percentage of Households Who:				Reduction in the Stock of Poverty (Percent)
	Remained Poor (A)	Escaped Poverty (B)	Became Poor (C)	Remained Non-poor (D)	
Andhra Pradesh, India (1976–2003)					
Sultanpurthanda	23.6	49.4	3.4	23.6	46.1
Bhojathanda	55.6	1.0	40.4	3.0	−39.4
Western Kenya (1975–2002)					
Buronya	15.3	47.2	5.6	31.9	41.6
Asere B	15.9	1.8	32.7	49.6	−30.9
Cajamarca, Peru (1994–2004)					
Alto Peru	9.1	23.6	12.7	54.5	10.9
El Aliso	51.5	13.6	13.6	21.2	0
Campo Alegre	9.4	6.3	17.2	67.2	−10.9

Western Kenya communities even as 18 percent of all households moved *out* of poverty.

Equally important is the need to disaggregate geographically. Aggregate statistics tend to gloss over and hide the considerable differences that exist among communities of the same region. While in one community larger numbers have escaped poverty, in another community, located quite close by, much larger numbers fell into poverty over the same period.

Table 3.2 reproduces some striking examples of such inter-community differences in three selected regions. Similar differences were in evidence in each of the other regions examined.

The first two rows of this table show how diametrically opposite trends have operated in two villages that are located just a few kilometers apart in Nalgonda District of Andhra Pradesh, India. Because 49 percent of households came out of poverty in the first village, Sultanpurthanda, while only 3 percent of households fell into poverty in this village, its stock of poverty fell by a total of 46 percent. Concurrently, in the second village, Bhojathanda, only 1 percent of all households moved out of poverty, while as many as 40 percent fell into poverty. The pool of poverty in Bhojathanda has grown much larger as a result.

National economic growth or the state government's policies do not help explain these disparate experiences. Micro-level factors better account for these stark differences. The exploitation of a local potential for lift irrigation helped many families escape poverty in the first village, Sultanpurthanda. In the second village, Bhojathanda, an insidious growth of salinity in the main drinking water source resulted in producing debilitating illnesses over time. Many individuals fell seriously ill. Several succumbed to their illnesses. Further losses were caused because cattle also died in large numbers.

Clearly, different kinds of assistance will be required in these two villages.[3] They happen to be located close to one another, but they have experienced very different trends. It is very important to know more about such geographic differences. Lacking this knowledge, we remain ill-prepared to provide assistance in the form and to the places where it will do the most good.

Overall, the stock of poverty may remain fairly constant, but that may not be because things are unchanging. As Table 3.2 shows, substantial movements into and out of poverty have occurred even in communities such as El Aliso in Peru where the overall stock of poverty remained virtually unchanged over the period examined. A total of 65 percent of all households were poor in El Aliso in 1994, and the same number, 65 percent, were poor in 2004—but not all people who had been poor in 1994 were still poor in 2004, and vice versa, not all who were poor in 2004 had been poor ten years earlier. A total of 13.6 percent of all households moved out of poverty over this ten-year period, and *another* 13.6 percent of households moved into poverty. The situation was hardly dull or static, although looking only at the stock figure—which did not budge—can result in depicting an unchanging situation.

Disaggregated poverty knowledge is essential for generating better policy designs. By facilitating the collection of disaggregated and decentralized poverty knowledge, the *Stages-of-Progress* methodology can help identify the natures of threats and opportunities in each specific location. Geographic poverty traps can be isolated.[4] Local potentials for growth can be tapped.

The results reported above are not, however, peculiar to the methodology adopted or the regions selected for study. Other scholars using other methods to study poverty flows in other contexts have independently arrived at quite similar results. In Asia, Africa, and North and South America, everywhere household and individual poverty has been tracked over time, the simultaneity of escapes

Table 3.3 A Common Finding

(1) Country/ Region	(2) Study	(3) Period	(4) Sample Size (households)	(5) Percentage Escaped Poverty	(6) Percentage Fell into Poverty
Bangladesh	Sen (2003)	1987–2000	379	26	18
Egypt	Haddad and Ahmed (2003)	1997–9	347	6	14
India (Rural)	Bhide and Mehta (2004)	1970–82	3,139	23	13
South Africa	Carter and May (2001)	1993–8	1,171	10	25
Uganda	Deininger and Okidi (2003)	1992–2000	1,300	29	12
Chile	Scott (2000)	1968–86	200	23	8

and descents has been found to be a recurrent feature. Table 3.3 reproduces results from a geographically diverse selection of recent studies.

These studies reported in Table 3.3 have considered different sample sizes, ranging from a small group of 347 households in a few communities of Egypt to over 3,000 households in rural India. Statistically representative samples for entire countries are included, alongside studies of particular regions or groups of communities. Different periods of time are considered, ranging from a short span of three years to longer periods of 14 years.

Commonly, however, these studies help illustrate the essentially dynamic nature of poverty. Everywhere, poverty was simultaneously created and overcome. In two of the six cases reported in this table, those from Egypt and South Africa, the numbers of households who fell into poverty exceeds the numbers of households who escaped. Poverty grew in these regions, even as many households escaped poverty. Other studies, not discussed here, have generated similar conclusions.[5]

We can no longer continue to think of poverty as a slow-changing stock. This ill-conceived image of poverty was an artifact of previously used methods of study. New methods have helped reveal how inward and outward flows constantly reconstitute the composition of the poor. Attending directly to these flows should be the central concern of anti-poverty policies.

Why Worry About Descents?

How seriously should one view the fact that people fall into poverty in considerable numbers? What part of the anti-poverty budget should be re-allocated
toward stemming descents?

In order to answer these questions more persuasively, additional information
is required about the nature—particularly about the persistence and depth—of
descents. Do descents into poverty always or mostly get reversed within short
periods of time? Are descents primarily experienced among people who live
precariously, teetering just above the poverty line? Are these mostly marginal
events, occurring within remotely located communities, or are communities at
the mainstreams of economic life also affected by adverse poverty flows?

Relatively little evidence concerning these issues has been available in the
past. Consequently—lacking evidence to the contrary—analysts and policy
makers have been prone to regard descents as temporary and marginal occurrences. Lifting people out of poverty has been their over-riding concern.
Descents were thought to be part of the less serious problem of transitory (or
temporary) poverty.[6] As we will see later in this chapter, while the terms chronic
and transitory poverty are critically important, they can be inappropriately
applied in the context of poverty flows. Descents into poverty can have short-
lived as well as longer lasting effects, helping produce both transitory *and*
chronic poverty. The question remains: How much of each type of poverty gets
produced as a result of descents?

Previous studies have not provided any compelling answers to this question.
While they have shown that descents into poverty are widespread, the question
of reversibility has not been directly addressed by investigations of the past.

Several studies show how, in addition to near-poor people, others who were
well off in the past also experienced descents. For instance, one study conducted
in KwaZulu-Natal, South Africa, found that quite large swings had been experienced by households belonging to both ends of the economic spectrum.[7]
Among households whose expenditure levels in 1993 were equal to *twice* the
poverty line, as many as 26 percent suffered precipitous descents, and by 1998
their expenditure levels fell below *half* the poverty line. On the other hand, 14
percent of those who were deeply in poverty in 1993 had expenditures in 1998
that were greater than twice the poverty line. Thus, it was not only people clus-
tered around the poverty line who fell into (or climbed out of) poverty.

Another study, undertaken in southern India, found a 'high incidence of reshuffling of households in the income ranking recorded between the two survey years [1971 and 1981]. One-third of all households in the bottom decile moved into one of the top five deciles, while one-quarter of those in the top decile slipped into the lower half of the household per capita income distribution.'[8] A third study, also undertaken in southern India, examined changes in rural households' ownership of their most precious asset, agricultural land, over 50 years. Remarkably, it was found 'that no less than 25 percent of the landless in 1920 had moved upward into the landed category by 1970.'[9] Downward mobility was even more significant: 44 percent of those who had significant amounts of land in 1920 had lost *all* of their landholdings by 1970.

The first few *Stages-of-Progress* investigations, conducted in Rajasthan, Gujarat, Andhra Pradesh, and Western Kenya, also found that along with those who were marginally above the poverty cut-off considerable numbers of formerly well-to-do people had also suffered descents.[10] Households who had previously had the capacity to purchase jewelry and acquire refrigerators now could not afford to send their children to school. Many had incurred high-interest debts. Several individuals were at risk of becoming bonded debtors, thereby jeopardizing any remaining chances they might have of escaping poverty in the future.

The fact that richer as well as poorer people suffer descents into poverty has thus been repeatedly demonstrated. However, little direct evidence has been available so far that can help establish the extent to which descents are reversed over time and the extent to which they tend to persist and harden, producing not transitory but chronic poverty.

A later group of *Stages-of-Progress* investigations addressed this question directly. These later studies examined two consecutive time periods. Tracking households over both periods made it possible to ascertain how many V-shaped movements had actually occurred: How many people who had fallen into poverty during the first period had moved out of poverty during the second period; and, vice versa, how many of the people who had escaped poverty during the first period had fallen back into poverty during the second period?

These results are, once again, of a good-news/bad-news type. In the majority of cases, escapes have endured: Most people who escaped poverty in the earlier period did not revert to poverty during the second time period. Unfortunately, the majority of descents have also persisted. Most of those who had fallen into poverty were not able to recover later.

Studying households in 36 Ugandan communities over two separate time periods, respectively, 1980–95, and 1995–2005, we found that 6 percent of all households had fallen into poverty during the first time period. Only one-third of these households (that is, 2 percent of the total number) managed to escape poverty during the second time period. The majority—two-thirds—of those who had fallen into poverty during the first period continued to be poor ten years later. At the end of the second time period, these households were still poor. Contrary to what one might have expected (and hoped), descents into poverty were only infrequently reversed. We examined the conditions, in 2005, of households who had experienced descents between 1980 and 1995. Of 344 such households, as many as 24 percent were not capable of obtaining food and clothing on any assured basis, and another 29 percent had removed their children from schools.

One such account of descent into persistent poverty was provided by Musebezi, a young man of Kikoni village in Ntumgamo district, Uganda.

> My father died and I had to drop out of school because we had no money to pay for school fees. My father's land was divided. My brothers and I received our shares. The piece of land that I inherited is too small for me to make a living by raising crops or animals. Furthermore, coffee has been affected by the wilt, and that has additionally reduced my income. Now my family depends on casual labor and on hiring land from other people upon which we can grow something.

Notice how multiple reasons for descent operated in this case, producing a cumulative long-term effect. The death of his father, who had been the major income earner of this household, had been followed by a customary division of land, which resulted in Musebezi inheriting an economically unviable fragment the productivity of which was further reduced by crop disease. Three negative events occurred in succession, with no means of protection available to Musebezi and many others like him. Few among the descents that occurred in this region were reversed in the following years.

Falling into poverty is not merely a temporary inconvenience. It has had long-term deleterious consequences for large numbers of households in each region studied.

Our inquiries in Peru, North Carolina, and Kenya generated very similar results. Like the Uganda study, each of these other studies also considered two adjacent periods of time. In each case, we found that the majority of those who fell into poverty during the first time period were still poor at the end of the second time period. Many among them had remained persistently poor for periods of ten years or longer.

Younger as well as older households have fallen into chronic poverty. As we will see in the next chapter, age of household head has relatively little explanatory significance, although particular life-cycle events, especially marriages and deaths, are importantly involved in many cases of descent. In fact, few household characteristics (apart from gender) help explain households' descents into poverty. Richer as well as poorer, smaller as well as larger, and surprisingly, educated as well as uneducated, households have suffered descents.

Rather than household characteristics, escapes and descents are better explained with reference to discrete events, as we will see in the following chapter. All households encounter ordinary events that raise the risk of descending into poverty. Successions of negative events have plunged even quite comfortably off households into chronic poverty.

A *micro poverty trap*, corresponding to a low-level equilibrium, tends to ensnare many households who experience descents.[11] Their asset stocks become so far depleted that income and consumption regularly fall below the poverty cut-off. Experiencing one or more negative events forces households to sell off some part of their assets. Selling only one or two cows or goats may not be so bad, but as successively more assets are sold there comes a point when a critical threshold is crossed.[12] Households falling below this threshold of asset ownership find themselves held within a micro poverty trap. Their capacity to earn becomes impaired to such an extent that it is nearly impossible to escape poverty in the future.

Because falling into poverty is not easily or often reversed, averting descents in the first place becomes all the more important. Consider the account related by Marcos Honorio Carrera of Cholocal in the district of Cachachi, Peru: 'I was much better off than my neighbors when my wife of 25 years became ill with cancer of the uterus. I was obliged to sell my animals, cows, oxen, and donkeys, and I also went into debt in order to care for her, and later, bury her. Today, old and sick, I have to find work as a day laborer.'

Marcos Honorio and several others like him have been reduced to the situation of the poorest people in their communities. They have been forced by events to liquidate their stocks of assets. As a result, reversing their descents into poverty has become an exceedingly difficult task.

Imagine what might have transpired instead if suitable forms of preventive assistance had been available. Thousands of other descents in these communities—and thousands of descents waiting to happen in the future—are unnecessary and eminently avoidable occurrences.

It is not only in remote or 'left-behind' communities that descents into poverty have occurred in large numbers. In all communities studied—no matter how remotely or how centrally they are located—escapes and descents have co-occurred, affecting households at different points in the wealth distribution. In capital cities and other current-day foci of economic growth, large numbers of people have fallen into poverty. In Nairobi, the capital city of Kenya, and in Mombasa, the second-largest city of this country, 10 percent of our random sample of households fell into poverty over the eight-year period, 1990–8. Less than one-third of these households were able to bounce back over the next eight-year period.

Evidence collected in industrialized countries shows how descents occur as well within these contexts. An examination conducted within 14 OECD countries refers to the 'two faces of poverty' that 'are evident in all of the countries analyzed, but their relative importance varies. On average across all countries, about 5 percent of the population, not previously poor, enter poverty each year.'[13] Within the communities that we studied in North Carolina, USA, 6 percent of all households became poor over the five-year period, 1995–2000. Less than half of these households were able to recover their previous positions over the next five years, during which time another 12 percent of all households became poor. Analyses conducted in other parts of the United States also demonstrate the co-occurrence of escapes and descents.[14]

In fact, the frequency of descents appears to have *increased* within the United States. 'Poverty entries and exits have changed over the past two decades, with the mid-1990s seeing an increase in both entries into poverty and exits from poverty. The number of people entering and exiting remained relatively constant from 1975 until the early 1990s, when both [trends] jumped dramatically.'[15] Observing these trends, Jacob Hacker has concluded that 'while the gaps between the rungs on the ladder of the American economy have increased, what has increased even more quickly is how far people slip *down* the ladder when they lose their financial footing. The chance that families will see their incomes plummet has risen.'[16]

Descents into poverty are frequent and widespread, they are not easily or quickly reversed in most cases, and they are experienced by better-off as well as not so well-off households and communities. Clearly, those who are only marginally above the poverty cut-off are more at risk of falling into poverty, but the danger of descent, the vulnerability to poverty, also extends upward along the prosperity scale.

Increasing Vulnerability?

Are these dangers becoming smaller or larger as the world becomes more connected and as average incomes grow in the developing world? In the United States, signs point toward increasing vulnerability, as discussed above. Are similar increases in vulnerability also afflicting people in the developing world?

It would be comforting if the risk of descent were decreasing over the years, as a result perhaps of economic growth, accompanied by improved social and physical infrastructure and better social protection. It is difficult, however, to come to any firm judgment on this question.

Hardly any data are available that can help discern whether the pace of descents has accelerated or slowed down. Data sets such as the Panel Study of Income Dynamics (PSID), a nationally representative sample of US families, and the European Community Household Panel make it possible to discern vulnerability trends within a group of OECD countries. Such longitudinal data simply do not exist for developing countries. Data tracking the same households over one period of time are rare enough. Tracking households over two separate periods has hardly ever been attempted.

Such multiple-period studies are necessary, however, for getting a grasp of whether and how the risk of descent has increased or decreased. They are also essential for persuading policy makers about the non-reversibility and serious-ness of descents.

As discussed above, two-time-period evidence was collected by the *Stages-of-Progress* studies that were undertaken in Uganda, Peru, North Carolina, and Kenya. Despite the obvious dissimilarities, a common and worrying trend was observed. In each of these places, vulnerability has risen sharply. Many more people fell into poverty during the more recent time period studied compared to the preceding period.

The study conducted in Uganda showed, for instance, that while the rate of escapes did not change appreciably between the first and the second time periods

Table 3.4 Escape and Descent over Two Time Periods in Uganda

	Communities of	*Percent of All Households Who:*	
		Escaped Poverty	Fell Into Poverty
1st time period	Central Region	15.6	6.4
(1980–95)	Western Region	10.0	4.6
2nd time period	Central Region	17.2	13.4
(1995–2005)	Western Region	10.4	11.6

examined, the pace of descents increased dramatically. Compared to the earlier time period, *more than twice as many* households succumbed to poverty during the later time period (Table 3.4).

A total of 6.4 percent of all households fell into poverty in communities of Uganda's Central Region during the first period (1980–95), but many more households—13.4 percent—fell into poverty during the second period (1995–2005). Similarly, in communities of Western Region, 4.6 percent of households fell into poverty during the first period, but more than twice as many—11.6 percent—fell into poverty during the second period.

Economic growth in Uganda was faster during the second period compared to the first period,[17] and everything else remained the same; poverty reduction should also have been faster during the second period, but because descents have been twice as frequent during the second period compared to the first period, the pace of poverty reduction has actually slowed down. The national stock of poverty increased from seven million to nine million between 1999 and 2002,[18] possibly because descents into poverty have also become more numerous within other Ugandan regions.[19]

The pace of descents has accelerated as well within the communities we studied in Peru. Four percent of all households fell into poverty during the 15-year period, 1979–94, but more than 8 percent fell into poverty over the next ten years, 1994–2004. Data from North Carolina, USA, give similar indication of rising vulnerability. While the pace of escapes from poverty changed relatively little, from 16 percent in the first sub-period (1995–2000) to 13 percent in the second sub-period (2000–5), the pace of descents shot up from 6 percent during the first sub-period to 12 percent during the second sub-period. The risk of descent had doubled within each of these quite dissimilar contexts.

Table 3.5 Percentage of Households Who Fell into Poverty in Different Livelihood Zones of Kenya

Livelihood zones	1st Time Period (1990–8)	2nd Time Period (1998–2006)
Livelihood zone 1	9	11
Livelihood zone 2	7	14
Livelihood zone 3	7	13
Livelihood zone 4	8	22
Urban zone	10	15

Notes: Livelihood Zone 1: Mixed farming high potential—food crops, tea, coffee, sugarcane, livestock. Districts: Nyeri, Kirinyaga, Butere Mumias, and Nandi.
Livelihood Zone 2: Mixed farming lower potential—food crops, livestock, and some cash crops. Districts: Kisumu, Busia, and Migori.
Livelihood Zone 3: Mixed farming marginal with livestock—food crops, livestock, palm, coffee, pyrethrum. Districts: Laikipia, Makueni, Tharaka, and Kilifi.
Livelihood Zone 4: Pastoral—livestock, some food crops. Districts: Marsabit, Tana River, and Wajir.

While the studies discussed above considered a specific set of communities, selected purposively in a few selected regions or counties, a follow-up study in Kenya, undertaken in 2006, adopted a different selection technique. Following a process of stratified random sampling, a group of 71 communities (rural villages and urban neighborhoods) were selected that are nationally representative in a statistical sense.[20] The results from this study (presented in Table 3.5) also show how vulnerability has increased appreciably in more recent times. In every one of five separate livelihood zones of this country—corresponding to areas with common agro-ecological conditions and livelihood options—considerably more descents into poverty occurred during the later time period compared to the earlier one.

These results point commonly toward a disquieting trend of rising vulnerability. Similar investigations in other regions and countries will help reveal whether or not any such general conclusion is warranted. However, evidence reviewed in the next chapter provides additional indication that growing numbers of people in diverse countries are becoming susceptible to micro poverty traps.

Be that as it may, one thing is for certain: Large numbers fall into poverty with a regularity that is disturbing. There are signs that these numbers might be growing larger still, but that might not be equally true in all places. Everywhere, however, descents are occurring in parallel with escapes from poverty.

Unfortunately, relatively little preventive assistance has been available in most contexts, and households facing impending descents have generally been left to their own devices. Conclusions from an investigation conducted in Zambia are illustrative in this regard: 'Despite the constant barrage of shocks and misfortunes that afflict Zambia's poor, there are few effective public policies and programs to promote security and address the needs of households who are exposed to frequent shocks. The programs that exist have low coverage and are under-financed and poorly implemented.'[21]

Lack of information about the frequency, intensity, and long-lasting effects of descents has resulted in producing a situation in which preventive measures have been under-funded in most countries. Now that more data on poverty flows have started becoming available, descents into poverty should be better appreciated and more effectively addressed.

Conclusion: Curbing Future Poverty

No collection of households—whether aggregated at the community level, at the regional level, or most of all, at the national level—rises out of or falls into poverty in unison. Under the same umbrella of macroeconomic policies and national growth rates, very different fates are experienced by neighboring households. Poverty is created, destroyed, and preserved, all at the same time. Everywhere, newly impoverished people live alongside those who have surmounted poverty and others who are chronically poor.

A considerable part of poverty is not inherited. In the 40 Peruvian communities studied, for example, members of more than one-third of currently poor households have not always been poor. They have become chronically poor within their lifetimes. Similarly large groups of households who have fallen into poverty inhabit each of the other regions investigated.

Could these and other descents into poverty have been prevented? Evidence advanced in the next chapter indicates that the reasons associated with descents can, in fact, be mitigated. Multiple actors—governments, NGOs, donor agencies, private foundations, social movements, and others—can do a great deal to reduce the flow of households into poverty.

Preventing poverty creation more effectively in the future will require doing things differently from the past. First of all, it will require changing the image that has so far principally informed our conceptions of poverty.

The faces of the poor are ever-changing, but our mental images, shored up by the available aggregate statistics, tend to depict poverty as a historical legacy: 'the poor are always with us.' Language reinforces this mental imagery. 'Poverty' becomes the problem, assuming a life of its own. We speak of 'the poor' as if we could tell apart members of some clearly distinguishable group, yet we have little idea of where to draw the boundaries of this group and of the processes driving change in the group's composition. Rather than dealing with any undifferentiated category of the 'the poor,' it is better to consider distinct sub-groups.[22] Reasons associated with the separate trajectories of different sub-groups of poor people need to be separately identified and addressed using context-appropriate measures. As John Toye has stated, 'we need to stop thinking about poverty in terms of a stock of poor people, often seen as helpless victims who need some kind of treatment, and to start thinking about poverty in terms of flows.'[23]

Any change in the stock of poverty is a resultant of two independent flows. Trying to explain the end result without looking directly at the constitutive flows makes little sense, especially since diverse flow combinations can produce the same end result. Disaggregating poverty in terms of escapes and descents helps to gain a better understanding of the influences associated with change. The budget for anti-poverty programs can be more effectively utilized when it is directed toward the streams of influence that matter most within each separate context.

Escapes and descents are separately responsive to different reasons, as we will see in the next two chapters. Defeating poverty requires mounting a two-front war: (a) preventing descents by alleviating region-specific micro poverty traps; and (b) promoting upward mobility through accelerating and augmenting escapes from poverty.[24] More effective preventive actions need to be taken in the future. It should prove less expensive to prevent poverty than to invest in poverty relief once people have become chronically poor. How much, for instance, do governments, donors, and others spend on housing and other welfare assistance that could have been saved earlier in the process through better preventive measures? Taking preventive actions will also serve as an additional stimulus for escapes from poverty. When people are less fearful of the possibility of descent, they will be more likely to take up initiatives that help improve their circumstances.

Future poverty needs to be dealt with before it comes into existence. A new category of analysis needs to be adopted, and new kinds of interventions must be employed. The newly impoverished (and those who are vulnerable to impoverishment for the same kinds of reasons) need to be acknowledged and assisted through context-appropriate interventions.

Researchers have directed attention toward two important analytical categories: chronic and transitory poverty. This distinction—between those who have been persistently poor and others who are shorter term residents in the pool of poverty—is an important one.[25] Over time, however, the distinction between chronic and transitory poverty tends to become blurred. Some among those who are entering poverty will bounce right back. For them, poverty will be only a transitory condition, but for many others—and in some cases, the majority of those who experience descents—poverty will abide, becoming a chronic condition. It is hard to tell in advance, simply by looking at them, who are in transitional poverty and who will go on to become chronically poor. Transitory poverty can become chronic poverty over time. Conversely, chronic poverty can be exited: People can transition out of poverty after having remained poor for long periods of time. Those who suffer descents can, at different points in time, occupy both categories: Transitory and chronic.

Dealing with the newly impoverished as either transitorily or chronically poor amounts, however, to shutting the stable door after the horse has bolted. The most suitable interventions in their cases are those directed toward *preventing* the initial descent. By neglecting to adopt policies that help restrict descents into poverty we are effectively giving up the fight against poverty even before we have started.

Stemming poverty creation must become an integral part of the anti-poverty agenda. In the following chapters, we will examine the reasons associated, respectively, with descents and with escapes, understanding how descents can be more effectively prevented, and how increasing numbers of escapes from poverty can be facilitated in different regions of the world.

CHAPTER 4

Reasons for Descent:
The Health Poverty Trap

Why do people fall into poverty? Are they lazy, uncaring, or dissipated? Do they fall victim, instead, to circumstances beyond their control? What reasons have been associated most often with past descents into poverty? What should be done in the future to reduce the risk of descent?

We examined these questions with the help of more than 10,000 household event histories. The sequence of events, including the timing of descent into (or escape from) poverty, was carefully reconstructed, so that events preceding descent (or escape) could be distinguished from other events that took place later on. Such event histories were recorded for thousands of households who fell into poverty and for thousands of other households who remained non-poor or moved out of poverty. Comparing event histories across different categories of households helped us learn more about how descents and escapes have taken place.

We found that discrete events, rather than any particular household characteristics, are closely associated with both poverty flows. While one set of events is related to descents into poverty, a different set of events is associated with escapes. This asymmetry of reasons between escapes and descents is a basic and recurrent feature. Other investigations, using other methodologies, have also uncovered evidence of asymmetry, albeit on a smaller scale. In an influential article examining poverty spells—periods of time spent in poverty by particular households—Mary Jo Bane and David Ellwood found that events associated with the commencement of a spell in poverty in the United States were different in nature from other events that helped end households' spells in poverty.[1]

Subsequent investigations carried out in other contexts have continued to provide support for this important finding.[2]

Two types of events—positive and negative—need to be distinguished. Positive events have a buoyant effect, improving households' economic prospects. Negative events drag households downward. Over longer periods of time, households tend to experience multiple events, some of which are negative while others are positive. The balance of negative and positive events that a household experiences determines whether it will move up or move down. In the next chapter, we will see how the balance of events is critically important; no single event usually accounts for as much.

Policy effectiveness lies in raising the overall buoyancy of a society by facilitating positive events while preventing negative ones. Two sets of anti-poverty policies need to be implemented in tandem. Countries and communities where preventive measures were put in place alongside other measures that facilitated movements out of poverty are the ones that have the lowest poverty rates.

In this chapter, we will look at the nature of negative events that have been associated with descents into poverty in each of the different contexts examined. The following chapter examines positive events more directly while investigating households' escapes from poverty.

Chains of Negative Events

Descents into poverty do not usually occur all of a sudden. In general, households fall into poverty in stages. Rather than any single momentous event, chains of ordinary events are involved.

One Indian village resident expressed it as follows: 'A single blow can be endured by most people, but when several blows fall one after the other then it becomes very hard for any individual to cope.' The ability of any household to suffer successive 'blows' is related to its initial wealth category, and households who live closer to the margin (and whose kinsmen are also relatively poor) can withstand fewer blows before succumbing to persistent poverty. However, the *nature* of negative factors is the same in each case. Relatively richer and relatively poorer households have fallen into poverty on account of similar types of negative events.

The nature of these events was identified in each separate context after evaluating and comparing a large number of event histories. Consider, for example, the experience of Heera Gujar, a farmer in Rajasthan, India, whose story of descent into poverty we read earlier, in Chapter 1.

> We were among the more prosperous households of our village. We owned land. We also owned many heads of cattle. But things changed for the worse, and today we are among the poorest people in our village, the recipients of community handouts on religious holidays.
>
> The bad days began when my father fell ill about 18 years ago. They say he was stricken by TB [tuberculosis]. We took him several times to the district hospital, about 35 kilometers away. Each time we spent a considerable amount of money. We must have spent close to 25,000 rupees on his treatment, but to no avail. When my father died, we performed the customary death feast, spending another 10,000 rupees. We sold our cattle, and we also had to take out some loans. We worked harder in order to repay these debts. Then, about ten years ago, my wife fell seriously ill, and she has still not recovered. We borrowed more money to pay for her medical treatments. More than 20,000 rupees were spent for this purpose. It became hard to keep up with our debts. Somehow we could make do for another two or three years. Then the rains failed for three years in a row, and that was the end of the road for us. We sold our land.
>
> Now, my sons and I work as casual labor, earning whatever we can from one day to the next. On some days, we find work. On other days, there is nothing.

Coding this account in terms of reasons—after first verifying it, like all other such interviews, with other members of this household and with the community group—we came up with the following sequence of negative events: ill-health and high health care expenses (on account of his father), social and customary expenses (related to the death feast), ill-health and high health care expenses again (on account of his wife), high-interest consumption debt, and rainfall failure. A succession of negative events contributed toward this household's descent into poverty, and they were unable to shake off these effects, gradually becoming persistently poor.

A contrasting experience is illustrated by the event history of the Daniel household. Residents of Kitovu Village of Mukono District in the Central Region of Uganda, Bukenya and his wife, Lutaaya, were desperately poor in 1995. Located at Stage 1 of the poverty ladder, they were barely able to feed themselves on any assured basis.

Following the example of his neighbors and with a little financial help from his relatives, Bukenya began to plant vanilla on a small plot of land that he possessed. As the returns from the vanilla crop started coming in, his wife, Lutaaya, began to invest in farm animals. First, she bought some chickens and, later, acquiring a few cows, she started a small dairy business, selling milk in the neighboring villages. It was at about this time that their household moved above the poverty threshold—and they have continued rising higher yet. Next, Bukenya opened a small shop in his village, selling foodstuffs and other daily necessities. He described himself proudly as 'a businessman' when we interviewed him at his home in the summer of 2005.

In sequence, help from relatives, diversification into commercial crops, and diversification through livestock constituted the reasons that contributed to this household's escape from poverty. Diversification through small business also helped, but it occurred after (and not before) this household's escape from poverty, so it was not included among the list of reasons involved in this escape.

Why were other households not able to take similar pathways out of poverty? Why could they not take up such seemingly obvious forms of diversification? Despite the availability of clear pathways out of poverty, why are so many people persistently poor?

A large part of the explanation has to do with the occurrence of negative events. Households who have become poor or who have remained poor have experienced more negative and fewer positive events. Analyzing the experiences of such households shows how most of them have exerted efforts to overcome poverty. The effects of these positive efforts were nullified, however, by the simultaneous occurrence of negative events. Serious illnesses and rainfall failure offset Heera Gujar's strenuous efforts to overcome the downward tugs that he had experienced. He worked harder, farming his land more intensively than before, but negative events kept occurring, pushed him backward time after time. Other poor households have been similarly beset by chains of negative events.

Observing continuing poverty in some households should not be taken to imply that nothing significant is happening within those households. Nearly all households, even the poorest that were interviewed, have been taking steps to lift themselves out of poverty. Like King Bruce's proverbial spider, however, two steps forward were followed by three steps backward for them. Unforeseen negative events have resulted in a reversal of fortune.

If only these negative events had been better guarded against in the past, poverty in these communities and many others would have been so much lower at the present time. More effective preventive measures are necessary for helping make people's self-help efforts more fruitful in the future.

How can people be better protected against the negative reasons that afflict them? A number of reasons for descent have operated within each of the different regions studied, and it is important to examine the nature of these negative reasons before discussing what should be done to mitigate their effects. No uniform preventive policy will be effective in every part of the world. The chains of negative events that push people into poverty differ in important respects from one region to the next.

One element of preventive policy is commonly required. Ill-health and high health care costs have contributed to the majority of descents examined in every context studied. In low-average-income regions, such as rural Rajasthan or urban Kisumu, as much as in higher-average-income regions, such as North Carolina in the United States, the majority of households who have become poor have experienced one or more serious health incidents. Households who have remained persistently poor have also experienced a disproportionately high level of health-related events involving major expenditures. The setbacks that these households have suffered include an important component of high health care costs.

Several other factors are also associated with falling into poverty, but in terms of frequency and magnitude, the effects of ill-health and health care expenses predominate in every region examined. Ill-health—when high treatment costs go together with loss of earning power—imposes a double burden on households and it has the biggest influence on becoming poor (and remaining in poverty).[3] Researchers who have examined these trends have concluded that a medical poverty trap is operating across multiple countries.

Thousands of families are living only one illness away from poverty, and thousands more have become deeply indebted on account of burdensome health care costs. Investing in more affordable and effective health care interventions is essential for reducing people's vulnerability to descents into poverty.

Other types of intervention are also required, directed toward other, context-specific reasons for descent. Different chains of negative events have been responsible for descents into poverty in diverse regions, as we will see below. Location-specific reasons for descent need to be identified before the mix of interventions appropriate to any given context can be ascertained. These reasons are discussed below for the different regions in which we undertook such investigations. The analytical procedures that helped identify these reasons are also briefly discussed.

Identifying Location-specific Reasons for Descents

At the time when we undertook our investigations, a total of 35,567 households resided within the 398 communities that we studied in five countries. Of these households, as many as 3,784 households (11 percent of the total) had experienced descents into poverty. What events and processes and what household characteristics help tell apart these formerly non-poor households from other households who have remained non-poor?

Reasons for descent were identified using the following procedure. Within each particular region where common stages of progress were identified, we looked to see what was similar among households who fell into poverty. What types of processes and events and what manner of household characteristics are widely shared among all households who experienced descent? In the next step, we examined events, processes, and characteristics associated with households who have remained non-poor. What characteristics, processes, and events are common to this second set of households?

Comparing across these two sets of factors—those common to descending households and those common to households who have remained non-poor—a particular sub-set of factors was identified. Factors included within this sub-set satisfy two criteria simultaneously. They are (a) commonly associated with the experiences of households who have fallen into poverty; and (b) commonly *not* associated with households who have remained out of poverty. This procedure, combining an analysis of similarity (within a category) and an analysis of difference (across categories), constitutes the crux of the comparative method. It is also the logic that underlies and empowers multiple regression analyses, which we conducted separately using *Stages-of-Progress* data.[4]

Proceeding in this manner—making comparisons systematically across different categories of households—helped identify quite clearly the proximate or micro-level reasons that are associated, respectively, with descent and escape. Higher-level reasons—national and international effects—were not always clearly known to the people whom we interviewed, nor indeed did we ask them to speculate about such distant causes. We inquired only about the particular events that people knew about with certainty, and we cross-checked this information with other household members as well as with a community-level focus group. Making the link between national policy and international events was a subsequent task, undertaken separately with the help of supplementary information.

Micro-level poverty traps could be identified more readily and accurately. The effects of factors belonging to five separate clusters were analyzed. The relative scope and importance of each cluster of factors varies across as well as within countries. Some factors are commonly important across all regions examined within a country; others have smaller areas of influence, sometimes only affecting one or two specific communities.

Ill-health and health care expenses constitute the first cluster of factors. The second cluster is related to household characteristics and other social and behavioral factors. Characteristics, such as family size, age and gender of household head, and level of education form part of this group, but social and customary expenses, including expenditures on funerals and marriages, are also included, as are alcoholism, drug addiction, and laziness. Not all of these factors are helpful for explaining descents. In fact, some among these factors have hardly any effect. Together, they constitute a broad and varied cluster of behavioral factors, which we examined separately within each context studied.

The third cluster includes land-related events that have considerable importance within rural and agrarian communities, including land division, crop disease, rainfall failures, and loss of soil fertility. The fourth cluster is a catch-all category that includes diverse region-specific events, such as debt bondage, which was observed in some parts of Gujarat, India, and family breakups on account of divorce, especially relevant in North Carolina, USA.

The fifth and final cluster of factors examined is composed of positive events, including employment, agricultural improvements, diversification of income sources, and business enterprises. As mentioned earlier, households tend to experience both negative and positive events. Considering the fifth cluster of factors helps examine the balance of events.

One Illness Away

Patterns of life and modes of social and economic organization vary across and within countries. Diverse kinds of downward tugs and different impediments to upward mobility have importance within each specific context.

Commonly, however, factors belonging to the first cluster were centrally implicated with descents into poverty. Ill-health and high health care expenses were associated with nearly 60 percent of all descents recorded in communities of Rajasthan, India, 74 percent of all descents examined in Andhra Pradesh, India, and 71 percent and 67 percent of all descents, respectively, in communities of Uganda and Peru. Among households who fell into poverty in 20 villages of Western Kenya, 73 percent cited ill-health and high health care costs as the most important reason for descent.

In Gujarat, an Indian state where annual growth rates in excess of 8 percent have been achieved for nearly two decades, as many as 88 percent of households who fell into poverty did so due to ill-health, hard-to-reach medical facilities, and high health care costs. Apart from one exceptional community, discussed later, where affordable and effective health care services are provided by a local NGO, health care costs were associated in the remaining 35 communities studied with the largest number of descents into poverty.[5]

Underlining the importance that health care has for poverty reduction, health incidents were more common among two groups of households—those who fell into poverty and those who have remained poor—and they were much less common among the other two categories of households (those who escaped poverty and those who have remained non-poor). In Uganda, for instance, 67 percent of households who fell into poverty experienced episodes of ill-health and were burdened by high health care expenditures.[6] Deaths of income earners, which have occurred mostly on account of diseases of various kinds, were importantly implicated in the cases of another 35 per cent of descending households.[7] Among households who have remained not poor—the comparison category for this part of the analysis—these two types of events were experienced by many fewer households. Only 12 percent of these households experienced episodes involving high health care costs, and only 4 percent experienced death of income earners.

Experiences such as the following were common to hear: 'I lost my husband to sickness ten years ago. I used to grow some crops for cash but now I am also sick, and the little that I make from tending my garden I use for buying the medicines that I need. Some of my grandchildren are sickly, and I may tell you some of my children died recently of disease.'

Communities located further away from health care facilities have, in general, experienced larger numbers of descents into poverty. People who live far away from government health centers either obtained no health care at all or they relied upon private facilities that charge higher fees. 'This seeming paradox of greater use of expensive providers by poorer people is aggravated by the deterioration of the public road transport system, to the point where nearly everyone has to walk (or be carried) to obtain medical treatment.'[8] Widespread absenteeism in public health care systems tends to make these problems worse by increasing the scope for unqualified private treatment providers.[9]

Research conducted in other regions of the world has also identified high health care expenses as a major factor responsible for the creation and the persistence of poverty. Evidence collected from many other countries—including Ethiopia, Haiti, Madagascar, Moldova, Sierra Leone, Senegal, and Vietnam—points unambiguously to the deleterious effects of ill-health and health care costs.[10]

'Illness causes more serious economic damage to households than crop failure,' a study undertaken in Cambodia concluded. 'It is impossible to pay large, lump-sum expenses for treatment just by earning additional income. This forces households to sell their land to cope with the expenses of illness. Illness—an idiosyncratic shock—can cause more serious long-term economic damage to households than community-wide crop failure.'[11] Even in times of famine, it has been found that ill-health, rather than starvation, results in causing more deaths and producing much greater physical and economic trauma.[12]

However, it is not only small farmers and agricultural laborers in developing countries who succumb to poverty on account of health-related factors. Our study in 13 North Carolina communities showed that health was primary among the reasons for descent into poverty. Households who fell into poverty had the lowest rate of health insurance coverage among all households: only 51 percent reported having any coverage at all. In comparison, health insurance coverage was much higher among households who remained non-poor (94 percent) and households who escaped poverty (84 percent). Serious health situations were often left unattended by members of households who did not have insurance coverage. People who desperately needed to see a doctor failed to do so quite often because they anticipated unbearably high costs. Outstanding debts are common among households who fell into poverty on account of health-related reasons.

Something other than greater average wealth is required in order to fix this important reason for descent into poverty. 'Health improvements are not primarily driven by income,' as Angus Deaton has observed.[13] We will return to this aspect later in this chapter while reviewing policy recommendations. Let us continue, meanwhile, with this examination of diverse factors associated with falling into poverty and remaining poor.

Variations Within and Across Countries

Table 4.1 presents the major reasons for descent within each of the different regions studied. While health-related factors are the most important ones in every region, other reasons for descent have more context-specific effects.

Social and Ceremonial Expenses

Expensive marriages and funerals have become common within some communities in the regions studied. Many households have taken out debts, often at predatory rates of interest, in order to fulfill the social obligations that they recognize and respect.

Ramji Lal, a farmer in Ajmer district of Rajasthan, India, explained why he organized an elaborate and expensive ceremony at the time of his father's death:

> People of our kinship group told us: 'Your father's soul will wait helplessly before the gates of heaven, unable to enter within. Unless you do the right thing by your father, that is, unless you arrange for an elaborate death feast, you will be condemning his soul to eternal punishment.' We were already poor at that time, but it is impossible to live with this kind of opprobrium, so we did what we had to do, and we are still repaying that debt 15 years later.

A report from Kenya relates how people here 'hold spectacular funerals designed to honor the dead and appease their spirits. They believe each person should be buried where they were born, and families hire expensive cars and travel hundreds of miles to bring the deceased back to their tribal homes,' slaughtering large numbers of cows and goats for the funeral feasts that follow. 'Honoring the dead can bankrupt the living,' the authors conclude.[14] An investigation conducted in South Africa found that households spend, on average, the equivalent of a full year's income for a funeral ceremony. More than one-quarter of all households were found to be in debt on account of funeral costs.[15]

Table 4.1 Principal Reasons for Descent into Poverty

Reasons	Rajasthan, India	Gujarat, India	Western Kenya	Andhra Pradesh, India	Central and Western Uganda	Puno and Cajamarca, Peru
	Share of Descending Households (percent)					
Poor health and health-related expenses	60	88	74	74	71	67
Marriage/dowry expenses	31	68		69	18	29
Funeral-related expenses	34	49	64	28	15	11
High-interest private debt	72	52		60		
Drought/irrigation failure/crop disease	18			44	19	11
Unproductive land/land exhaustion			38		8	
Number of observations	*364*	*189*	*172*	*335*	*202*	*252*

Note: The total of percentages reported in each column adds up to more than 100 because more than one reason was involved in most cases of descent. Health-related reasons were equally prolific in North Carolina communities, but other reasons were quite different from the ones reported here. These data are examined in the text.

In communities studied in different parts of India, elaborate marriage ceremonies and dowries have contributed to many households' descents into poverty. There are indications that instead of abating in the wake of economic growth and the consequent societal changes, the amounts involved in dowries have actually increased with the passage of time.[16] More than two-thirds of all households experiencing descents in Gujarat and Andhra Pradesh, and about one-third of such households in the third Indian state, Rajasthan, were encumbered by such customary expenditures. Similar reasons have also operated, with varying degrees of intensity, in particular parts of Uganda and Peru.

Economic aspects, related to employment and productivity growth, are not the only ones that matter for the reproduction of poverty. Non-economic aspects, related to social customs and societal norms, are also centrally implicated. One might be tempted to conclude that poor people have only themselves to blame. Knowing their conditions, why don't they do away with ostentatious ceremonies and elaborate wedding feasts?

As discussed later, changing social expectations and norms is a collective, rather than an individual, undertaking. Simply decrying a practice will not help effect these changes. Expectations of rightful behavior need to change. Sustained actions by collective actors are required. Customary and ceremonial expenses have been successfully reduced in different parts of the world. Non-government actors, including social movements, have played noteworthy roles.

Household Characteristics

In addition to looking at events and processes at the household level, we also examined various household characteristics, including family size and asset holdings, and the gender, age, and education of the household head. The analysis showed that, apart from gender, other household characteristics are not consistently associated with producing either negative or positive effects.

Consider *family size*. Different views about the effects of family size have been expressed in the literature, with some analysts emphasizing the handicaps imposed by large family size and others stressing the benefits to rural households of having a larger number of sturdy workers.[17] In Rajasthan, India, as in the other regions studied, the evidence was mixed in regard to family size. Small family size was an important factor in the experiences of 16 percent of all households who escaped poverty: They had fewer mouths to feed. Conversely, large family size was associated with the experiences of another 8 percent of escaping households. Because they had more hands to work, they could more successfully diversify their sources of household income.

When one adds up all these numbers and looks at the aggregate picture across regions, large family size goes together more often with downward rather than with upward mobility, but considering only the aggregate picture tends to obscure the complex reality hidden beneath. Small and large family sizes are both associated variously with escape and descent, and it is impossible to say without more detailed knowledge how the effect of family size might work out in any particular case.

In some instances, large family size was a by-product of health events leading to death. Many children whose parents succumbed to HIV/AIDS were taken in by other relatives, resulting in an increase in the numbers of mouths to feed. In most regions studied, however, large family size did not have such one-sided effects, working variously positively or negatively for different groups of households.

Surprisingly, the *education* level of the household head was *not* significantly associated with descents into poverty. One would have expected more educated household heads to have experienced significantly fewer descents into poverty, but the data showed that more educated and less educated households have suffered descents in roughly equal proportions. We will read more in the following chapters about why education does not have a uniformly positive impact for households' levels of prosperity. The basic point is that education is not, by itself, enough to guarantee a good job. In contexts where a weak institutional infrastructure acts to limit the availability of knowledge about career opportunities, more educated people have not always been able to find higher paying jobs. Education counts for much less within such institutionally impoverished contexts, while family connections and other social networks can count for much more.

Examining other household characteristics, we found that *age* of household head made relatively little difference to the probability of experiencing a descent into poverty. Younger as well as older households have all been vulnerable to descents, and the same sets of negative events have mattered. Life-cycle events (those that occur at particular stages in an individual's life) do matter, however, and incidences such as deaths and marriages have been implicated with descents into poverty, especially when heavy expenses on the associated ceremonies were also involved, as discussed above.

Among all household characteristics examined, *gender* had the most consistent effects. Female-headed households are at significantly greater risk of falling into chronic poverty. Members of a random sample of 133 female-headed households were interviewed in Gujarat. Among them, as many as 74 percent have remained persistently poor, and another 15 percent have fallen into poverty, making for a total of almost 90 percent who were poor at the time of investigation. In male-headed households, the comparable poverty rate was much lower: less than 7 percent of such households fell into poverty over the same period.

Asset ownership can serve as insurance against descents. Households who possessed more assets in the prior period were better able to guard against descents into poverty. Building up households' assets at the present time can help alleviate the risk of descents in the future.

In general, we found that household characteristics other than gender and asset holdings have relatively little explanatory value for poverty dynamics. A specific set of events has mattered much more. Chains of events, and not just a single event, were associated with most cases of descent.

Debt

In addition to health incidents and social expenses, *high-interest private debt* has contributed to descents in a large number of cases, as seen in Table 4.1. In most cases, debt did not constitute an entirely separate reason. It resulted from and helped exacerbate other reasons for descent. A very large part of debt incurred by poor families in India has arisen on account of high health care expenses. Results from communities studied in Andhra Pradesh, India showed that rather than ill-health or debt considered singly, it was the interaction of these two factors—the simultaneous presence of both health care costs and high-interest debt—that was most significantly associated with descents into poverty. In fact, the odds of a non-poor household falling into poverty increased by more than four times when both ill-health and debt formed part of its event history.[18] Inquiries in other parts of India and in rural Vietnam have revealed similarly that medical expenses are a major reason for large-scale indebtedness.[19]

Debt has taken on an especially destructive form among communities studied in Gujarat. Many poor households have become bonded debtors, pledged to perform labor on their creditors' fields whenever called upon to do so. Owning more than half of all agricultural land in the village, richer persons are dependent upon poorer ones for supplying the additional labor power required to farm their lands. When poorer persons ask for loans to bail themselves out of financial emergencies, they frequently become entangled in relationships involving bondage.

> Major expenditures that sometimes become unavoidable can only be made by selling the labor power of one or even all household members for advance payment. The price that has to be paid for the loans received is high because the debt relationship that they enter into leads to further under-payment and detracts from their freedom of action.[20]

People who, through such labor obligations, service the debts that were contracted by their parents (and often, their grandparents) are forced to work for the employer to whom these debts are owed. Because they are not free to move in search of better opportunities, prospects for individual advancement are virtually non-existent for them.

Incidences of debt bondage were not encountered in anywhere close to the same numbers within the other two Indian states that we studied, even though much slower rates of economic growth have been experienced in these states. It was somewhat troubling to observe that the greater industrialization and faster economic growth in Vadodara District of Gujarat were accompanied by a much higher incidence of debt bondage. As many as 44 percent of all households who have remained poor in villages of Vadodara District were found to be involved in debt bondage relationships, while many fewer households, 18 percent of those who have remained poor, were involved in such relationships in the more 'backward' Panchmahals District of the same state. Economic growth does not automatically result in making reasons for descent less influential. Specific actions are necessary for this purpose.

Like many other factors associated with descents into poverty, indebtedness has more pronounced effects in some regions and fewer or no effects in other regions. High-interest private debt is more widespread in the communities studied in India (and also to a considerable extent in North Carolina). Indebtedness was not a prominent reason for descent in the regions examined in Kenya, Uganda, or Peru, probably because private moneylenders rarely operate within these regions. In India, however, and in some other countries studied, high-interest private debts are most often contracted with private moneylenders. Exorbitant rates of interest, as high as 10 percent per month, are paid.[21]

Agriculture-related Factors

Agriculture-related factors, including drought, crop disease, irrigation failure, and land exhaustion, constitute the last set of factors examined in Table 4.1. Such factors were particularly important within some of the developing country regions examined.

These factors were not equally important in the case of North Carolina, where *job losses* were the most frequently cited reason for descent. A total of 66 percent of all households falling into poverty in North Carolina either lost a job or suffered a reduction in working hours. Importantly, each of these households also mentioned at least one health-related problem, such as an illness, an accident, high medical expenses, or disability. Beyond the impact on income, job loss very often implied the loss of health insurance benefits, which in turn increased the vulnerability of the household concerned. A combination of job loss, insurance loss, and serious illnesses was associated with the majority of descents into poverty in North Carolina.

In the other four countries studied, agriculture-related factors have contributed considerably to descents into poverty. Specific sub-regions have been especially affected by these reasons.

Location-specific Reasons

The same reason for descent can have significantly different effects not just across countries but also within countries and smaller regions. In Uganda, for instance, land division played a key role for descent in communities of Western Region, but it was not significant for communities of Central Region. Conversely, land exhaustion was a significant descent-related factor in Western Region but it was not important in communities of Central Region. Irrigation failure was an important reason for descent in Andhra Pradesh, India, but its effects were pronounced in communities of Nalgonda District and less visible within the other two districts (Khammam and East Godavari).

Similar inter-regional variations in reasons for descent were also apparent among communities of Peru. Funeral expenses were associated with a considerable number of descents in Cajamarca communities but with many fewer descents in communities of Puno. Land division contributed to 38 percent of all observed descents in Puno communities, but it did not feature as a notable factor of descent in Cajamarca.

The fact that location-specific reasons matter a great deal has important consequences for the design of public policies. To the extent that reasons for descent are similar across an entire state or region, policies can be developed that have larger geographic scope. Standardized policies will have less effect in respect of those reasons for escape and descent that vary across regional boundaries. Decentralized and region-specific policies will perform better.

Within each particular region, the policy mix to be implemented must be customized to deal with local variations in micro reasons for descent. A mix of centralized and decentralized policies and programs will be more effective, resulting in producing a polycentric response, as discussed later.

Personal Shortcomings

Before concluding this section, it is worth discussing one last set of factors, which we found *not* significantly associated with descents. As mentioned in Chapter 1, attributes such as alcoholism and laziness do not distinguish clearly between those who fell into poverty and those who remained (or became) non-poor. Alcoholism can, no doubt, become a serious social evil, and laziness, where it is evident, can only be condemned,[22] but to attribute either of these features especially to those who are poor requires evidence more than ideology. Such evidence was lacking in the regions investigated.

To be sure, we did find evidence of drunkenness within several communities. However, alcoholism or drug use did not appear to be associated preponderantly with those households who have suffered descents into poverty (or who have remained poor). Households who escaped poverty and others who have remained consistently non-poor were implicated in occasional drunkenness in similar numbers. Equally, laziness was not distinguishably associated with those who have remained poor or become poor. In each separate study that I conducted, beginning with the first Rajasthan study, I probed these aspects with some interest because I was keen to find the extent to which the incidence of poverty can actually be blamed upon poor people's dissipation and lack of initiative. Each time, I found hardly any evidence in support of any such view.[23]

Across all categories of households, laziness was mentioned as a contributing factor in less than 4 percent of all cases, and drunkenness or drug addiction were cited as a contributing factor for less than 5 percent of all households interviewed. In household interviews and especially in community meetings, cases of drunkenness and laziness were spoken of openly, sometimes with the help of easy-to-follow signs and euphemisms. It is possible that some households successfully hid this information from us, but I have no sense that such dissimulations were frequent or that they were particular to any one category of households.

The vast majority of poor people do not become poor or remain poor because of bad habits or on account of lack of ambition. People fall into poverty most often on account of negative events that are beyond their individual control. Precipitators of poverty, such as ill-health, high health care expenses, social and customary expenditures, crop failures, commodity price fluctuations, and high-interest private debt, were much more often involved with immersing and preserving households in poverty. Protecting households better against such negative events is an essential component of any strategy to reduce poverty.

Unless descents into poverty are better controlled, the pool of poverty can never be emptied. The rest of this chapter will elaborate upon what needs to be done, beginning with better health care. In addition to exploring further the grassroots-level evidence that we collected, I will draw upon evidence obtained by other scholars studying diverse levels of societal aggregation.

Alleviating the Health Poverty Trap

'There is growing evidence of households being pushed into poverty when faced with substantial medical expenses, particularly when combined with a loss of household income due to ill-health.'[24] Very large numbers of people are falling into poverty with a regularity that needs to be much better recognized and controlled. However, 'this negative impact of health systems on households that can lead to impoverishment' has been ignored for too long.[25] It needs to be centrally addressed, not only as a public health issue, but also as a key part of the agenda for poverty reduction.

Why is ill-health so often a reason for impoverishment? The emergence of new diseases, including HIV/AIDS, provides some part of the explanation. However, the continued occurrence of diseases known in the past has also produced deleterious effects for very large numbers of households.[26] The episodes of ill-health examined within the regions studied included everyday diseases such as gastro-enteritis, malaria, and worm infestations; workplace injuries and road accidents; and calamitous diseases, including HIV/AIDS, but also cancer and tuberculosis.[27]

More than the prevalence of diverse diseases, however, rapidly increasing expenditures on medical treatments are producing a growing number of descents. Household surveys undertaken in 59 countries of Asia, Eastern Europe, and South America indicate that catastrophic payments on health care—expenditures that are far in excess of these households' capacities—are on the rise, becoming common across a large group of countries.[28]

The human body is often poor people's main productive asset, an indivisible and, in most cases, an uninsured asset, which unlike most other assets can flip or slide from being an asset to being a liability.[29] The resulting dependence of survivors, including orphans, upon other household members contributes further to descent in many cases.

No asset risk threatens poor people's livelihoods more than health risk. Health expenditures consequently have high priority for poorer people.[30] 'Health status is given priority over other expenditures' was the finding of a study of the urban poor in four countries. 'Poor households pay at least twice their income share for these services as non-poor households.'[31] Ill-affording to make these expenditures, but likely to become even worse off if they do not, large numbers of households are forced into poverty on account of large (and growing) health care expenses.

Data from other countries also show how the costs of medical services have grown enormously. As 'China's health services were commercialized, as part of market-oriented economic reforms, the costs of health care have risen sharply.'[32] Per capita incomes doubled between 1990 and 1999, but the cost of medical care increased faster. The average cost of visiting doctors rose by 625 percent, and in-hospital treatment became five times more expensive, resulting in producing an 'increase in the number of people who fell into poverty by exhausting their income and savings to pay for medical treatment.'[33]

A single visit to a hospital or doctor can end up with 'total costs approximately [equal to] one-half of a person's monthly average income... Nearly half of those suffering from health problems did not see a doctor for treatment... The average cost of in-hospital treatment approximates or exceeds a person's average annual income.'[34]

In India, as well, expenditures on medical treatments account for a large and growing share of the household budget.[35] Our survey of households in Gujarat,

India, showed that 76 percent of them needed to consult a doctor at least once during the year preceding the survey. More alarmingly, in 20 percent of all households at least one member needed to be hospitalized. The average expenditure incurred in these cases was 31,000 Indian Rupees (about US$750), which is more than what the average person in this region makes during an entire year.

The story in these emerging economies is not very different, however, from what has been occurring within the United States. More than one-half of all personal bankruptcies in the United States arise on account of unbearably high medical expenses.[36] 'Every thirty seconds, someone files a bankruptcy claim that is due in part to medical costs and crises.'[37]

As the example of the United States shows, health care services do not automatically become more affordable or easier to access simply as a consequence of economic growth. Higher average wealth does not guarantee better medical care for all people. On the other hand, very substantial improvements are possible even at much lower levels of national income.

A report produced by the United Nations shows how 'countries at similar levels of income display huge variations. For example, Honduras and Viet Nam have far lower levels of neonatal mortality than India and Pakistan. Indeed, at a lower rate of income and a comparable rate of economic growth, Viet Nam has now overtaken China on improvements in child mortality. Similarly, at a lower level of income and with far lower growth, Bangladesh has overtaken India.'[38]

The historical and institutional context has to be seen in which economic growth and health improvements have co-occurred within some presently richer countries. In many of these countries, including Sweden, Japan, and South Korea, building new hospitals and training more medical professionals was undertaken in parallel with the installation of more effective financial risk-mitigation mechanisms. In many presently low- and middle-income countries (and in some richer ones), the infrastructure of hospitals and clinics has expanded rapidly. However, institutions for risk mitigation and risk pooling, such as social insurance or tax-financed health services, have not been developed in parallel. The result is a higher financial burden for households and individuals, who have to pay from out of pocket, even for severe and chronic illnesses.

A comparative examination of health data from 11 low- and middle-income Asian countries shows that in countries where a higher proportion of health expenses are paid from out of pocket, larger numbers of people fall into poverty.[39]

More than 75 million people fall below the low threshold of US$1-per-day every year on account of high health care expenditures, accounting for 3 percent of the total population of these countries. However, this proportion varies from 0.05 percent of the population in Malaysia (where out-of-pocket expenses add up to less than 40 percent of all health care costs) to 3.7 percent of the population in India (where out-of-pocket payments make up 80 percent of total health care costs). In Thailand, Indonesia, and Sri Lanka, as in Malaysia, the proportion of out-of-pocket payments is comparatively low, because effective health coverage schemes have been put in place. In comparison, the risk of descent into poverty is much higher in India, China, and Bangladesh, where vast swathes of the population still have no health care coverage.

Across other countries, as well, 'rises in out-of-pocket costs for public and private health care services are driving many families into poverty and increasing the poverty of those who were already poor. The magnitude of this situation, known as the medical poverty trap,' needs to be urgently appreciated and more effectively addressed.[40]

Expanding the coverage of health insurance schemes is necessary for reducing the persistence and creation of poverty. Research is required that can help identify the natures of insurance schemes that will be effective within different contexts. It may not be possible or necessary that centralized, government-run schemes are run everywhere or that modes of private insurance popular in different parts of Europe are replicated within developing countries. Growing attention is being paid in this connection to various micro insurance and community-based alternatives.[41] Reviews of existing schemes show that while many among them have been effective in providing financial protection and reducing out-of-pocket spending, the quality and efficiency of care provided has not invariably improved.[42] Initiatives to further improve the working of micro health insurance schemes are continuing in different parts of the world. I had the opportunity to see at first hand the schemes being implemented by BRAC, an NGO, in different parts of Bangladesh. More such initiatives are required to be taken up. Their outcomes need to be carefully evaluated and learned from.

While important, even essential, health insurance is not, however, enough by itself to contain the rising financial burden of health care. More effective regulation is required in addition.

The increased commercialization of medical services coupled with weak or absent regulation has resulted in a proliferation of fly-by-night operators, over-prescription, over-charging by private providers, spurious drugs, and other such avoidable social evils. Without taking account of these developments it is hard to explain why the financial burden of health care costs has risen so sharply, especially within developing countries where

> Pharmaceutical drugs now account for 30 to 50 percent of total health-care expenditures, compared with less than 15 percent in established market economies. Private drug vendors, especially in Asia and parts of Africa, tend to cater for poor people, who cannot afford to use professional services. These vendors, who are often unqualified, frequently do not follow prescribing regulations. In parts of India and China, [such unqualified] drug vendors can be found on nearly every street corner. Limited access to professional health services and aggressive marketing of drugs on an unregulated market have not only generated an unhealthy and irrational use of medicine, but also wasted scarce financial resources, especially among poor people. Cultural access is a special problem that encompasses lack of responsiveness and disrespect shown towards disadvantaged groups of people and widespread use of informal, so-called 'under-the-table,' payments.[43]

As health systems are privatized with little or no regulatory discipline and no concurrent investments in risk-pooling institutions, ever larger numbers of people have become vulnerable to the risk of falling into poverty. 'The commodification of medicine invariably punishes the vulnerable,' observes Paul Farmer.[44] Protecting the vulnerable and others liable to becoming vulnerable requires more effectively regulating the markets for health care. A report prepared for the Chinese government concludes that 'government should use its power to regulate medical services in order to influence the behavior of providers. The purposes of such regulations are (1) ensuring the fairness of market exchange in the delivery system; (2) correcting market failures in the delivery system; and (3) ensuring equity in the delivery of medical services.'[45]

Preventive medicine, including better sanitation and hygiene and safe drinking water, is needed in addition to the provision of cheaper and more effective cures. Regular medical check-ups are necessary. They will help detect problems at an early stage, rendering unnecessary many expensive late-stage interventions.

Conditional cash transfer programs, being implemented within a growing group of countries, can be helpful in bringing about some of the required changes.[46] Directly, these programs can stimulate the demand for medical services by making it incumbent upon the recipients of cash transfers to attend health clinics on a regular basis. Indirectly, by requiring that these services are, in fact, made available to program beneficiaries, they can also help improve their supply. Sustained over longer periods of time such programs can help improve health care behaviors on the parts of both the providers and the patients. However, simply waiting for these outcomes to arise in the natural course of events may not prove to be enough. Regulation and oversight are necessary in addition to stimulating demand and building infrastructure.

A wide-ranging response is necessary for alleviating the worsening health poverty trap. Risk-pooling and social insurance are very important, but so are better provision and improved oversight. More complete epidemiological maps need to be assembled. They will help to determine more precisely the natures of diseases that need to be targeted within each specific region. Regular information flows can help guard consumers of these services better against the possibility of malpractices by providers.

Addressing Context-specific Negative Events

Providing better health care services is critically important for controlling descents into poverty, but other reasons for descent are also important, and these context-specific reasons will also need to be addressed. Breaking the chains of negative events at multiple links will more assuredly prevent future poverty from arising.

Social and customary expenses are second only to health care, contributing to poverty in large numbers of households in the regions examined. People spend enormous amounts of money, relative to what they possess, on organizing ostentatious weddings and elaborate death feasts. It is easy for outsiders to say: 'But these things must stop!' It is harder for the individuals concerned to make these changes. Immersed as they are within particular cultural and social settings, they must do what is expected of them by others who share the same social norms.

One example helps point up outsiders' reactions to such events. Ira Weiss, Chairman of the Bangalore-based internet company Babajobs.com (about which we will read more in a later chapter), indignantly reported the following incident in an email message sent to me:

> One of our field staff, who has completed ten years in a Tamil-medium school and two years in an English-medium school, is getting married. She is 25 years old and earns 7,500 Rupees per month [equal to 150 US

dollars at that time]. She is borrowing 50,000 Rupees for her wedding: 30,000 for jewelry and 20,000 for the party. Her father is a partially-employed painter, and I doubt that the family's total monthly income (five earners, one child still in school) is more than 30,000 Rupees. I was appalled. I asked her why she was spending so much, and she said she had to have jewelry so that people didn't think her family was poor. I wanted to yell at her, 'But you *are* poor, what are you wasting these scarce resources for?'

I know I bring my cultural biases to the situation. To my wife and me, if people are your friends they won't care if you don't buy conspicuous items. And if people aren't your friends then why bother to impress them? When I was growing up in Los Angeles we used to joke that 'Los Angeles is where you buy things you don't need, with money you don't have, to impress people you don't like.' Who would have thought that statement to be applicable to lower-income Indians as well?[47]

I share Ira's anguish and his concern for the young lady and her family, but he does bring an outsider's sensitivities and biases to apply to this quite different cultural context. Calling attention to the problem is only the first of many steps.

Changing social norms and values and altering human behaviors requires building sustained collective actions. Governments may be able to do relatively little, especially in a primary role, toward reducing the significance of social norms. Legislation outlawing many such customs has been enacted in India and elsewhere, but these laws have generally proved hard to implement.

Social movements have made better and longer lasting impressions. An account from some Rajasthan villages is illustrative. Nearly all caste groups in southern Rajasthan are vulnerable to descent on account of marriage and funeral expenses. One exception is constituted by scheduled tribes of Dungarpur district,[48] among whom we did not find a single case of descent brought on by death feasts or wedding ceremonies. There is no other caste group in these villages of Rajasthan for whom such social expenses were not involved in descents including, surprisingly, scheduled tribes of the adjoining district, Udaipur. Scheduled tribes of Dungarpur are alone in this respect. They abjure death feasts entirely and spend relatively small amounts on marriages. They adopted these reforms after getting involved with a powerful social reform movement, which acquired roots within these communities beginning in the early 1970s.[49]

Other examples, from other regions and countries, also show how a longer term collective effort is necessary. Individually, people are virtually powerless to bring about the reforms required. Different kinds of initiatives—undertaken by cooperatives, NGOs, private foundations, and other non-governmental actors—have helped resolve the collective action problems involved in changing norms related to appropriate celebration of landmark occasions, such as funerals and weddings.

In Bangladesh, for example, the Grameen Bank requires its borrowers to sign a pledge not to pay or expect dowry as an effort by the poor to get out of this drag on their economic conditions. Burial societies have been functioning in Botswana and some other countries that share funeral expenses after standardizing these at low levels. In Sri Lanka the Death Donation Societies have played a very important role, because everyone accepts a common pattern of low-level expenses as adequate commemoration meeting social expectations.[50] Similar examples have been reported as well from other parts of the world. Community-based funeral associations in some parts of Ethiopia and Tanzania have helped their members cope more effectively with the expenditures involved.[51]

Institutional innovations of these kinds, involving shared risks and lowered expenditures, are also required to deal with a third set of negative factors, related to high-interest debt. Rotating credit associations and self-help credit groups have the potential for providing credit when needed at relatively low cost.[52] However, such groups do not function everywhere. They were not much in evidence within the communities that we studied. Further, the few credit associations that did exist have not usually advanced credit for consumption purposes, being mostly concerned with enhancing production.

The potential for helping stave off descents—by helping reform social norms over the longer term, and in the interim, by helping underwrite cheaper loans for necessary health care and ceremonial expenses—needs to be exploited more fully by expanding co-operatives and self-help groups. Because close-knit rural communities have intimate knowledge about the situations of individual households, it should be helpful to expand and strengthen networks of community-based groups.[53] Micro credit operations of different kinds constitute an important component of the steps needed to prevent future poverty creation.

Different threats and risks are more salient in diverse parts of the world. Policy outcomes can be improved by examining the most common sequences of negative events influencing households within each particular region. The comparative advantages of different actors need to be harnessed for this purpose. Banks, private foundations, individual volunteers, and other actors have important roles to play in addition to governments, NGOs, and donor agencies.

Conclusion: Prevention First

This investigation of micro reasons for descent shows that while poverty reduction schemes have focused on raising poor people's incomes, attention should also have been paid to the opposite side of the ledger, related to household expenditures. Unprotected risks, resulting in large household expenditures, have made the difference between remaining non-poor and falling into poverty.

Multiple, context-specific, reasons have contributed to the descents that were experienced in different regions. Because descents are generally brought on by a chain of events, occurring sequentially rather than precipitately, multiple opportunities are available for helping people in need *before* they become acutely or chronically poor.

Better health care services are critical for preventing the large-scale creation of future poverty. Millions of households are living precariously, one illness away from poverty. Providing them with more affordable, accessible, and efficacious health care services will help prevent large numbers of impending descents. Suitable health insurance mechanisms are essential for this purpose. Effective regulation is also necessary, with more consumer choice and more information on these choices, and easier access to this range of alternatives. It would be a better world if people did not have to sell their homes and other assets simply in order to pay for the medical treatment of a loved one.

Other policy supports are also required to help people guard themselves better against other, context-specific, reasons for descent. Identifying the reasons for descent and escape that matter most within each particular location is the essential first step. Once the reasons for escape and descent operating within any particular context have been properly identified, then specific groups of people can be more effectively assisted. Of particular importance are those households who have already experienced one or more negative events. The cumulative effect of yet another negative shock would be most deleterious in their case. Female-headed households also need special consideration. Compared to other households, those headed by divorced, widowed, or separated women are at greater risk of impoverishment.

Richer as well as poorer societies need to take steps to prevent the creation of future poverty. Reasons for descent do not disappear simply because a society has grown richer on average. Greater wealth is not a guaranteed route to health improvements, nor is low wealth necessarily a barrier to progress. Richer countries have not always supplied effective health care provision to all citizens. Other countries, poorer on average, have performed better on occasion.[54]

Other factors of descent, including customary expenses, crop disease, land exhaustion, and indebtedness, are also not resolved simply on account of faster economic growth. Everything else being the same, a faster growth rate is certainly better than a slower one. More resources get generated as a result of more rapid economic growth. However, translating resources into results requires intervening actively using locally-appropriate preventive measures.

Stronger social safety nets need to be built that are different in important respects from the safety nets of the past. Providing supportive measures—helping people in poverty—is very important, but preventive measures are also needed. Perversely, however, 'since the early to mid-1990s the coverage of social insurance in developing countries has stagnated or declined,'[55] and assistance has been provided in most cases after people have fallen all the way into dire poverty. Surely, the message to people in need of assistance cannot be: 'Keep falling further. We can't assist you yet. Come to us when you have passed below the official poverty line.' Pre-emptive and protective assistance is essential. We should seek to cure only what we cannot first prevent.

Once the emergence of new poverty has been more effectively controlled—once the stable door has been secured, the drains shut off, the leaks repaired (choose whatever metaphor you prefer)—then one can focus more fruitfully on raising people out of poverty, with greater confidence that these efforts will not be compromised. Soon-to-occur descents will not then refill the pool of poverty.

When the risks of descent are lowered, people's incentives to invest in the future will also be raised. The successes achieved will more often endure. In the following chapter, we will begin to look at the reasons that have helped people escape poverty.

CHAPTER 5

Reasons for Escape: Diversification and Agriculture

Turning now to the happier half of the story, let us look at escapes from poverty. What kinds of household strategies and what natures of external aids have helped people move out of poverty in the past? What can we learn from investigating these experiences that can help facilitate more—and better—escapes from poverty in the future?

It is important to note that in the regions examined escapes from poverty have not usually occurred suddenly or without advance preparation by the household concerned. None of the households who escaped poverty won a lottery. No other windfall benefits were usually involved. People planned and invested efforts over long periods of time, carving out the pathways that took their households upward by degrees.

Parents invested in their children's school and college educations so that their sons and daughters could have better prospects in the future. Farmers labored for years on their agricultural fields, leveling land, digging wells, and constructing irrigation canals, so that low-value crops could eventually be replaced by higher-valued ones. Others invested cautiously and incrementally in small business enterprises—retail shops, household dairies, service-provision operations, and the like. Putting aside more pressing and immediate needs, people reposed their faith and pledged their resources toward building more secure futures. They learned from the examples of others in their communities who have carved out similar pathways in the past.

Entire regions were not suddenly benefited, nor did entire communities move upward in unison. Some households in each community moved out of poverty. Simultaneously, other households fell into poverty or remained poor. Large-scale (or covariate) events affecting entire countries or regions do not help explain these parallel and opposite trends. Specific idiosyncratic factors— ordinary events associated with particular households—better distinguish between those who rose out of poverty and others who could not.

No single event was usually determinative over the longer term. Sequences of positive and negative events were experienced by most households. The balance of events has been emphasized before. It is illustrated in this chapter with the help of an example drawn from Gujarat, India. Parts of this state were hard hit by an earthquake that occurred in January 2001. Thousands of livelihoods were suddenly in tatters. Instead of having long-term pernicious effects, however, the impact of the earthquake was moderated over time. Five years after the earthquake, many fewer people were poor in the worst-hit areas than had been poor five years before this momentous event. Several ordinary events assisted people's rise out of poverty, helping them overcome the devastation they had suffered.

Working gradually, and often going unnoticed by outside observers, ordinary and seemingly commonplace events have also assisted escapes from poverty in each of the other regions studied. The nature of these ordinary events has varied considerably across different groups of communities. Within the same country, and often within the same state, different reasons for escape and descent have operated.

It is worth noting that formal jobs in the private or the public sector did *not* constitute the principal pathway out of poverty in any of these developing country regions. Formal jobs—as this term is usually understood, implying enforceable contracts, legal protections, and agreed-upon tenure—were available to only a small percentage of people. Instead, the urban informal sector served in many regions as the most important pathway of escaping poverty. In other regions, and at other times, agriculture provided the more promising escape routes. Different strategies were associated with households' investments in agriculture. Crop diversification was prominent within some geographic areas. Investing in livestock produced higher returns in other areas.

It is heartwarming to consider that large numbers of people escaped poverty within every region examined. Disappointingly, however, hardly anyone who escaped poverty became rich. People who moved out of poverty via the informal-sector route became watchmen, gardeners, lorry loaders, cooks, nannies, shop assistants, or street vendors in some city, small or large. To find even such low-paid and precarious occupations, many traveled great distances from their homes. Others, who remained behind and farmed their lands more intensively, also achieved relatively small gains in the most part. The tiny tracts of land that poor households typically operate have limited the gains that they derived from agriculture. Still others, who selected to follow the small business route, were also constrained. Low capital stocks coupled with meager credit lines limited the extent to which they could rise above poverty.

As a result, hardly anyone who escaped poverty has become part of what Manuel Castells regards as 'the network society,' implying by this term a social structure made up of networks powered by modern information and communications technologies.[1] Only a tiny proportion of individuals who made their beginnings in poor communities have risen to higher-paying positions. Hardly any among them finds a mention within telephone directories or yellow pages; virtually none has an email account.

Much more attention needs to be paid in the future, not just to raising the numbers of those who escape poverty, but as well to improving the nature and the quality of individual escapes. Better self-advancement opportunities need to be made available to capable people from poorer communities. Much higher priority needs to be given to strengthening these presently weak micro–macro links. There is a risk otherwise that two separate economies—two flat worlds—will evolve in parallel, with very few people moving across this divide.[2] Already, such a trend is beginning to become evident. Inequalities of different kinds are growing.

Disappointingly, education has not served as a reliable avenue toward more substantial material progress. Despite investing in higher education many young adults have been unable to advance very far. Several factors are implicated in this lack of achievement. Lack of information is critical among them. Below-potential achievement has resulted in many cases from lack of knowledge about alternative opportunities and career pathways. I will return to this aspect in the following chapter, arguing in favor of investing in information institutions. Before coming to that point, let us take stock of the reasons that have assisted escapes from poverty in the regions examined.

Poverty Escape Strategies: Informal Sector Occupations and Agriculture

Table 5.1 brings together the principal micro-level reasons for escape in each region. It does not report these figures for North Carolina, where a shorter and different list of positive reasons has operated, as discussed below.

In general, more than one positive reason was associated with each household's escape from poverty. The cumulative effect of multiple positive stimuli pushed households above the poverty cut-off, helping offset the downward pulls made by negative events.

Notice how diversification of income sources—through the urban informal sector and separately through crops and livestock—served as the most important avenue of escape in every developing country region studied. In fact, diversification of livelihood sources is a more widespread household strategy, associated both 'with success at achieving livelihood security under improving economic conditions as well as with [preventing or alleviating] livelihood distress in deteriorating conditions.'[3]

Households have diversified their income sources employing multiple means. Many have simply diversified their agricultural portfolios. Others have started small business enterprises on the side, or they have gone looking for paid work in a city.

In North Carolina, escape routes of these kinds had relatively little importance. Instead, obtaining a formal-sector job—with formal protections, paid benefits, and legal safeguards—was the most important pathway of escape from poverty in this region, benefiting 56 percent of all households who escaped poverty. Such jobs were available to much smaller proportions of households in other regions. Other types of pathways matter relatively more.

The Growing Urban Informal Sector

Informal-sector work has served as a major avenue for upward mobility, serving large proportions of households who escaped poverty within every developing country region examined. For as many as 77 percent of all people who escaped poverty in the 71 Kenyan communities examined, the urban informal sector provided important income supplements. In each of the other developing country regions examined, the informal sector has played a similarly prominent

Table 5.1 Principal Reasons for Escaping Poverty

Reasons	Rajasthan, India	Gujarat, India	Kenya (country sample)	Andhra Pradesh, India	Central and Western Uganda	Puno and Cajamarca, Peru
			Share of Households Escaping Poverty (percent)			
Diversification of income (informal sector)	58	35	77	51	52	44
Diversification of income (crops and livestock)	39	29	64	48	41	69
Private-sector employment	7	32	9	7	9	8
Public-sector employment	11	39	11	10	6	5
Government/NGO assistance	8	6	3	7	3	4
Number of observations	*499*	*285*	*388*	*348*	*398*	*324*

Note: The total of percentages reported in each column adds up to more than 100 because more than one reason was involved in most cases.

role. In the Ugandan communities studied, 52 percent of all people escaping poverty utilized the informal-sector route.

Characterized by 'easy entry, little unionization, no legal minimum wages, weak safety standards at work, low physical capital inputs, low returns to labor, and mainly small (often family-based) units,[4] the informal sector is made up of an array of enterprises producing a variety of goods and services.[5] An authoritative review shows how 'the bulk of new employment in recent years, particularly in developing and transition countries, has been in the informal economy.'[6] In Africa, informal work accounts for almost 90 percent of all new work opportunities created between the mid-1990s and 2005. In Latin America and Asia, as well, the major share of new work opportunities has been created within the informal sector. As the result, the share of informal workers in the non-agricultural labor force has grown. At the beginning of the twenty-first century, this share ranged from 51 percent in Latin America and the Caribbean to 65 percent in Asia to 72 percent in sub-Saharan Africa.[7]

Juakali is a term of common usage in Kenya. It refers to the sprawling informal economy, functioning beyond the reach of most labor laws and social security requirements, where you can have your wristwatch mended, your clothes stitched, or your motorcycle repaired at low cost. The vast majority of people in Kenyan cities derive their livelihoods from this shadowy informal economy. Using some connection, a kinsman or a friend from their village, new migrants from the countryside find a toehold within this sector.

Mostly, quite modest natures of gains have been made by people who took up positions within the informal sector. Prospects for more substantial advancement are limited because 'work in the informal economy cannot be termed "decent" compared to recognized, protected, secure and formal employment. Most cases of child labor are to be found in the informal economy, often in the most hidden and hazardous forms of work, including forced labor and slavery. On the whole, average incomes in the informal economy are much lower than in the formal economy. The working poor are concentrated in the informal economy.'[8]

Hernando De Soto has provided many important insights related to the operation of the informal economy in Peru and elsewhere.[9] The precarious lifestyles of people in this sector; the disrespect shown to them by employers and government officials, the lack of attention by mayors and national governments; and the consequent blockage of capital in assets that, because they are unrecorded, cannot easily be sold and therefore lose value—these pathologies and many others afflict people immersed in situations of informality.

There is, however, no better alternative for many. For people who live within rural areas, the city quite often contains the most viable pathways out of poverty. Within cities, a vast and growing informal sector has served as the principal creator of new positions and opportunities.

Few Formal Jobs

Economic growth has undoubtedly provided some dividends to poorer people, but instead of arising in the form of secure jobs in the formal sector, these benefits have come mostly by way of informal sector employment and improvements in agriculture. Even in Gujarat, India, where per capita incomes have grown very rapidly, only 9.5 percent of all households in the communities studied were able to escape poverty, while more than 50 percent have remained persistently poor. A little less than one-third of all households who escaped poverty—or just over 3 percent of all households in these communities—found formal employment in the private sector, and another one-third were employed in formal positions by the government.[10] The corresponding numbers are considerably lower in the other regions studied.

Industrial growth in Andhra Pradesh, another state of India, has also not resulted in making formal jobs a viable pathway out of poverty. The 12 villages that we studied in Nalgonda district of this state are located at varying distances from a cluster of privately owned cement plants. However, less than 10 percent of all households who escaped poverty in any of these villages were benefited by a formal job of any kind. Relatively few jobs have been created by industry. Further, the conditions of employment are such that securing a job does not always enable the household concerned to move out of poverty. Informality characterizes the situations of many who are employed within the formal sector. Local residents who work in the cement industry are quite often hired by intermediaries and contractors (and not directly by the cement factories), and they are paid, often for years on end, on a day-to-day basis, with no benefits and no security of tenure.

Industrial growth helps its host region in many ways, but banking upon such growth does not appear to be a viable strategy for poverty reduction. Relatively fast industrial growth was not good enough for this purpose in Gujarat and Andhra Pradesh, nor has this particular pathway worked any better in any of the other regions. Growth in formal-sector employment was not the major remover of poverty in communities of Uganda and Peru. Quite similar trends were observed in Kenya. Even in Nairobi and Mombasa, the largest cities of this country and its main centers of manufacturing, the vast majority of households escaping poverty relied upon finding *Juakali* positions.

Examinations conducted within other countries have produced similar findings. Even where manufacturing output has grown rapidly, employment growth has lagged far behind.[11] For China, analysts have observed how 'industrialization in the period under globalization has been remarkably employment-hostile. The output elasticity of employment in China's industries fell drastically. More capital-intensive technologies [were adopted]…The process of transition has been characterized by very slow growth of employment.'[12] Similarly in India, despite rapid economic growth, total formal sector employment has not increased. Already quite low as a proportion of the vast population of India, employment in the formal sector (private and public) has actually fallen further—from 28.2 million persons in 1997 to 27.0 million in 2003.[13] Over the ten years preceding 2005, 'the change in the organized or formal sector employment was nil or even marginally negative.'[14]

Agriculture

Because employment in the formal sector has not increased by much in India, and it has only slowly increased in other developing countries, diversification of income sources—through agricultural and non-agricultural means—has provided to poorer households their most important pathways for escaping poverty. People pursuing diversification have taken up a range of different activities. Non-agricultural means have been more prominent in some regions. In other regions and communities, improvements in agriculture paved the way to escape.

Crop diversification was principally important within some locations, while livestock diversification was more important in other regions. In Peru, crop diversification was more important in communities of Cajamarca, being associated with 41 percent of all escapes from poverty, but livestock diversification was more important in communities of Puno region, accounting for 52 percent of all escapes from poverty.

Rosalia Muñoz Saldaña, a resident of a community in Puno, had the following to say in this regard:

> Twenty-five years ago, I always had livestock: cattle and small animals. I also harvested crops, but for me, livestock is the one thing that helped most. Livestock, especially cattle, helps. When we need something in the family, we can sell an animal. It also helps for my business of cheese. Raising more animals, we are better off. The problem is that there is not more pasture, and we need more irrigation infrastructure.

Agricultural developments, including crops and livestock, were also important for escapes from poverty in other developing country regions. In Kenya, as in Peru, livestock mattered comparatively more in some regions, particularly in the northern part of the country, while crop-based improvements were more important in the southern and western regions. Similarly, in Gujarat villages, diversification within agriculture was considerably important, with dairy activities helping elevate the economic status of many households, especially within particular parts of this Indian state.

Multiple Context-Specific Reasons

Households have adopted multi-stranded strategies. In addition to making investments in agriculture, households in both Peruvian regions sent one or more of their members to work at a trade or to find an occupation within a city. Rural households in Cajamarca have benefited proportionately more than those in Puno from remittances sent back by such city-based individuals.[15]

In Rajasthan, India, some people have taken up additional activities within their village, rearing livestock, opening a micro grocery shop, or working for wages in some local mining operation. Simultaneously, other household members have sought new sources of livelihood in cities. Many among them have traveled considerable distances, going as far away as Mumbai, Bangalore, Chennai, and Pune, several hundred kilometers away, where they have worked as ice cream vendors, laborers, masons, sign-painters, tea stall assistants, truck drivers, and waiters. Mostly younger males move to the city for this purpose, and in nearly all cases they travel by themselves. The positions they occupy in the city are hardly secure, so it is better for all concerned that dependants remain behind in the village.

Diverse activities were taken up by households in different regions of Andhra Pradesh. Broadly, two types of activities were involved. First, some households set up tiny businesses of their own or they took recourse to the urban informal sector. These types of activities were more frequent in villages of Nalgonda and

Khammam districts. A second type of diversification (within agriculture) was more important in villages of East Godavari district of the same state.

Different natures of diversification have been more important, therefore, within each particular region examined. Different policy supports are required to promote escape through diversification in various parts of the same country.

Household Characteristics and Community Features

In addition to looking at events of a positive and negative nature, we also examined the effects of different household characteristics. We found that only one household characteristic—gender—was consistently associated with escaping poverty. Other household characteristics—including household size and the age and education level of the head of household and other adult members—had more mixed effects, being neither consistently associated with escapes from poverty nor consistently a feature of descents. Community characteristics, such as relative remoteness and population size, also did not associate clearly with a greater frequency or proportion of escapes. Infrastructure provision did make a difference, however. Communities that are better served by physical and communication infrastructures have experienced proportionately higher numbers of escapes.

Education is the first household characteristic that we examined. Contrary to what we had expected earlier, we found that education did not always result in producing upward mobility. Not all those who escaped poverty were educated. Conversely, not all who gained education were able to find a job or otherwise improve their economic situations. Contacts providing information were often critical for successful job searches. 'We need resources, not free things,' one interviewee in Vance County, North Carolina, stated, referring above all to informational resources. Individuals and households who lacked information and contacts were less able to use education as a pathway out of poverty.

Other studies have found similarly. For instance, education was found to have a larger positive effect in Uganda when it was combined with access to infrastructure and to job opportunities.[16] In India, analysts have found that education is not by itself significantly associated with escapes from poverty.[17] In conjunction with other factors, however, particularly when given assistance by helpful social networks, educated individuals have been able to achieve considerably larger gains.[18]

Investments in education alone are unlikely to be sufficient for raising poor households out of poverty. Particularly within situations where institutional and information gaps are large, investments complementary to education are additionally required, as we will see in the next chapter.

Among other household characteristics, we found that age of household head did not significantly raise or lower the odds of escaping poverty. Life-cycle events, such as deaths and marriages, do make an important difference, raising the odds of falling into poverty, as we saw in Chapter 4—but other events matter as well.[19] In general, age of household head had relatively little to do with escaping poverty. Younger as well as older households escaped poverty in roughly equal proportions.

Household size also did not have any consistent relationship with escaping poverty. As examined in the previous chapter, the effects of household size are more complex and varied.

One other household characteristic—*gender* of household head—was consistently and negatively associated with escapes from poverty. Female-headed households have fared much worse than other households. Such households have faced additional stresses, and they were more likely to become poor or remain poor. While the nature of negative reasons is not different for female-headed households, a greater frequency of negative events has tended to increase their odds of impoverishment. Compared to other households, female-headed ones are in greater need of antipoverty assistance, as discussed in the previous chapter.

Moving from household characteristics to community-level features, we found that population size and relative remoteness are not significantly associated with escapes from poverty. Communities that are located closer to big cities and commercial centers did not experience significantly higher proportions of escapes. Many smaller communities, including those located at considerable distances from the mainstream of commercial activity, had a higher-than-average record of escapes.

Transportation links have made an important difference. Communities that were not connected by all-weather roads and bus or train services have fared poorly on average. Other communities, located further away in terms of physical distance but served by regular transportation links, recorded more escapes. Connections matter critically. In addition to physical connections, such as roads or train services, links of information have also improved individuals' prospects for upward mobility, as we will see later.

Community organization and social capital have also helped produce positive effects, especially within some among the different regions that we studied. In the Puno region of Peru, for instance, these positive effects were clearly visible. Community organizations of this region have helped households in multiple ways, first, by enabling investments in land-based activities, especially livestock, and second, by helping households cope better with illnesses and other negative events.

Both forms of community assistance were illustrated in the account narrated by Victor Tapara Ancco:

> When I was a child, my father and my mother were shepherds who worked for one landowner. We never had any land of our own. My brothers and I could only go to primary school and no further. We also grew up working as shepherds. I got married, and my wife was also a shepherd. Six years ago, the community awarded me with a piece of land and some cattle. Little by little, I have bought more cattle, and now I sell milk to the community cheese plant. One's own land always helps to be better off, we can have more livestock, and we can live more peacefully. The community also helps when someone is sick or in need. It is through their support that I am better off today.

In some villages of Rajasthan, India, effective community organizations and higher levels of social capital have enabled people to make more productive investments in forests and pastures.[20] In other villages and in other regions examined, the effects of social capital were less pronounced.

Government and NGO Assistance

Direct programmatic assistance from government agencies or NGOs did not form a significant part of households' experiences of escape within any of the regions examined.[21] Overall, very few households, less than 10 percent in all, received any such assistance, and few among these recipients of government or NGO assistance were able to escape poverty. It is possible that people are more willing to speak glowingly of their own roles, and they will minimize the role played by outside assistance, but most households who escaped poverty had, in fact, received no direct government (or NGO) assistance, and indirect forms of assistance—such as electricity, water supply, roads, schools, etc.—were available as well to other households, who remained persistently poor or who fell into poverty.

The wrong conclusion should not be drawn from these results. It should not be inferred that government and NGO assistance is not required; the requirement is urgent and widespread.

The more important issue concerns the *kinds* of assistance provided. What natures of activities are promoted by external assistance programs? For what reasons are particular activities preferred over others? Is the choice of program activities preceded by any careful study of what actually helps people escape poverty in the region?

Knowing contextually-relevant reasons for escape and descent is a precondition for effective program design, but rarely have external assistance programs identified and targeted context-specific reasons. In the most part, programs of assistance have followed a pre-determined and broad-brush logic, one that is dictated by people far removed from (and often ignorant about) diverse and changeable local conditions. Further, as Jeffrey Sachs has emphatically and correctly pointed out, the total quantum of assistance provided by governments and international agencies has been miniscule compared to the need.[22]

Aid budgets need to grow. Simultaneously, the thrust of donor assistance and government programs needs to change radically. Identifying, and then targeting, context-specific negative and positive reasons needs to become a guiding principle for assistance programs of the future. There is no magic remedy that will be equally efficacious in all parts of the developing world. Standardized programs extended across large numbers of regions and countries will very likely continue to have relatively little positive effect. Programs that are designed after gaining knowledge of locally operating threats and opportunities will more effectively tilt the balance of events in the right direction.

It is noteworthy that households who have never experienced poverty were exposed to the same kinds of positive influences as other households who escaped poverty. These positive factors—including diversification of income sources, improved agricultural productivity, and progress in small business enterprises—helped consistently non-poor households offset the negative effects of illnesses and social expenditures. On the other hand, households who remained poor or who fell into poverty experienced a different balance of positive and negative events.

Influencing the balance of local events is the critical task of public policy and donor assistance. That the balance of events matters more over time than any single event, no matter how large and calamitous it may immediately seem, is illustrated below with the help of an example taken from Gujarat, India.

The Balance of Momentous and Ordinary Events

A severe earthquake, measured at 7.7 on the Richter scale, devastated parts of Gujarat in 2001. In order to identify changes in people's poverty status and to evaluate and help redesign programs of assistance, we conducted a study five years later at the behest of the women's cooperative movement, Self-Employed Women's Association (or SEWA). The *Stages-of-Progress* methodology was used for this study, which was undertaken over four months in 2006. Event histories were compiled for a total of 2,660 households belonging to 50 communities in three districts of this state.[23]

The epicenter of the 2001 earthquake was located in Kutch district of Gujarat. More than 20,000 people were killed, another 160,000 were seriously injured, and about 70 percent of all buildings in this district were partly or fully destroyed, including the homes of more than 1.5 million people. All at once, households in Kutch district were devastated. Although the effects of this earthquake were also felt in the adjoining districts of Patan and Surendranagar, death and damage occurred on a much smaller scale.

One would have expected that a disaster of these proportions would produce long-term poverty effects, casting many households into persistent poverty, especially in Kutch, with smaller dips occurring in the two adjoining districts. Surprisingly, however, a different nature of trends was observed. From five years before to five years after the earthquake, that is, between 1996 and 2006, the proportion of people experiencing poverty *fell* by 13 percent in villages of Kutch. Over the same period, the stock of poverty *rose*, respectively, by 12 percent and 2 percent, in villages of neighboring Patan and Surendranagar Districts. In the district that was worst affected by the catastrophe, there was a net reduction in the stock of poverty. In two less badly affected districts, the numbers of people in poverty increased.

No sudden spurt in economic activity occurred after the earthquake in Kutch, nor were the rains continuously bountiful in subsequent years. No single sizeable event seems to account for this observed paradox in poverty trends. Timely assistance provided by a variety of agencies certainly helped households cope with the immediate effects of the disaster. Over time, however, a collection of ordinary events was more closely implicated with households' movements into and out of poverty.

The ordinary events that mattered most in these communities included marriages, sicknesses, births and deaths, employment, investments in land or a business—occurrences that are very significant for the household concerned but that do not constitute, individually or collectively, some unusual or striking episode for an entire community, far less for an entire region. Ordinary events of a positive nature, such as an informal-sector job or a successful business investment, helped take households upward. Other ordinary events, such as illnesses or expensive ceremonies, exerted downward tugs on households. The balance of these ordinary events determined the final outcome for each particular household.

Figure 5.1 demonstrates graphically the importance of viewing the balance of events. The variable 'net events,' shown on the horizontal axis of Figure 5.1, is simply a net count of ordinary events. It measures the sum of all positive events less the sum of all negative events experienced by a particular household over the ten-year period examined in this study. The vertical axis reports the number of stages by which a household improved its status in 2006 compared to

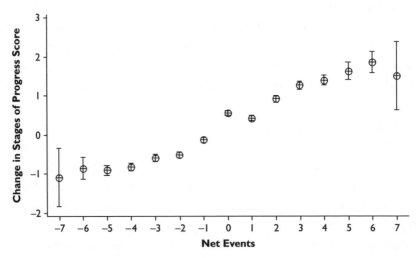

Fig. 5.1 Relationship Between Household Events and Change in Status (95% CI for the Mean).

Note: Change in Stages of Progress score (on the vertical axis) is calculated as a household's stage in 2006 minus its stage in 1996. Net events (on the horizontal axis) is calculated as the number of all positive events less the number of all negative events experienced by a household over the ten-year period, 1996–2006.

1996. Negative numbers refer to those households whose stage of progress in 2006 was lower than it had been in 1996, that is, they suffered a reversal of fortune. Positive numbers represent an improvement of status over this ten-year period.

A regular relationship is apparent in Figure 5.1 between the net number of ordinary events that a household experienced and the extent of change (positive or negative) in its economic situation. Households who continued to experience negative events after the earthquake became worse off compared to where they had been five years before the earthquake. Households who could avoid negative events while experiencing positive ones improved their economic situations—despite the earthquake.

The effects of a one-time calamitous event have not been determinative over the longer term. Successions of ordinary events have eroded or enhanced its influence over a period of time.

Immediately, the earthquake had a devastating negative impact, and it is likely that households would have progressed even further if the earthquake had not taken place. But other—less visible and less frequently noted—events also made a difference. What mattered ultimately was the balance of events.

Policy effectiveness lies in attending more closely to the balance of ordinary events. Too often, however, policy makers tend to get fixated on grand and sweeping causes. Smaller events that take place below the policy radar get hidden from their view. As a consequence, many useful policy levers remain undetected.

Much more attention needs to be paid in the future to the minutiae of individual lives and to the balance of ordinary events. New systems of poverty monitoring are required for assisting with these purposes.

Changes Over Time and Across Space

Reasons for escape and descent do not remain static. They can change significantly, especially over longer periods of time. Some previously influential factors can become less important, while some other factors can gain in influence and scope. Thus, program designs that are useful at the present time may not be equally efficacious in the future. Policy effectiveness lies in keeping current our knowledge of positive and negative reasons. Context-specific reasons for escape and descent need to be tracked on a regular basis.

Table 5.2 Variations Across Space and Time (an Example from Uganda)

CENTRAL REGION	WESTERN REGION
FIRST PERIOD (1979–94)	
Negative reasons	
Health care expenses	Land exhaustion
Crop disease	
Positive reasons	
Job (private)	Job (private)
	Land improvement
SECOND PERIOD (1994–2004)	
Negative reasons	
Health care expenses	Health care expenses
Deaths of major income earners	Deaths of major income earners
Marriage expenses	Large family size
Crop disease	Crop disease
	Land exhaustion
Positive reasons	
Diversification (informal sector)	Job (private)
Land improvement	Land improvement

Table 5.2 presents some results from Uganda that show how reasons for escape and descent have changed with the passage of time. Two separate regions, Central and Western, were considered for this analysis as well as two separate time periods, 1979–94 and 1994–2004. In order to facilitate brevity and enable comparison, only the identities of statistically significant factors are reported here.[24] The balance of events was considered by viewing both positive and negative events.

Notice how negative reasons that were significant during the first time period continued to remain significant during the second time period. In addition, other negative reasons gained significance during the second time period. It should come as no surprise that almost twice as many households fell into poverty during the second time period as compared to the first time period (as seen earlier in Table 3.4 of Chapter 3).

Health-related reasons for descent were not significant in Western villages during the earlier time period. During the later time period, health-related reasons became significant in both regions. Inadequate health care has increased in importance as a reason for descent into poverty.

A second cluster of descent-related reasons includes large family size and marriage expenses. Neither of these negative reasons was significantly associated with descent during the first time period in the Central or the Western Region. However, during the second time period, large family size became a significant factor of descent in Western villages, and marriage expenses became a significant factor of descent in the Central villages.

A third cluster of negative factors includes land-related reasons: land division, land exhaustion, and crop disease. Here the story is more mixed. Land division played a key role for descents in Western Region during both time periods, but this reason was not significant within Central villages in either time period. Land exhaustion became significant in the Western region during the second period, but it has not been an issue in the Central Region in either time period. Crop disease has remained a significant reason for descent during both time periods in Central villages. In Western villages, this reason only became significant during the second time period. Thus, negative reasons have varied both spatially and over time.

Positive reasons have also differed between these two regions of Uganda and across the two time periods considered. In communities of Western Region, the same two positive reasons—jobs in the private sector and land improvement—were significant during both time periods. In communities of Central Region, reasons for escape changed considerably between the first and the second time period. Private sector jobs and business gains were significant during the first time period. In the second time period, private sector jobs lost significance, while diversification of income sources (through the urban informal sector) gained significance.

These results help reinforce a finding presented earlier, namely, that reasons for escape and descent vary geographically. As important, these results show how reasons for escape and descent change over time. Older threats and opportunities can become less important; newer threats and opportunities can arise.

Adjustments to policy designs need to be made on both counts. Policies must be geographically variegated, targeting context-specific threats and opportunities. Further, policy designs must be amended over time in response to changes in reasons for escape and descent.

Efforts must be made to identify at regular intervals the most influential positive and negative reasons operating within each particular region.

Institutions need to be put in place that can help policy makers acquire this ground-level information on a continuous basis.

A network of poverty monitoring stations—akin to weather stations—can help considerably in this regard. By identifying region-specific reasons for escape and descent and by keeping track of these reasons as they change over time, such poverty monitoring stations can help make policies and programs more responsive to current and emerging concerns. I will discuss this point further in the concluding chapter, expanding further upon this proposal for poverty monitoring stations.

Meanwhile, it is important to probe in more detail the nature and quality of individual escapes. Why have most escapes from poverty been narrow and insubstantial affairs? Why have more individuals not gone further ahead? Some answers to these questions were provided earlier in this chapter. Some additional considerations are examined below.

Restricted Upward Mobility

Consider once again Table 2.1 of Chapter 2 in which sample stages of progress (from one set of Kenyan communities) are depicted. Notice how a considerable distance still remains to be traveled after people move out of poverty and before they become prosperous. In this Kenyan case, four stages of progress are located between the poverty and the prosperity cut-offs. In Uganda, similarly, an intermediate zone, consisting of four stages of progress, straddles the space between poverty and prosperity. Similarly wide intermediate zones— between poverty and prosperity—were reported as well within the other regions studied.

Households who have moved out of poverty in the past have mostly moved into these intermediate zones. The distance that exists between poverty and prosperity—four stages in the Kenyan case and in the Ugandan case—was covered in full by only a small proportion of households who escaped poverty.

On average, those who escaped poverty in these Kenyan and Ugandan communities improved their status by 3.4 stages. Thus, even if they had started out just below the poverty cut-off—and many started their climbs from further below—the majority of those who rose out of poverty were unable to rise past the prosperity cut-off. Those who could not previously afford to send their children to school can do so now; they can also purchase small animals, like chickens and goats; and some among them can go further yet, making improvements to their homes. But most of them still cannot afford to buy more land, construct a brick house, or purchase a refrigerator. In other regions as well, households' movements out of poverty has been marked in most cases by relatively small improvements in living conditions.

Two accounts from Uganda give some indication of the nature and extent of the changes involved. Namwandu Wanyana Kizindo, a female resident of Katega Village, provided the first account: 'My husband died in the war in Luwero. I started brewing *waragi* [the local alcohol]. I got a reasonable amount of money from it, and I was able to start up a small piggery project. This project is still paying me. I also generate some money from making and selling mats and baskets.'

Mwera, a resident of Lwanda Village in Luwero District, narrated the second account: 'After the bush war ended, I worked hard in agriculture. I grew coffee, which had a market then. Now the most selling item is bananas, which makes local brew, and I am seriously doing that. The difference between other banana growers and me is that I make the beer myself instead of selling the bananas. Therefore, I earn some more money than them.'

In neither of these cases, nor in the majority of other cases of escape from poverty, did the household concerned experience any vast increase of income or wealth. A preponderance of small gains was commonly observed in all of the other regions studied. Such communities and such natures of escape from poverty are hardly atypical. The bulk of world poverty—more than 75 percent by some estimates—continues to remain located within rural communities. Analyses show that while 'the share of US$1-a-day poor living in urban areas rose from 19 percent to 24 percent over 1993–2002, even so, it will be many decades before a majority of developing world's poor live in urban areas.'[25]

Left to themselves, people in rural communities will continue to tread pathways similar to the ones that were taken earlier. Some households will seek to diversify their incomes through agriculture. Others will look for informal positions within a city. As a result—unless some more effective interventions are mounted relatively soon—escapes from poverty will continue to remain in the most part insubstantial, and often, precarious, affairs.

Why have more substantial gains not been made by larger numbers of households? Considering the nature of involvement that poorer people have with agriculture and the informal sector provides us with an important set of clues.

Limitations in Agriculture

Consider agriculture first. It is notable that even as industries and services are often hailed as the engines of modern economic growth, agriculture has served as one of two principal pathways out of poverty. The figures reported in Table 5.1 show how agricultural improvements of different kinds were associated with a very large number of escapes, ranging from 29 percent in industrializing Gujarat to as many as 64 percent in Kenya.

Evidence from a broader swathe of countries shows similarly how, compared to the industries and services sectors, growth in agriculture has had more beneficial effects for poorer people. Commenting on this aspect, the World Bank's *World Development Report 2008* observes how 'Cross-country estimates show that GDP growth originating in agriculture is at least twice as effective in reducing poverty as GDP growth originating outside agriculture.'[26]

With so many of the world's poor people continuing to live in rural areas, it is hardly surprising that analyses have commonly highlighted the poverty-reducing role played by agriculture. It has been computed that as much as 84.5 percent of all poverty reduction in India during the second half of the twentieth century can be attributed to rural growth, particularly growth in the agricultural sector, with growth in manufacturing having much smaller effects.[27]

For China, where some of the most impressive gains in poverty reduction have been witnessed, especially from the late-1970s through the end of the 1980s, agriculture has been calculated to account for '77 percent of the decline in national poverty rates.' By contrast, trade reforms are not even a 'plausible candidate for explaining China's progress against poverty.'[28] As the focus of China's economic strategies has shifted from the countryside to the global economy, the poverty-reducing effects of economic growth appear to have declined considerably. 'From about the middle of the 1980s—the beginning of the shift in China's development focus away from the rural economy and toward integration with the global economy—China experienced increasingly more dis-equalizing and less poverty-alleviating economic growth.'[29]

Analyses conducted in many other developing countries have regularly reaffirmed the same point: Growth in the agricultural sector has been pivotal for reducing poverty.[30] These country-level examinations paint a picture that is similar to what we saw earlier with the help of our micro-level investigations. Rather than the manufacturing or services sectors, agriculture has provided the more important pathway out of poverty.

Unfortunately, the extent to which different households can get ahead with the help of agriculture is limited by the amount of land that they possess. The data we collected shows that, in general, poor households—both those who have remained persistently poor and others who have fallen into poverty—operate very tiny parcels of agricultural land. Average land-holding among poor households was less than 1.5 acres in the Ugandan communities studied. In communities of Cajamarca, Peru, average land-holding among poor households was only 1.4 acres. In Vadodara district of Gujarat, it was 1.1 acres; in Nalgonda district of Andhra Pradesh, 0.72 acres; and in East Godavari district of the same Indian state, poor households held on average only 0.48 acres. Given that each household has six members on average, per capita landholdings are miniscule in size. Many rural house-holds, who are dependent on agriculture for a living, possess no agricultural land of their own. As many as 27 percent of poor households in rural Andhra Pradesh communities and 21 percent of all poor households in rural Cajamarca communities are landless.

Table 5.3 reproduces from our statistically representative study of Kenya the average landholdings of poor households in different livelihood zones.[31] Notice how even in the pastoral districts of Livelihood Zone 4—where the potential for crop farming is relatively low—the extent of land held by poor households is no more than 2.6 acres on average. In the more fertile areas of Livelihood Zones 1 and 2, the average poor household's landholding is smaller still, no more than 1.5 acres in Livelihood Zone 1 and 1.75 acres in Livelihood Zone 2. Per capita land-holdings among poor households are nowhere more than one-half of an acre.

Not a great deal of advancement through agriculture can be achieved given this tiny asset base. With each passing generation, even these small land-holdings are likely to be further sub-divided. As a result, the already small

Table 5.3 Kenya: Average Land Cultivated by Poor Households (in Acres)

	Livelihood Zone 1	Livelihood Zone 2	Livelihood Zone 3	Livelihood Zone 4
Households who have remained persistently poor	1.0	1.6	2.2	2.6
Households who became poor between 1998 and 2006	1.5	2.1	2.6	2.4

potential for self-improvement will become progressively smaller. Already, such a trend is visible in India. A government report observed that while productivity per worker in agriculture has increased only marginally, per capita area operated has decreased substantially, falling by more than 50 percent between 1960 and 2003.[32]

The Low Glass Ceiling in the Informal Sector

Those who have opted to take the informal sector route have also faced their share of difficulties and privations. Despite being widely important, as we saw above, this sector has rarely served as a conduit to prosperity. On the contrary, people who took the informal-sector route have mostly joined the swelling ranks of the urban near-poor. Many among them live in dwellings 'constructed out of crude brick, straw, recycled plastic, cement blocks, and scrap wood,' where they 'squat in squalor, surrounded by pollution, excrement, and decay,' as Mike Davis has described.[33]

A survey of informal sector workers in New Delhi, India, found 'a high degree of uncertainty, irregularity, and lack of socioeconomic security. Irregular employment means irregular income, and fall-back options are few. Income depends on hours worked, and loss of hours due to illness means a fall in income.'[34] In Mumbai, another rapidly growing city of India, informal sector workers were found occupying positions such as

> cart pullers, rag-pickers, scullions, sex workers, car cleaners, mechanic's assistants, petty vendors, small-time criminals, and temporary workers in petty industrial jobs requiring dangerous physical work ... They often sleep in (or on) their places of work, insofar as their work is not wholly transient in character. While men form the core of this labor pool, women and children work wherever possible, frequently in ways that exploit their sexual vulnerability.[35]

Reports from other developing countries paint a picture of similarly unpropitious circumstances. Bangladesh's large apparel industry, which has provided as many as 1.5 million (mostly informal) jobs, is reported to be composed of

> 3,300 inadequately regulated garment factories, some of which are among the worst sweatshops ever to taunt the human conscience. Holidays mandated by law are a myth. People are expected to work virtually every day. Overtime pay, another legal requirement, is also a myth. Most wages range from $25 to $50 a month, or as little as six cents an hour. Children earn less. 'When we'd

complain, they'd lock the door so we couldn't get out,' said one sewing machine operator. 'If someone complained too much, they were fired.' Factories are often makeshift enterprises in Dhaka's decrepit downtown buildings. Electrical wiring is frequently a jangle of overloaded circuits.[36]

In the areas we studied, the situations of the individuals concerned were not qualitatively different from the ones described above. Overall, less than 10 percent of all households escaping poverty via the informal sector route have crossed past the intermediate zone. In the remaining 90 percent of cases of people escaping poverty, the city on the hill remains still a distant dream.

Why have so many escapes from poverty nevertheless taken place through the informal sector route? One explanatory factor is related to the nature of employment growth. Some countries have experienced little or no employment growth in the formal sector, as discussed above. But even in contexts where better opportunities have been available in larger numbers, institutional discontinuities have effectively limited poor people's access to higher return niches. 'Most people have been going into the informal economy because they cannot find jobs or are unable to start businesses in the formal economy.'[37] Large amounts of capital are often required to enter more lucrative sectors, so poorer people, lacking access to credit sources, are effectively denied access.[38] Information is another critical and missing resource.

> Markets where information is highly imperfect and asymmetrically held are often biased against the poor, for whom and from whom credible information may be scarcer and more difficult to process and certify. In such circumstances, the rich have many advantages—information for them and about them is less of a problem.[39]

Because upward mobility has been restricted in different ways, people from poorer households have no option except to find places for themselves within the growing informal sector, quite often taking up dirty, dangerous, and semi-legal or illegal occupations, with no insurance against workplace injuries, no legal protections, and no security of tenure. Thus, while the kinds of diversifications currently ongoing can help reduce the numbers in poverty, they will not result in producing a society of the prosperous. The numbers of near-poor people will continue to increase. In the two closing decades of the twentieth century these numbers grew by 600 million worldwide (see Chapter 1).

Conclusion: Slim Improvements

In each of the diverse regions and communities investigated, large numbers of formerly poor households have escaped poverty. No particular household characteristic (other than gender) is consistently associated with escapes from poverty. Rather, a particular set of events is involved. Ordinary events, rather than momentous ones, were more often implicated in escapes and descents within the regions and communities examined.

Different types of ordinary events have mattered more within each particular context. No uniform set of interventions will help promote escapes from poverty everywhere. Context-specific forms of assistance will be more effective. Locally relevant threats and opportunities must be investigated before programs of assistance are given shape. Not only do reasons for escape and descent vary geographically; they also change significantly over time. Keeping policy effective requires staying abreast of these changes. One cannot simply continue doing what was done earlier or 'replicate' what worked well somewhere else.[40]

New systems of poverty monitoring are required that can help map reasons for escape and descent on a regular basis. Using this knowledge, policies and programs need to evolve, reflecting ongoing changes on the ground.

More attention needs to be given as well to improving the *quality* of escapes from poverty. In the past, poverty was overcome by large numbers of people, but prosperity was achieved by relatively few. Secure and formal jobs were available in only a small number of cases. Even within regions that experienced rapid economic growth, low-paying and precarious informal sector positions were more important for escapes from poverty. Agriculture helped additionally in many instances of escape. However, the potential for improvement via the agriculture route has been limited by poorer households' typically tiny asset holdings. As landholdings diminish further on a per capita basis, even more limited possibilities for progress will remain.

People who live within rural communities are not unaware of these facts. Very few look anymore to the village as a place where their sons and daughters can build viable careers. A large-scale transfer of talent is under way, with smart and educated young men and women from rural households seeking opportunities in city-based occupations. Unfortunately, most of them, even the more educated ones, have failed to obtain any higher-paying niche.

Most individuals escaping poverty have gone on to serve in subsidiary occupations. They have been assisted by the growth of the modern economy, and they have helped build this growth, but their roles and their contributions have been marginal in most cases. Working as maids and gardeners and construction laborers and small farmers, they have no doubt played an important part, but very few among them have become drivers of mainstream processes of economic growth. Their peripheral—and in many cases, shadowy—roles are responsible for the low glass ceiling under which many still remain.

Newer and better trails out of poverty will need to be blazed. Individuals, especially the more capable ones, should have access to a better set of opportunities. What needs to be done in order to support this higher-order objective? The next chapter addresses these issues.

CHAPTER 6

Connecting Capability
with Opportunity:
Investing in Information

We saw in the previous chapter how agriculture and the urban informal sector have provided the principal pathways out of poverty. Many people who took these pathways rose above the lower poverty cut-off, but relatively small improvements were made in most cases. How should the prospects for upward mobility be raised in the future?

Few answers are as yet available in the academic literature, although a growing body of research is concerned with these questions. Researchers belonging to diverse disciplines are examining issues related to social mobility, equal opportunity, and income inequality,[1] showing how these concepts are related in practice. Opportunity is more widespread in societies where an individual's expected level of achievement is 'a function only of his effort and not of his circumstances.'[2] Family background and class of origin count for less in such societies; individuals' capabilities and hard work count for more. Social mobility is higher within societies where opportunities are more equitably and widely distributed, where even the poorest and humblest have a real chance to rise high. In turn, when capable individuals from poorer households are able to advance further, inherited inequalities are progressively reduced.

Thus, a society that enables more poor individuals to rise, not just above the lower poverty line, but all the way up to the city on the hill, will experience lower inequality over time. Conversely, inequalities will tend to grow in societies where capable individuals from poor communities are unable to rise to higher paying positions.

By more effectively utilizing its overall talent pool, a society that promotes social mobility should also achieve faster economic growth. On grounds of efficiency, as much as for reasons of equity, therefore, equalizing opportunity should be seen as an important societal goal. 'In today's globalized world, with competition largely on the basis of skills and ideas, countries need to cultivate latent talent wherever it might reside. Motivated and talented children from poorer households deserve the opportunity to excel as much as their wealthier peers.'[3]

Little practical guidance is available, however, regarding how opportunity can be widened and social mobility enhanced. Research in these fields is still at an early stage. Investigations undertaken so far, mostly within industrialized countries, have helped generate knowledge about the *extent* of social mobility in different societies.[4] Comparatively little work has been done, however, that can help explain *why* these trends have arisen.

Differences in individuals' social mobility prospects have been assessed by examining how sons (and, less often, daughters) fare compared to their fathers. In general, a robust correlation has been found to exist. Richer and higher status fathers tend to have richer and higher status daughters and sons, while poorer and lower status children tend to go together with poorer and lower status parents. However, the closeness of this correlation—the extent of social mobility across generations—varies considerably across different Western countries.[5] 'Some countries have relatively open class structures and hierarchies that are readily breached by upwardly mobile persons from less privileged origins; other societies are relatively closed to intergenerational mobility.'[6]

Researchers examining intergenerational changes in income have found that 'mobility is lower in the United States than in the United Kingdom, where it is lower again compared to the Nordic countries. Persistence is greatest in the tails of the distributions,' that is, the richest and poorest fathers have, respectively, the richest and poorest children.[7] Initial examinations in a small group of developing countries have shown that parents' and children's earnings are more closely correlated in these contexts compared to the West.[8]

As yet, few explanations have been provided that can help account for these different trends. Why—for what reasons of institutional history or current policy—is income or class mobility higher in some countries and lower in other countries? A review of this literature points out that 'research on inequality of opportunity has been overwhelmingly oriented toward empirical description, with the consequence that convincing explanations of cross-national variations are lacking.'[9] The task of explaining social mobility patterns—and understanding how they can be purposively influenced—remains as yet substantially incomplete.

Individual factors have been examined and found to have varying degrees of influence. Researchers have found, for instance, that 'IQ cannot explain why children from less privileged social strata systematically perform more poorly than others or why children from privileged families systematically perform better.'[10]

Education can certainly help raise social mobility prospects. However, the effects of education appear to be contingent and contextual. While 'educational achievement is a major mediating factor in class mobility, modern societies are not meritocracies in the sense that, once educational qualifications and other "merit" variables are controlled, class of destination is no longer dependent on class of origin. To the contrary, a significant and often substantial dependence remains.'[11] Very similar social mobility patterns are seen to prevail across countries with dissimilar levels of public investment in education and different national educational systems.[12] While individual advancement is rarely possible without at least some amount of education, having more education provides no assurance of greater economic success.[13]

Researchers have examined many other sources of influence, including early childhood nutrition and child rearing practices, race- and neighborhood-related factors, school quality, state-supported daycare centers and pre-school programs, personality traits, health conditions, and cultural capital.[14] Each of these factors can make a significant difference for social mobility.

Calculations show, however, all of these factors collectively explain no more than one-quarter of the observed intergenerational correlation in earnings.[15] Given the present state of knowledge, 'the transmission of economic success across generations remains something of a black box.'[16]

More insights will emerge as this body of work is carried further.[17] Newer and different types of research enterprises will help us learn more about how poorer children can be enabled to compete more effectively in their intellectual weight-class. Barriers to progress and viable means of overcoming these barriers need to be urgently identified. In addition to preventing descents into poverty, enhancing social mobility prospects—raising the quality of individual escapes—is a critical feature of poverty policies of the future.

Two Sets of Inquiries

In an effort to nudge the frontiers of this knowledge—to learn more about who makes it to high positions, who does not, and why—I conducted two sets of original inquiries. First, I looked at a sub-set of high-achievers—newly recruited software engineers in Bangalore, India—and I inquired about the social origins and educational backgrounds of these new recruits. How many among them have backgrounds of poverty? What can be learned from studying these experiences?

Second, I looked within rural communities of India, Uganda, and Peru, and I identified the natures of jobs and positions that different individuals in these communities have achieved in the past. I asked, in particular, about the highest positions—in any walk of life—that individuals from these communities had achieved over the ten-year period prior to my investigations. By studying the experiences of individuals who have climbed appreciably higher, and by comparing these experiences with those of others in the same communities, I tried to learn more about the nature of factors that have enabled superior achievements in the past.

These two sets of inquiries, conducted, respectively, from the top down and the bottom up, helped me learn about many important facts. I did not come upon any slum-born millionaires or even any slum-born software engineers. Similar to what we saw earlier from the poverty data, these additional inquiries tell a story of limited upward mobility. Relatively little progress has been made by poor households in the course of one or even two generations.

Low-level achievements in the past have produced low aspirations among individuals currently preparing for employment. In turn, low aspirations produce low achievements in the future. A low-level equilibrium is the result.

Breaking this cycle of low achievements and low aspirations is critical for raising social mobility. Different kinds of interventions are required. Among these interventions, information has a very important role to play. In many other cases, the roads that lead to higher paying positions are not traveled because they are not known.

Information about career pathways is not a freely available resource nor is it simply a by-product of education. I met several educated men and women in diverse communities who continue to live in conditions of poverty. Several others, not equally educated, have overcome poverty and risen higher. Differences in information availability account in part for these different outcomes. People who were informed about a broad range of opportunities more often found positions commensurate with their capabilities. Others, less well informed, aspired to and (if they were lucky) achieved low-level positions.

I found that ignorance about career opportunities and pathways most often arose on account of institutional gaps. Information-providing institutions— such as employment exchanges, career counseling services, college guides, and the like—are virtually non-existent in the communities where poor people typically live. As a result, people learn about opportunities and pathways almost entirely from other people who form part of their social network. Individuals whose social networks provide richer and more complete information come to know about the roads that lead to more rewarding careers. In other cases, latent talents fail to flourish as a consequence of inadequate roadmaps.

Such a situation cannot be allowed to persist. Investments in better information provision are critical for a just society. They will not fully resolve the problem of limited upward mobility, but they are a necessary component of any workable solution.

Diverse impediments exist that need to be tackled simultaneously. A complementary package of interventions, including education, health care, and information will provide a more considerable boost to social mobility. Physical connections—such as roads, bridges, and telephone and internet links—are very important. Social inclusion—sometimes denied on grounds of gender or community—is essential to enforce. Information provision is also necessary; cognitive connections are a necessary resource.

The Bangalore data, presented next, first made me aware of the importance of information. Supplementary inquiries conducted within rural communities of three countries, discussed later, showed me how lack of information has limited people's aspirations and lowered their incentives to invest.

Who Became a Software Engineer?

Bangalore, home for much of India's software industry, is a hub of globalization, off-shoring, and out-sourcing. Many higher-paying jobs are located within this fast-growing city. Many poor people inhabit its slums and sidewalks.

I based my study of recently recruited software engineers within three software companies of Bangalore.[18] I am indebted to the chief executives, human resource managers, and other employees of MindTree, Philips, and Sasken— three software companies of different sizes—who generously agreed to take part in this study.

Human resource managers in each of these companies compiled a list of software professionals recruited at the entry level over the previous five years. Fifty such individuals were selected through random sampling from each participating company, making for a total sample size of 150. A pre-tested survey instrument was administered online to these individuals. A total of 102 individuals completed this survey, resulting in a very encouraging response rate of 73 percent.[19] Interviewing human resource managers of four other software companies, I learned that recruitment practices are fairly similar across this industry. Thus, the patterns reported below should not be dissimilar to those prevailing more widely within the software industry.

Different economic and social backgrounds characterize newly hired software professionals. The diversity of India finds reflection in this group of new recruits. Different regions, languages, and caste and ethnic groups are represented.

Compared to rural households, however, urban ones are better represented. While more than 70 percent of India's population lives within rural areas, only 11 percent of software professionals grew up in rural areas and attended rural high schools. Being educated in a city appears to convey a distinct advantage. Apart from the quality of education, there are also other benefits to living in a city, as we will see below.

We assessed economic conditions in these software engineers' households of birth by asking about 15 different assets. This list of assets included relatively minor assets, such as bicycles and radios, as well as higher valued ones, such as commercial properties, farm machinery, and stocks and bonds.

Not a single software engineer in our sample grew up in a household that was entirely without assets. Not one grew up in an urban slum. However, quite restrictive economic conditions were faced in several cases. A total of 14 percent of respondents grew up in households who possessed no assets other than one bicycle or one radio. Despite being embedded within an increasingly unequal society, the software industry in India has helped equalize opportunities to some extent.

Table 6.1 Software Engineers in Bangalore: Parents'
Education Levels (Percent of Respondents)

Level	Father	Mother
PhD	3	1
Masters (or equivalent)	32	13
Bachelors (or equivalent)	47	37
High School	17	29
Less than High School	0	19

Children from households with straitened circumstances do have a chance of rising high, these results indicate. However, what differentiates those capable but economically less well-off children who make it to higher paying positions from hundreds of others who do not?

The data pointed toward a peculiar factor that is common to a vast majority of successful cases—and very uncommon for Indian society as a whole. More than any other factor, the level of their *parents' education* clearly distinguishes those who have become software engineers. Table 6.1 provides these results.

A total of 80 percent of interviewed software engineers have fathers who are college graduates (46 percent of fathers have a bachelor's degree, another 31 percent have a master's degree, and 3 percent have doctoral degrees). Not one father has less than a high school education. Additionally, as many as 51 percent of respondents' mothers have college degrees, while another 29 percent have high school diplomas. Thus, 80 percent of mothers have a high school education or better.

This combination of college-graduate fathers and high-school-graduate mothers is rarely found in India. National statistics show that among Indians of the same age group as the parents of newly recruited software engineers (that is between 45 and 70 years), less than 7 percent of all males are college graduates, and less than 4 percent of all females have a high school diploma (or any higher qualification). Considering rural areas alone, these percentages are lower still. No more than 3.5 percent of all rural men between 45 and 70 years have a college education, and less than 1 percent of rural females of this age group have completed high school.[20]

Thus, if having two educated parents is a 'requirement' for gaining entry to better paying jobs, then at best somewhere between 4 to 7 percent of all Indians will qualify. The rest, more than 90 percent, will most likely not advance very far. This range of figures may seem startling at first, but it is not very different from what other observers have independently deduced.[21]

Why should parents' education have such a strong association with upward mobility? Several avenues of influence are suggested by the emergent literature on social mobility in industrialized countries. First, as parents, particularly mothers, become better educated, early childhood nutrition and upbringing practices tend to improve. Second, educated parents are better able to monitor their child's progress at school, reinforce what is taught in the classroom, hold teachers accountable, and provide emotional and practical support.[22] Third, educated parents transmit higher levels of cultural capital—habits, dispositions, and social skills—thereby enabling their children to fit more easily within higher social strata. In industrialized societies, in multiple ways, parents' education makes a difference to individuals' social mobility prospects.

In developing societies, parents' education matters even more. In addition to providing all of the other positive influences listed above, educated parents also serve as their child's most important source of career information. In environments where knowledge about career opportunities is mostly propagated by word-of-mouth, where no information institutions are at hand, having two educated parents—who are socially networked with other educated and well informed people—is the best source of career guidance that any individual can hope to get.

In follow-up interviews that I conducted with a selection of young software engineers in Bangalore, I asked specifically about the roles that had been played by their parents. One young man informed me as follows:

> There was some guidance from my [relatively less educated] parents. That was mostly about: You should study well and do well. There was no clear-cut career guidance—[indicating] this is the line of work that you should go into—which could help me decide what is good for me. I think that kind of environment was just not there. It was more like: Study well and do well, so you can get into a good job. What that good job could be was never made clear.

Another young respondent expressed similar thoughts:

> There are a set of people who are from more educated families. I know my friends whose parents were teachers or professors or doctors. Their children have done their bachelors, masters, or Ph.D. degrees, because that is what they were brought up to do. They were always very aware of what they wanted

to be...People like me? All of us want to get into jobs. We want to start working. We have no clear objective. No clear idea is given to us by our parents. Education is not the biggest hurdle; it is the clarity of vision that one grows up with.

Interviews with other young software engineers and with young residents of different rural communities helped me learn more about how people's vision had been limited in some cases and widened and sharpened in other cases. A very important difference was made by how easily and reliably information about career pathways could be obtained.

In communities such as the ones I investigated, knowledge about higher paying job opportunities is hard to come by. Many capable young people do not get to know about the range of opportunities that exist, where to go, how to apply, and what kinds of preparation to undertake in order to compete successfully with other candidates. Attending a high school or college in a rural area does not automatically fill these information gaps. Rarely, if ever, do schools provide any such information. Every individual must fend for himself or herself.

My children, growing up in the United States, were privy to a barrage of career-related information. They had access not only to dedicated counselors at school, but also to several career-related publications, to libraries and internet resources, and to numerous friends and their parents. The children whom I meet in developing-country communities have access to few information resources. They live on the wrong side of a wide information divide.

'I knew that there probably were many job opportunities,' another newly recruited software engineer informed me, 'but I did not have any access to the information required. Even today, no newspaper comes into my village.'

In such circumstances, it is the exceptional (or exceptionally lucky) individual who is able to rise high. Vasundhara is one such exceptional individual. She grew up in a village in southern India, part of a family that was neither poor nor prosperous, living between the upper and lower poverty lines. Economic conditions were tight in her family. Because she is a woman, Vasundhara faced additional obstacles.[23]

Despite these limitations, Vasundhara succeeded in becoming a software engineer, finding employment in one of the best-reputed and highest-paying companies of Bangalore. How was she able to make this impressive leap? Here is what Vasundhara told me.

I studied in my village until Class 5, that is, elementary school. Then I went to the neighboring village, where my grandparents lived. I studied there until I finished Class 7. There, one of my teachers recommended to my father to send me to an urban high school.

This teacher had detected that Vasundhara was especially talented. In multiple ways, not least through information provision, he helped Vasundhara succeed.

He went and obtained the official application form and actually processed the entire application. He was the one who initially informed my father about this possibility and then continued to urge us on. With his guidance, I wrote an examination meant to pull in the talent among rural children who are 11 to 13 years old.

She performed extremely well at this competitive examination.

And then I was funded by the government and went to attend [an elite] public school in a big city. That is where I completed my high school. Initially, when I got that admission, my parents were reluctant to put me into [what for them was] a very new thing. But my teacher helped here also. He told them that it would be safe for me: He had relatives living in this city.

After graduating from high school, and with the help of another fellowship, she attended a well-regarded engineering college, following which she went to work in the software industry. None of this would have been possible without the critical first step.

Vasundhara is quick to acknowledge the role played by her former schoolteacher: 'I will thank him all my life. But for him, my education would have ended when I was 14 years old. He helped me make the connections that opened my eyes.' In turn, she is helping other individuals connect with appropriate opportunities. She collects information about diverse higher paying opportunities and she shares it with young people in her village whenever she visits.

I wished after hearing Vasundhara's story that every village schoolteacher could be like the one that she had, inspiring young people and actively steering them toward better opportunities, but I realized that I was merely being wishful. Exceptional individuals like Vasundhara's former schoolteacher can make very important differences, but communities and countries cannot wait for exceptional individuals to come around.

Instead of relying upon the luck of the draw, *information institutions* need to be built, so that all who desire it can obtain career-related information regularly and close to hand. Why can't smart village kids, such as the hundreds whom I met, have access to newspapers, libraries, counselors, role models, and mentors (and specialized interactive web sites)? It cannot be only because of shortage of funds. Public libraries began to be widespread in England and the United States as early as the seventeenth century.

The connection between information resources and economic development needs to be visualized more clearly. In more ways than one, lack of connection is the critical impediment. This lesson was reinforced by my inquiries in rural communities.

A Low Glass Ceiling

Supplementary inquiries were undertaken within a group of 165 diverse rural communities of India, Uganda, and Peru. Within each such community we inquired about the highest positions—in any walk of life—that residents, both current and former ones, had achieved over the previous ten years.[24]

Table 6.2 provides the results obtained from 20 communities of Karnataka, a state in the southern part of India that has Bangalore as its capital city. I had thought that because of the proximity to Bangalore at least a few software engineers would have emerged from within these communities, but the results of these inquiries were disappointing in general.

In all, nearly 60,000 people inhabit these 20 Karnataka villages. During the ten-year period preceding the inquiry, a total of 397 individuals graduated from high school. But not one among them became a software engineer. The highest positions achieved in most communities were those of schoolteacher, army recruit, and police constable. These positions are important; schoolteachers,

Table 6.2 Highest Positions Achieved in 20 Karnataka villages (1996–2006)

Schoolteacher (20)	Village Council Secretary (2)
Police Constable (11)	Driver (2)
Jawan (Soldier) (8)	Messenger (2)
Clerk Typist (6)	Engineer (2)
Lawyer (4)	Veterinary Assistant (2)
Land Records Assistant (3)	Nursing Assistant (1)
Accountant (3)	Doctor (1)
Lineman (2)	

army recruits, and police constables make very significant contributions to the societies in which they live. But why should capable and hardworking people not be able to choose from among a wider range of career choices, exploring a richer set of opportunities? Only rarely, however, did people from these communities achieve any higher paying position. One medical doctor, two engineers, and four lawyers represent the highest paid positions achieved collectively by these thousands of village residents over an entire decade.

In a second Indian state, Rajasthan, I conducted similar inquiries within a larger group of 71 village communities—and I obtained very similar results. More than 1,000 residents of these villages graduated from high schools during the ten-year period examined. Yet, only one among them became a software engineer, one other person became a civil engineer, one became a medical doctor, and one individual is practicing as a lawyer in the district court. Others who did manage to get full-time jobs mostly joined at very low levels in some government agency, while many—most of those who graduated from high school and several who completed college—were unable to find any full-time position and had to content themselves with occasional work.[25] The situation was no different in a third Indian state, Andhra Pradesh.

I repeated these inquiries in communities of Uganda and Peru, only to uncover a very similar result. A tiny number of people from these communities were able to obtain any high-paying position. Among all residents of 36 village communities studied in Uganda, two individuals became medical doctors over a ten-year period, two others became school teachers, two people got positions in commercial banks, and one was hired as a laboratory technician in a government hospital. These were the highest positions in any walk of life that anyone from these 36 villages achieved over this ten-year period.

In 20 communities of the Puno region in Peru, four people became school teachers over the ten-year period examined, and one became a nurse practitioner. In addition, one exceptional individual, who was assisted by a distant uncle, left to study at a university in Argentina, and became a biological chemist. In 20 communities of the Cajamarca region of the same country, one individual became a civil engineer, one works at a small cafe in Lima, one other became an electrician, one is sergeant-major in the country's army, four are school teachers, and one is a salesman of veterinary medicine. In most communities, the highest positions achieved were those of president or deputy of the village council.

Separate investigations are required to find out whether social mobility is equally low within other developing countries. However, the regularity of this finding across four countries in three continents could well be suggestive of a more general trend.

Other available evidence also points in a similar direction. Studies show, for instance, that Latin American countries 'are not on the way to becoming 'middle-class societies,' that is, societies that are more egalitarian. On the contrary, there is every indication that the occupational structure has become the foundation for an *unyielding and stable polarization* of income.'[26] Higher income occupations account for only 9 percent of the workforce, 14 percent are in the intermediate category, and the rest, the vast bulk of these countries' workforces, are stuck within the lowest layer. The average earnings of people trapped within this lowest layer, 'a large and disparate mass accounting for three-quarters of all employed workers, are not sufficient to raise a typical Latin American family above the poverty threshold. People compensate by increasing the occupational density of their households.'[27]

Diversification becomes a survival strategy, as we saw in the previous chapter. No single job or occupation suffices to provide a living wage. Multiple household members work at multiple low-paying occupations. 'The general strategy is *isang kahig, isang tuka* (literally, one scratch here, one peck there)... Even those who are lucky enough to have regular employment as factory workers, workmen, drivers or office employees often earn less than the official minimum wage.'[28]

Partly because of these trends, inequality has increased within many developing countries. 'Inequality in China was markedly higher at the end of the 1990s than it had been in the early part of the 1980s. The best available estimates suggest that inequality in India has also been rising. In Bangladesh, Nepal, and Sri Lanka, recent and reliable data show very large increases in inequality.'[29] Across many parts of Latin America, initially high inequality has grown higher.[30] 'The limited statistics for sub-Saharan Africa show that high levels of income inequality have persisted since the 1970s,' becoming worse in many countries in more recent times.[31]

Apart from being unsupportable on normative grounds, such a situation is unsustainable in practice. Rising inequality makes it harder to reduce poverty in the future.[32] Vast and growing gulfs in achievement and opportunity are detrimental to the future of democracy.[33] 'A society characterized by extreme inequalities and the lack of opportunities can become a breeding ground for violence and crime.'[34] Political stability and social peace are more firmly grounded where people are not filled with hopelessness. For all these reasons, much more needs to be done for widening opportunity and raising social mobility.

Information, Incentives, and Aspirations

How can capable people from poorer communities become better connected to a wider and richer set of opportunities, becoming partners in building economic growth rather than 'beneficiaries' of special projects? As mentioned before, knowledge about these aspects is only recently being acquired. It is worrisome, however, that relatively little action is being taken on the knowledge that has been gained. The pattern of low achievements is being perpetuated. Low aspirations are being generated as a result.

Follow-up investigations that I conducted within two groups of rural communities in India showed that the aspirations of those currently attending high schools replicated the pattern of past achievements in these communities. We asked more than 1,000 young village respondents, aged 14–22 years, in two Indian states, Rajasthan and Karnataka, what they aspired to become after completing their studies—what positions they wished to achieve.

We divided these reported career aspirations into two broad types: those that could be classified as high-paying positions, and others that are clearly low-paying ones. We took a rather generous view of the first type of positions including within it, for example, everyone aspiring to become an accountant, doctor, engineer, lawyer, and business manager, regardless of what type of accountant or lawyer they hoped to become or what type of business they intended to manage.

Table 6.3 provides these results. A very large number of young people believe that, despite working hard, they can at most become a village schoolteacher or police constable.[35] Very few people have any better prospects in mind.

Around 40 percent of young adults in both states, Rajasthan and Karnataka, aspire to become schoolteachers. Another large group of young people—26 percent in Rajasthan and 34 percent in Karnataka—aspire to become low-level government employees, such as police constables, bus conductors, typists, and messengers. A third large chunk hopes to become low-level army recruits. In total, 87 percent of young villagers in Rajasthan and as many as 91 percent in

Table 6.3 Percentages Reporting Different Career Aspirations

	Rajasthan	Karnataka
High-Paying Positions		
Accountant	Less than 1%	Less than 1%
Business Manager	Less than 1%	Less than 1%
Doctor	2%	2%
Engineer	3%	4%
Lawyer	2%	1%
Senior Government Official	3%	1%
Other Well-Paid Positions	1%	2%
Low-Paying Positions		
Schoolteacher	43%	39%
Army Recruit	13%	5%
Policeman	11%	12%
Other Low-Level Government Positions	15%	22%
Other Low-Paid Private Occupations	5%	11%

Note: A total of 1,456 respondents aged between 14 and 22 years were interviewed.

Karnataka aspire only to such low-paying occupations. Most of them know of no other positions that they could or should aspire to achieve.

'Individual desires and standards of behavior are often defined by experiences and observation. A person's behavior is conditioned by the experiences of other individuals in the cognitive neighborhood. These experiences may be all-important.'[36]

In the absence of institutions providing career information, people's horizons become limited to the positions that they see in their immediate vicinity. Schoolteachers, low-level government employees, and army recruits make their presence felt in these villages. The pathways that lead up to these positions, being often trodden, become better known. Other occupations appear only hazily on villagers' cognitive horizons. Aspirations are constrained as a result.

A particular incident that occurred in Andhra Pradesh helped me understand better how fear of the unknown can limit what individuals aspire to achieve. In a village of this state, I met Chandru, a gifted young man, at that time about 15 years of age. My colleagues were involved in a community meeting, but knowing no more than a few words of Telugu, the language spoken in this area, I went out for a walk in the village. I had walked a short distance, when, hearing a shout from behind, I turned around to find Chandru coming after me. His right leg, crippled by childhood polio, was supported by a stout wooden stave.

'*Telugu woddu*,' I apologized. 'I know no Telugu.'

'I speak English!' Chandru declared with some pride. He studied in the 9th grade at the village school.

'What is your favorite subject at school?' I inquired.

'Mathematics,' he said, without hesitation.

I wrote out some math questions in my notebook, quite simple ones to begin with, which he answered in a flash. My next few questions were difficult ones, and the ones I wrote later were harder yet. Each time, Chandru responded accurately and quickly.

Then, turning the notebook around, he penned some questions for me. His boldness must have left me gaping, or maybe I was forgetting the mathematics I have learned, but the second of his three questions left me bewildered. I faltered and paused helplessly. Luckily for me, Chandru's father came looking for his son, saving me from the further embarrassment that would surely have ensued.

Like most others of his generation who live in villages in India, Chandru's father has no formal education. (Very few village schools existed when he was a child.) He speaks not a word of English. A conversation between us became possible only because Chandru stepped in to translate. We spoke initially about the crops and the weather and desultorily exchanged other pleasantries, but as soon as I could politely change the subject I came out with the question that was uppermost in my mind.

'What do you wish for this son of yours to become when he is older?'

'He reads every mathematics book that he can find,' Chandru's father told me, 'and he wants to become an engineer. But no one who lives in this village can guide him about how one can become any such thing. What does one do? Where should one go?'

'Besides,' he added pensively, 'it is likely to be very expensive. I have just finished paying for two daughters' weddings, and I am carrying a heavy load of debt.'

Surely, I thought, if lack of money was the major impediment, then some means of financial assistance could be found. Visiting the state capital a few days later, I tried hard to locate a likely source of assistance. With the help of former colleagues, now highly placed in government offices, I came to learn about a fully-funded government fellowship. Further entreaties helped me obtain copies of the stipulated procedures and application forms.

Late that night, in a considerably elevated mood, I wrote a detailed letter of explanation, which I mailed to Chandru the following morning. Naively, I thought that the likelihood of getting external funding would help change this family's decision.

In fact, my little intervention made hardly any impact. Chandru's father was unmoved by the possibility of a free college education. The highest hurdle in his mind was not related to finances. The mere thought of his son becoming an engineer seemed like an impossible dream.

'It is not for the likes of us,' he stoically maintained when I went to see him a few months later. 'No one from here can become an engineer. No one ever has.'

He was factually correct in one important respect: No one from this village community, or for that matter, from any community within a ten kilometer radius, had ever become an engineer—nor had anyone become a doctor, lawyer, engine driver, or architect.

How one can become an engineer was not publicly known. Of all those whom Chandru's father could rely upon for career advice, not one person could provide useful answers to critical questions, such as: What does it take to gain admission to an engineering college? What becomes of those who fail to make the grade? Such information was not available either in the schools of this area or in any other institution, public or private. The ignorance that resulted was responsible in large measure for the low achievements and low aspirations that prevailed.

Economist William Easterly has emphasized the role played by incentives, claiming that where the 'incentives to invest in the future are not there, expanding education is worth little.'[37] Incentives are linked to possibilities and alternatives. When the range of possibilities visualized is itself impoverished, people's incentives to invest are reduced.

Inequality of opportunity is sustained in contexts where information about career options is available only from other members of one's social network. In such societies, as Arjun Appadurai notes, better off individuals tend to 'have a more complex experience of the relationship between a wide range of ends and means, because they have a bigger stock of available experiences...Poorer members have a more brittle horizon of aspirations… and a thinner, weaker sense of pathways.'[38]

There is no natural law, however, which dictates that knowledge about alternative career pathways can *only* be gained from other members of one's own social class. More equal societies have invested in building public institutions that are responsible for providing career-related information to all.

Employment offices, privately operated or government-run, function in every large and small town that I visited in Sweden. Government-operated employment offices, *Arbetsförmedlingen*, have been in operation for a fairly long time. More recently, privately operated employment exchanges have started operating in parallel. Additional guidance and vocational training opportunities are provided at high schools and through trade unions and the mass media.[39]

In Kenya or Uganda, in India or Peru, such facilities are simply unavailable to the vast majority of people. Employment exchanges are hard to find, and where they exist, they function poorly, providing hardly any job-related guidance, and acting solely as registration bureaus. One must possess the information one needs to apply for a job *before* coming into these offices. It is not surprising that poorer people in these countries 'have a thinner, weaker sense of pathways,' and their career aspirations are so often limited to the kinds of low-paying positions that others in their communities have achieved in the past.

Individuals who have suffered from the non-availability of career-related information recognize the critical importance of this resource. Here, for example, is what one software engineer from a less well-off rural household told me.

> QUESTION: Suppose you had a pot of money, and you wished to help young people in rural areas. What would you do?
> ANSWER: I don't need much money for doing this. I would just give more knowledge to the people. This is what you need: You need to create the balance, the urge in people to become whatever they want to become. You just have to make it visible to them—what are the possibilities, what they can achieve if they take this approach—and confidence that they themselves can do it. That would be enough.

He was overstating his case in order to make his point with greater conviction. Information is necessary, but it can never be enough. Information provides the initial spark, helping individuals gain a better idea of the road ahead.

Whether they are able after gaining these ideas to prepare for the careers they wish to pursue depends as well upon the presence of other enabling factors.

Conclusion: Investing in Information

'Information imperfections are pervasive in the economy: indeed, it is hard to imagine what a world with perfect information would be like.'[40] Economists have shown how information asymmetries influence actors' behaviors in the marketplace, producing sub-optimal results in a variety of situations.[41]

Lack of information about career options also produces sub-optimal results. Capable individuals aspire to achieve only low-paying positions, because these are the only positions about which they are able to learn.

The people whom one can ask for advice—along with the sources that one's parents can consult—limit the career possibilities that one is able to identify and pursue. Parents' education can count for a great deal in such situations. The experience of software engineers in Bangalore, India, reviewed above, indicates how having two educated parents has helped some individuals overcome the information deficit. Similar trends have been noted as well within other low-information contexts.[42]

What should be done in respect of capable and hardworking young people whose parents are *not* well educated? One might take the long view and hope that since educational attainments are rapidly increasing, this problem will resolve itself in one generation or two. But a generation or two is a very long time to wait. Can something more effective not be done at the present time?

Examples from diverse countries show that investing in appropriate institutions can help promote equality of opportunity. We reviewed above the example of information institutions in Sweden. Some other examples are also available. In South Korea, where impressive rates of growth were achieved together with rapid poverty reduction, public policies were designed to achieve 'equitable growth in capabilities.'[43] Promoting social mobility was a critical policy concern. Improving public education constituted one part of the government's response. Building linkages—physical and cognitive ones—constituted another important part. Vocational training, career guidance, and job placement were all part of the package of assistance provided by the South Korean government.[44]

The provision of regular and reliable information through a variety of means—role models, mass media, career counselors, web sites, and the like—can help connect talent better with opportunity, thereby promoting faster growth along with greater equity. New forms of institutions can and should be pioneered that make use of diverse technologies.

One such example is provided by Babajob.com, a self-supporting commercial venture launched in Bangalore that is intended to connect employers and job-seekers. The basis of their economic viability lies in successfully bridging the information gap. Sean Blagsvedt, the driving force behind this effort, explained why he quit his lucrative job with Microsoft Inc. in order to promote this vision:

> Most people find jobs through people they know—namely their extended social network—and most employers would like to hire a person whom someone they trust can vouch for. Babajob.com is an attempt to digitize this process to efficiently 'get the word out.' It is an experiment, a possible solution to provide all levels of job seekers with better job opportunities, while efficiently helping employers find suitable employees. We don't know if this will work, but we do collectively believe that the idea is interesting enough, that we simply had to quit our day jobs to give it a shot.[45]

Initially an internet-based provider of job-related information, connecting employers and job seekers in the city of Bangalore, Babajob.com has expanded its activities, utilizing multiple media outlets, arranging for health insurance as well as jobs, and intending soon to extend operations to other Indian cities. An article in the *New York Times* reporting on the early achievements of Babajob. com noted how 'more than 2,000 job seekers had already registered. The listings are a portrait of India's floating underclass, millions and millions seeking a few dollars a day to work as chauffeurs, nannies, gardeners, guards, and receptionists.'[46] Higher paid positions have been filled more recently. Another such example, also headquartered in Bangalore, is LabourNet. According to its web site (www.labournet.in), this organization 'is a professionally managed social enterprise which aims at improving earning opportunities, working conditions, skills and security for workers in the unorganized sector, who constitute over 90 percent of India's work force.'

By making available information about more rewarding career pathways, companies concerned with information technology can help connect talent with opportunity. It should not require a great deal of investment to develop interactive web sites where young people can inquire about the pathways available and the nature of preparation required by each. In fact, such web sites can also help identify individuals with superior capabilities, thereby helping companies find promising future employees at an early stage. The proliferation of internet cafes across small towns in the developing world, and the commitments of governments to provide broadband links in schools across the countryside, suggest that such interventions will bear rich fruit in the future.[47]

Other types of technologies can also help. Radio programs can be designed that help children and young adults learn about different career pathways. Virtual employment exchanges can be run using television programs and mobile telephones. Using other modes of communication—through textbooks and lessons at schools, by means of a lecture series—young adults and their parents can be assisted to overcome the information divide.

As remarked earlier, information is a necessary requirement but not a complete remedy. Several factors, in addition to information, also hamper the life chances of capable individuals growing up in poor communities.

Low-quality education provided in public schools is a notable impediment. Schools located in rural areas and urban slums very often deliver low-quality instructions. Teachers are quite often absent from duty or careless about their tasks.[48] Students emerging from these institutions are inadequately prepared to compete.

Yet only rarely do we come across instances of parents and students agitating for better performance by teachers at school. It is not that they are unconcerned about the educational outcome. Quite often, they know of no better standards. Low aspirations are adequately served even by under-performing teachers, who are rarely called upon to account for their lapses. As aspirations are raised through the provision of better information, and as parents become better informed about their rights as consumers, accountability will be better enforced in public schools.

Developing better role models is critical for these purposes.[49] When one individual from a poor community succeeds in becoming an airline pilot or a software engineer, others will more likely begin to dream of becoming the same. The urge to succeed, the initial spark, will be greatly strengthened when the road ahead becomes clearer. People who are more confident that they can achieve bigger and better things will more often expect and demand better services from the providers.

Many interesting experiments are ongoing that should help develop better role models for the future. Inspired by its farsighted chairperson, H. M. Abed, the NGO, BRAC, launched its *Medha Bikash* (talent development) program in Bangladesh in 2005. Capable high school graduates from poorer households are assisted with fellowships for attending college, given specialized lessons in English and computer skills, and provided with career counseling. *Shanti Bhavan*, a residential school in India, selects talented young children from the poorest rural households and provides them, free of charge, with a first-rate education, nurturing aspirations for higher paying careers.[50] These and other similar initiatives, undertaken in different countries, need to be catalogued, studied over time, and their lessons carefully analyzed and disseminated.

Other types of research will also help. Several questions are worth pursuing, some of which will require taking directions different from those that have been taken in the past. It should be useful, for example, to investigate how many CEOs of private companies, how many senior government officials, sports stars, musicians, theater personalities, etc., have experienced poverty at some point in their lives. How were they able to overcome these odds? Investigating these and other related questions is hardly a stupendous task, but it will help generate important information that is currently unavailable.[51] It will also help compare how societies that have actively promoted equality of opportunity, including by installing information institutions, have fared in comparison to other societies.

All of these tasks will be more easily and more effectively achieved when the goals of the development enterprise are revised to accommodate a more encompassing vision. There is need for a 'broader view of economic development seen in terms of expanding social opportunities.'[52] Institutions and policies that can help make this vision come to life need to be identified and supported.

CHAPTER 7

A Two-pronged Strategy: Protection and Opportunity

New directions and strategies are required for reducing poverty. Newer tactics and tools are also necessary. In the concluding chapter of this book, we will draw together lessons from previous chapters and consider what needs to be done in practical terms.

The prognosis is optimistic. Poverty *can* be reduced much faster—and more securely, in other words, without reversals. But we must begin by acknowledging that a search for sweeping remedies would be ill-conceived. In order to do something meaningful and lasting, poverty must be understood first in elemental terms. People, and not countries, become poor and escape poverty. Investigating the diversity of human experiences is essential for understanding how poverty begins and how it ends.

Information reviewed in Chapter 3 shows that people everywhere are simultaneously moving in opposite directions. Looking only at national stocks of poverty has the effect of obscuring these constitutive flows. Regardless of how well the national economy performs, some people overcome poverty while other people become poor. This simultaneous ebb and flow is the essence of poverty dynamics. It is at the core of what needs to be influenced in order for poverty to be removed. National stocks of poverty cannot be reduced until the constitutive flows are brought under control. In turn, poverty flows cannot be influenced until the reasons associated with each case are identified and addressed.

The parallel flows related to poverty are asymmetric in terms of reasons. One set of reasons is associated with descents into poverty, but a different set of reasons is associated with escapes. Thus, not one, but two, sets of poverty policies are required: one set of policies for preventing descents into poverty and another set to accelerate and augment escapes.

More than any characteristic of the individual people involved, discrete events are associated with both poverty flows. Events of an economic nature are not the only ones that matter. Social and cultural factors also make a big difference. As a result, raising poor people's incomes is not all that is required for reducing poverty. Events that raise people's expenditures also need attention. We saw in Chapter 4 how heavy expenditures—on health care and on social and ceremonial occasions, such as funerals and weddings—have pushed many households into poverty. The effects of such events, which result in producing future poverty, must be reduced. Concurrently, another set of events and processes—those that facilitate escapes from poverty—must be catalyzed and their effects enhanced.

No universal, best strategy is available for these purposes. Reasons for escape and descent vary across space and over time, as we saw in Chapter 5. Diverse threats exist and different opportunities are available in different parts of the same country. A mix of strategies tailored to suit particular contexts is required for reducing poverty more effectively. Localized inquiries, identifying context-specific reasons for escape and descent, are an essential first step.

Objectives and Strategies

Looking at stocks and not at flows—and analyzing aggregate statistics without looking at individual experiences—has resulted in several missed opportunities and strategic errors. More than a few course corrections will need to be made in order that assistance is provided more effectively in the future.

Preventing Future Poverty

First, much more attention should be paid toward preventing future poverty. Many people are poor today who were not poor in the past. Evidence reviewed in Chapter 3 shows that as many as one-third of all presently poor people were not born into poverty. They became chronically poor because of a particular set of events. Different descent-inducing events have operated in each of the different regions investigated. Acting on their own, individuals have very little control over these events. Societies must act collectively to protect people against descent-inducing events. Poor as well as non-poor people need to be better protected.

Preventive policies are essential, all the more since the risk of falling into poverty appears to be growing. We saw in Chapter 3 how descents into poverty have become more frequent. Larger numbers of people have fallen into poverty during a more recent time period compared to a period in the past. The events that induced descents in the past are causing renewed damage. In addition, new reasons for descent have appeared on the scene. Most of those who fell into poverty in the past have remained poor. Relatively few were able to bounce back. Many people who lived comfortable lives in the past have become the chronic poor of today. Many people who are not poor today will become the chronic poor of the future—unless something effective is done.

Preventive assistance must become a norm of poverty reduction. Protecting both poor and non-poor people against the damage caused by negative events is essential. Why wait until *after* someone has become desperately poor before offering assistance? Poverty creation must be nipped in the bud.

Installing context-specific safeguards against descents into poverty is an essential aspect of future assistance efforts. Improving health care is critically important in this regard, as we saw earlier in Chapter 4 and as I will discuss in more detail later. Particular location-specific responses are also necessary. A polycentric approach is proposed in the next section.

Putting the Horse Before the Cart

Policies and programs to combat poverty should be given shape only after contextually relevant reasons for descent and escape have been identified. This sequence of events would appear to be both logical and necessary, a matter of putting the horse before the cart.

Unfortunately, the reverse sequence is only too common. Rather than starting with an examination of the problem and its genesis, particular solutions are investigated first. Too often, poverty action and poverty research tend to be focused on solutions currently in the limelight.[1] Is X or Y best? Is micro finance the magic bullet? Will mobile phones, or adult education, or dry tillage—or whatever else that happens to be currently in vogue—serve as *the* answer to poverty?

Fashions and fancies come and go in the world of development practice. Solutions are proposed and examined energetically—but relatively few efforts are made to understand how the problem has come into being, or how it was actually resolved by the people who overcame poverty in the past.

Implemented on a large scale, even very worthwhile solutions get discredited because they do not work well everywhere. New grand solutions come to take the place of old ones, only to go out the same way as the previous solutions. Developing solutions is important, but figuring out which to employ and where requires an understanding of the specifics of particular situations.

Closed-ended investigations, looking at the efficacy of individual solutions, must be complemented by more open-ended inquiries. The beginnings and ends of poverty must be investigated directly. Implementing solutions based on best guesses is hardly optimal. We need to start by gaining knowledge, as Easterly has advised, 'of local conditions and some ways to get feedback from the poor who will find out (and are already finding out) the variable and complicated answers.'[2] Methods of investigation that assist with problem identification, pointing out looming threats as well as available opportunities, must be built up and implemented.

Attending to the Events that Matter

An enterprise that has looked primarily, and sometimes exclusively, at monumental causes and broad-brush solutions needs to include an examination of smaller scale events and everyday conditions. Macro reasons, affecting large regions or entire countries, are certainly important to investigate and address. Micro reasons, operating over smaller regions, also have very important effects.

Depending upon the circumstances facing any particular group of people, it might be either large-scale events or everyday ones that could make the bigger difference. In situations where banks are failing, or locusts are invading, or civil war is breaking out, it does little good to focus attention upon the smaller problems in life. But where life is more humdrum and consistently meager—as it is for many poor people in large areas of the world—details of everyday life need to be attended to more closely.

Ordinary events made the difference between escape and descent within the communities investigated in five diverse regions of India, Kenya, Uganda, Peru, and North Carolina, USA. Epic or macro-level events do not help account for why some people moved out of poverty in these regions while others simultaneously became poor.

Chains of ordinary events—such as deaths and marriage, illnesses and injuries, crop diseases and social customs—have pushed and are pushing millions of households into poverty. Breaking these chains at their most critical stages is essential for reducing future poverty. Identifying the nature of ordinary events that have mattered in the past will help in designing better assistance programs for the future. It will also help align external assistance more closely with the ongoing efforts of ordinary people.

Going Beyond Immediate Needs

A negative image of the poor—portraying them as lazy, or dissolute, or otherworldly—does not do justice to the facts on the ground. The vast majority of poor people do not sit idly by, waiting for programmatic benefits to arrive. Instead, they make spirited efforts to break out of poverty. Unfortunately, these efforts are too often compromised by negative events. Poor households can take two steps forward, investing a great deal of labor and time in an effort to break out of poverty, but a serious illness might then occur or a crop disease might break out, pushing them back to where they started. Continuing poverty is the result, in most cases, of just such a negative balance of events.

The fundamental objective of a more effective assistance strategy consists in tilting the balance of events in the right direction by encouraging and assisting people's positive efforts while helping to limit the effects of negative events. Addressing poor people's most immediate and visible needs is important, but it is hardly enough.

Poverty is not just about lack of food and inadequate housing. A dynamic perspective, considering poverty flows, shows how these manifestations of poverty come about. Investigating poverty flows shows that:

Poverty = frequent downward tugs + restricted upward mobility.

People remain in poverty because they have few protections against negative events. Simultaneously, their prospects for upward mobility are severely restricted. Shortages of food are experienced because frequent downward tugs draw people into situations of poverty. Unless these downward tugs are reduced in frequency and intensity, more people will need food assistance and housing support in the future.

Addressing the underlying forces—the *reasons* for descent—is critical for altering the conditions that continue to reproduce poverty. In parallel, the provision of opportunities for upward mobility needs to be substantially increased. Once the forces that reproduce poverty are brought under control, the need for immediate assistance will be reduced.

Raising the Bar

The objectives of poverty-reduction policies have been expressed most often in aggregate terms. Reducing the *numbers* of people who live below the poverty line is seen as the primary goal. When considered in relation to the totality of poverty in the world, this goal seems only fair: It would be a better world if fewer people lived below the US$1-a-day level.

A different rationale emerges when these goals and objectives are considered, instead, from the viewpoints of particular individuals. Capabilities vary quite considerably among individuals who are poor. Many are quite capable of rising very high above the poverty line. Only a blinkered vision would set the goal for potential Nobel Prize-winners or star athletes in terms of rising past US$1 a day.

Which goals—whose viewpoints—should inform the design of assistance programs? Should programs be designed that serve only the aggregate goal, helping raise ever larger numbers above US$1 a day? Or should assistance be aimed, not only at reducing the aggregate numbers in poverty, but also at nurturing talent, enabling people to rise as high above the poverty line as they are individually capable? I take the latter view in this book, believing that while the goal of reducing mass poverty is critically important, it cannot overshadow the parallel need for improving poor people's opportunity structures. Certainly, all poor people should be assisted. The basic needs of all should be met in full. However, providing only a few days' wage labor or a couple of goats to highly capable but poor individuals is hardly the best thing that a just society can do for them.

A dynamic vision focused on individual capabilities needs to be adopted. As Nobel Laureate Amartya Sen has persuasively argued,[3] individual capability needs to be recognized and encouraged, even as the conditions of poverty are removed for all. Independent India's first Prime Minister, Jawaharlal Nehru, wrote in 1961: 'I have no doubt that there is a vast reservoir of talent in this country. If only we can give it opportunity!'[4] Policy tools are urgently required to help convert this vision into reality in India and other developing countries.

Opportunity and *protection* constitute the two prongs of a future strategy. Enhancing opportunities for upward mobility—that is, making it possible for individuals to rise as high as their talents and dedication allow—while simultaneously protecting people against the damage caused by negative events: These are the objectives to which different actors in the struggle against poverty must contribute.

No single actor is capable of doing all that is necessary. Influencing specific reasons for escape and descent is better accomplished by using the energies and resources available to multiple actors. In addition to governments and NGOs—the agencies most often charged with the tasks of poverty reduction—social movements, private foundations, academic institutions, for-profit businesses, media agencies, individual volunteers, and grassroots groups can all make very important contributions.

Tools and Tactics

New methods of investigation are required to support these future assistance efforts. New tactics—including better methods of targeting, regular monitoring of context-specific reasons, and polycentric policy responses—will help make better use of the available resources.

Identifying Context-specific Reasons

Longitudinal data sets similar to those existing in the United States and Western Europe need to be constructed within developing countries. These data-collection methods need to be supplemented with others that inquire directly into context-specific reasons for escape and descent. Because studies conducted in the past have rarely identified such reasons, little knowledge has been gained about what factors need to be suppressed and what other factors need to be promoted. Lacking this knowledge, programmatic interventions have been risk-prone; many have failed in important respects.[5]

I have made the case above for new methodologies that can help identify the nature of events—large-scale as well as ordinary—that matter most within particular contexts. While no particular research methodology is best suited for all circumstances, adopting a participatory approach has several advantages. Ideas about what constitutes poverty, and what are viable and honorable ways out of poverty, differ in important respects from one social context to another.[6]

People's strategies and their aspirations are intimately tied up with the ideas that *they* hold about what constitutes poverty. Beginning by learning about these ideas and the strategies to which they give shape can help develop more effective assistance programs that complement, and do not displace, people's ongoing efforts.

The *Stages-of-Progress* methodology, developed for the studies reported in this book, represents one such methodological advance. It helps develop a clear scale of measurement rooted in shared, context-specific, social understandings. Micro reasons for escape and descent are dependably identified. Variations across locations and over time can be tracked. At relatively low cost, such investigations can be undertaken.[7] More precise and better targeted interventions can be designed as a result.

Targeting Reasons Before People

New tactics are required along with new methods of investigation. The thrust and direction of targeting policy has to change. In the past, programs have focused attention on *whom* to target, ignoring *what* to target, which is a mistake.

Targeting people is likely to be of little consequence unless reasons for escape and descent are targeted first. The logic behind this assertion is equally valid for both tasks of poverty reduction.

Let us consider descents first. We cannot really predict who will fall into poverty, but we can with greater confidence identify the reasons responsible for descents. So it makes better sense in respect of controlling descents to target reasons first and foremost.

Now consider escapes from poverty, and recall the nature of reasons associated with escapes. Improved yields from agriculture, jobs in the informal sector, and, to a smaller extent, full-time and protected jobs in the private or public sectors: These reasons for escape were the most important in the contexts examined. More than 90 percent of all households who moved out of poverty followed one or more of these pathways. Making similar pathways available to other poor people will require promoting education, irrigation, and information provision. Practically speaking, these interventions cannot easily be made available to any particular sub-set of people while excluding all others interested in obtaining the same provision. Entry into public schools cannot feasibly be denied to any child who is interested to learn. Information about jobs and opportunities cannot be passed selectively to more deserving beneficiaries while bypassing others. Irrigation canals cannot simply flow into poorer people's farms without also crossing through tracts owned by others in the same watershed. It is not administratively practical, or politically feasible, or even patently fair.

Targeting reasons before people would make better sense, therefore, in respect of promoting escapes from and preventing descents into poverty. Instead of the targeting practices currently in vogue, a three-step method of targeting will produce better results. First, actionable reasons for descent and escape must be identified within each context. Second, the appropriate interventions should be designed and put in place. Third, and last, efforts must be made to direct these programs toward the people who need them the most.[8]

Developing Polycentric Responses

A similarly pragmatic view needs to be taken in respect of another concern, related to centralized versus decentralized (or standardized versus location-specific) modes of program administration. While some analysts have pronounced clearly in favor of one or another of these modes, others have refused to make a binary choice. Elements of both centralization and decentralization need to be combined, according to this second group of analysts: Some issues are better dealt with in a centralized fashion; for some other issues, location-specific remedies are more effective.[9]

The logic of micro reasons supports such an eclectic vision, showing how policy responses of varying geometry are concurrently required. Reasons for escape or descent operate variously over areas of larger or smaller size. Some reasons, such as ill-health and high health care costs, can have countrywide significance. Other reasons, such as a potential for lift irrigation or customary costs related to funerals, can have more localized effects.

Thus, instead of an entirely centralized or a completely decentralized set of programs, it is preferable to develop polycentric responses. The reach of each selected intervention should match the scope of the threat or opportunity that it addresses.[10]

The Grameen Bank in Bangladesh provides one example of a polycentric response, dealing with some issues at the base level of organization, composed of a five-member local group, and addressing threats and opportunities that are common to wider areas at progressively higher organizational levels. In an essay that he wrote for a volume on illustrative cases of rural development, Muhammad

Yunus, Nobel Laureate and founder of the Grameen Bank, discusses the nature of these arrangements and the rationale that motivated him to develop a poly-centric response.[11] Other cases in the same volume, notably, the example of Six-S, a development support organization that operated in parts of Francophone West Africa, also illustrate the benefits of taking a polycentric approach.[12]

In order to develop the set of polycentric responses that is appropriate to any given context, micro-level inquiries, pinpointing local threats and oppor-tunities, need to be undertaken first, as discussed above. Such inquiries need to be undertaken on a regular basis, because reasons for escape and descent tend to vary not only across geographic regions; they also change significantly over time.

Regularly Monitoring Reasons

Some reasons for escape or descent that were previously critical can have little or no effect at a later date. Other reasons can emerge and acquire new influence, as we saw in Chapter 5.

In order that policy designs continue being effective, reasons for escape and descent must be tracked regularly. Sporadic surveys undertaken at irregular intervals will not suffice. Institutions need to be developed and put in place that can help acquire the required information on a continuing basis.

A network of poverty monitoring stations is required in order to keep track, reliably and regularly, of changing opportunities and threats. Like weather stations that are based in particular locations but which help track climate for an entire country, strategically located poverty monitoring stations will help map context-specific reasons for escape and descent that are relevant to a wider region. Multiple research methodologies can be implemented by the staffs of these stations, helping generate knowledge about diverse facets of poverty. Poli-cies and programs can be designed based on reliable information about current conditions, rather than imitating 'best practices' derived from other contexts.

Building such a network of poverty monitoring should not be overly costly or time consuming. Several new and lower cost methods of measuring and moni-toring poverty have been developed in recent years.[13] Additional economies can be generated by making poverty monitoring stations a part of the existing estab-lishment of poverty studies. Diverse grassroots studies are carried out in many countries, for instance, national stocks of poverty are calculated at regular inter-vals, people eligible to receive program benefits are identified, and monitoring and evaluation exercises are mounted by different organizations. The task of poverty monitoring can be combined with such ongoing investigations, saving on expenditure all around.

It can be organized in different ways and known by different names, but some such effort is essential for the future. Diverse agencies—universities, NGOs, government departments, and private research organizations—can take responsibility for poverty monitoring stations in different parts of a country. By investigating micro-level reasons at regular intervals, say, every four or five years, policy responses can remain current and effective, staying abreast of changing circumstances on the ground.

The benefits of more effectively using anti-poverty resources are many, including averting needless human misery. The costs involved in poverty monitoring stations will be more than recovered when resources are put to better use, helping produce deeper and longer lasting change.[14]

Is All of This Hard Work Really Necessary?

Won't economic growth automatically take care of poverty? A rising tide lifts all boats, it is said. So shouldn't the focus simply be on raising the aggregate economic tide? In conversations held across the world, such views are only too often expressed. It is important to carefully evaluate the evidence.

Arguments suggesting that poverty will go away as a result of economic growth are based upon comparisons of aggregate countrywide data.[15] A robust empirical regularity has been demonstrated by such cross-national statistical analyses: More often than not, national economic growth tends to go hand-in-hand with lower national poverty stocks. However, what is true in general may not be true in any specific case. 'The same rate of growth can bring about very different rates of poverty reduction.'[16] Thus, the effects that national economic growth will have for poverty in any specific country or region or community cannot be foretold with confidence.

An important reason for this uncertainty lies in relating a macro (or country-level) result with a micro (or individual-level) occurrence—without tracing the intermediate links. As discussed in Chapter 1, growth is an aggregate national outcome, while poverty is an individual's or household's situation. In order to make a causal link from growth to poverty reduction, it is necessary to identify the intermediate links between macro and micro, between changes in the national economy and improvements in individuals' material circumstances. How exactly are the beneficial effects of growth transmitted to influence particular individuals? Why did some (but not other) poor individuals escape poverty in the past? What intermediating gates opened up for them but stayed closed for others who have remained in poverty? Very little is known at present in relation to these questions. However, until the nature of these intermediate links is better specified, the theory linking growth and poverty reduction will remain incomplete and uncertain.

Any particular rate of economic growth can be achieved following quite different processes.[17] Considering only the similarity in rates—and not the difference in processes—gives little idea of what is actually at work. The nature of growth processes—and the nature of different people's involvement with these processes—needs to be examined in detail before any reliable predictions can be made.

Poverty is reduced when downward tugs become fewer in number; simultaneously, restrictions on upward mobility must be removed. How economic growth can help remove poverty in some country must be explained in terms of how it affects individuals' prospects for escape and descent.

Why descents into poverty occur, and how they can be prevented, cannot be explained, however, in terms of economic growth rates. Recall the nature of reasons associated with descents into poverty. Health care is commonly the most important reason, but health care does not improve simply as a by-product of economic growth, nor does worse health care necessarily follow from a lower rate of growth, as we saw in Chapter 4. Other factors of descent, including customary expenses, crop diseases, land exhaustion, and indebtedness, are also not resolved simply as a side-effect of growing aggregate wealth.

Something other than growth is needed to avert households' descents into poverty. Large numbers of people have fallen into poverty in the three regions studied in India, even when economic growth proceeded apace. Large numbers also fell into poverty in North Carolina, despite its much higher level of average wealth.

Countries that have succeeded in reducing poverty to single-digit figures have not simply banked upon economic growth. Japan is sometimes mentioned as an example of a country that grew its way out of mass poverty. Dramatically high rates of growth were, in fact, achieved in post-war Japan, and aggregate poverty also fell drastically, but Japanese government officials did not simply sit back and wait for growth to do their work. Quite early on, they sponsored studies that directly investigated poverty flows. Not surprisingly, these studies revealed 'the causal inter-relationship between poor health and poverty,' showing how 'illness was a major cause of impoverishment.'[18] In response, the Japanese government implemented a comprehensive health coverage package. It also instituted many other preventive measures—well before high-speed growth was achieved.[19]

The poverty rate in Japan is 2 percent at the present time, among the lowest rates found in any country of the world. By the same measure, more than 13 percent of the US population is poor. Despite having achieved, through growth, one of the highest per capita incomes in the world—almost US$45,000 per year—the United States has not overcome the problem of poverty creation because reasons for descent, in particular health care, have not been effectively addressed.

Developing countries cannot afford to wait to achieve similar levels of per capita income. In fact, given global resource constraints, such levels may be simply unattainable.[20] But even if similarly high levels of per capita consumption were to be somehow achieved, the problem of descents would not automatically go away.

Looking for any grand or mono-causal theory of poverty reduction is a misguided enterprise, a 'pervasive illusion,' according to Jeffrey Sachs.[21] Can anything—economic growth or anything else—be a sufficient cure for what is brought into being on account of one set of factors and diminished on account of a different set?

All else being the same, it is clearly important to do what is necessary for accelerating the rate of economic growth, but waiting for growth to occur is not good anti-poverty policy. As Ravi Kanbur states, aggregate-level 'correlations between per capita income and poverty are beside the point, because the real dispute is about the consequences of alternative policies.'[22] If we are serious about reducing poverty, then we need to introduce specific policies based on localized examinations of how poverty begins and how it ends.

Preventing Descents: Health Care First

Pursuing the goal of faster poverty reduction requires intervening pro-actively, first of all by preventing the accretion of future poverty. Rather than any one momentous event, chains of everyday events have been more closely associated with descents into poverty in the regions studied.

Different types of events have mattered more within each particular region. However, ill-health and high health care costs have played a major part everywhere, being associated with the majority of descents. Other reasons also matter, but they tend to have more localized effects. Social and customary costs, arising from funerals and weddings, were associated with descents in some parts of India, Kenya, Uganda, and Peru. High interest debt was a factor of descent in North Carolina and regions of India. Drought due to irrigation failure was particularly important in one part of India. Land exhaustion, crop failures, and commodity-price fluctuations were important factors of descent in parts of Uganda and Kenya. Different policy mixes will need to be implemented in each particular region.

Commonly, health care needs attention everywhere. Millions of households are only one illness away from chronic poverty.

Poor health is not simply a consequence of poverty; it is a profound cause. Unless we can come to grips with the ravages of ill-health, and unless we can address the widespread need for access to high quality health care in an affordable manner, that is, without people losing their shirts or becoming bonded debtors, there is little hope for resolving the problem of poverty.

No country in the world has succeeded in reducing its stock of poverty to single-digit figures without making affordable and high quality health care available to its residents. We reviewed above the example of post-war Japan. Similar pathways to poverty reduction become apparent after examining the experiences of other OECD countries.

Studies show that poverty has been removed fastest within the sub-group of rich countries that have provided better public health care and other social benefits. Economic growth rates have not mattered equally. 'Australia's growth performance has been much touted, yet it is the only country in which absolute poverty increased. There are also cases, such as Sweden, France, and Germany, in which mediocre economic performance has still resulted in considerable absolute poverty reduction between the early 1980s and 2000.'[23]

The difference was made in large part by better health care. Vulnerability to descents—and along with it the overall stock of poverty—is lower within the sub-group of OECD countries that provide universal health care coverage (Norway, the Netherlands, Germany, Sweden, Austria, Canada, and Denmark), and higher within a second group of countries where health care coverage is less widespread (Australia, Ireland, and the United States).

Achieving higher average levels of wealth is not a precondition for implementing better health care coverage. Several examples exist of countries in which improved public health care was made available at a very early stage of economic development. In addition to Japan, Sweden and Denmark are other notable examples. 'Until the end of the 19th century, Sweden was a poor backward agrarian country on the outskirts of Europe,'[24] but a public law to subsidize voluntary sickness funds was passed as early as 1891. In Denmark, similarly, 'the state began to subsidize health care funds in 1892. The number of fund members rapidly increased. At the beginning of the 1890s, the Danish funds covered less than one-tenth of the population, but by 1930 their coverage was two-thirds.'[25] Some current-day developing countries, such as Colombia, Costa Rica, Cuba, Thailand, and Malaysia, also have reasonably effective health care systems in place.[26]

Other developing countries need to improve their health care coverage urgently. They cannot wait until they achieve any particular level of wealth.

Some quite disturbing trends are coming to light that need to be tackled expeditiously. In China, for instance, 'two-thirds of the population lacks any type of health insurance, and about half of the sick do not seek professional medical treatment at all.'[27] Cooperative medical systems, which used to be available to 90 percent of the rural population, now serve fewer than 5 percent of all villages.[28] Families' long-term incomes fall by 13 percent, on average, because of every major health incident.[29]

Similar trends have become apparent in India. It is calculated that an additional 3.24 percent of the total population, or approximately 32.5 million people, are plunged into poverty every year on account of high medical expenses. 'Not only households just above the poverty line but also many households well above the poverty line' are regularly pushed into poverty on account of the high costs of health care.[30] Analysts observing these trends have concluded that further reductions in poverty are not possible in India without *prior* improvements in health care.[31]

Commentators who applaud the rapid economic strides taken by China and India should take note of the large-scale human tragedies that are occurring in parallel. 'The official Chinese news media are regularly filled with accounts of the desperate choices that people are regularly forced to make over health care, of brothers who must draw lots to see whose serious illness will be treated because their family cannot afford to treat both, or of a father who sells a kidney to treat an ill son.'[32] A similarly grim picture is emerging in many other developing countries.[33]

Across a large part of the earth, the crushing burden of health care payments needs to be brought under greater control. A combination of measures is required. Extending the network of hospitals and clinics, expanding health insurance coverage, and enacting and enforcing effective regulation are all important components of the required response.

Evidence from different parts of the developing world shows how poor people are willing to pay for health care coverage, provided that it is made available affordably, effectively, and accountably.[34] Presently, however, many poor people pay very high amounts from out of pocket for medical treatment. The coverage of health insurance schemes must be extended, if necessary by using public subsidies. Colombia provides one example of a national health insurance policy that can help.[35] Other workable models have been developed in other places, which need to be studied and adapted to suit the specific conditions of each country.

Alongside better insurance coverage, consumer protection and quality control are required. Information asymmetries, arising between providers and consumers, coupled with the immediacy of the need for attention, can place consumers of health care services at a clear disadvantage. As one especially perceptive observer puts it, 'health care is not like other products or services (when your child gets sick, you don't go shopping for the best bargain).'[36] In such situations, unregulated providers can (and unscrupulous providers do) take advantage of poor people in urgent need of medical attention. In some instances, there is outright fraud.

Codes of behavior enforced by civil society groups, along with laws and regulations implemented by national governments, are required that can help bring about higher standards of accountability and assure people that they will receive high quality care at a fair price. Consumers of medical services must be made aware of these standards and regulations and given access to forums where complaints are heard and remedial action can be taken.[37]

Better and more complete epidemiological maps also need to be constructed. It is necessary to identify the specific types of health incidents that tend to impoverish families in each particular location.

Fixing health care is primary among measures required to stem the creation of poverty, but other region-specific measures are also necessary. Because events of diverse kinds are involved—including social and cultural together with economic ones—multiple actors have important roles to play. We saw in Chapter 4 how high funeral and marriage expenses have been brought under control in one part of India. Persistent efforts by members of a dedicated social movement helped alleviate this long-standing reason for descent. Similarly, burial societies and funeral associations have helped their members overcome this reason for descent in parts of Bangladesh, Botswana, Ethiopia, and Sri Lanka. Similar actions on a broader front will help reduce these risks of descent in different parts of the developing world.

A collage of responses to descents is required, involving diverse agencies. Public–private partnerships are necessary, as are partnerships across a wider set of actors, including some who have not been conventionally associated with poverty reduction, such as social movements, hospitals, and for-profit businesses.

Equalizing Opportunity: The Parallel Objective

The results reviewed in Chapters 5 and 6 show that many people have moved out of poverty, but in the majority of cases improvements were slim. Relatively few people escaped poverty as a result of finding a regular job. Agriculture served as the principal engine of escape in some regions, but progress through agriculture was limited, largely on account of shortage of land. In search of better opportunities, many people made their ways from agrarian settings to cities near and far, but only a tiny minority found positions that come together with enforceable contractual agreements and with the benefits and protections underwritten by law. The informal sector provided the most important route for escaping poverty. Street peddlers, maids, lorry loaders, and other such low-paid and uncertain positions predominate in the accounts that we heard.

Restricted upward mobility is a defining condition of poverty. Despite their best efforts, poor people are unable to rise high. Hardly anyone from a poor household or poor community rose to become a highly placed executive, businessperson, media or sports personality, public official, or medical doctor. Not one among the software engineers we interviewed in Bangalore grew up within a poor household.

Leveling the playing field is not only desirable for reasons of fairness and equity, it is also necessary for maintaining public peace and promoting social harmony. The collective narratives that hold societies together invariably reward those who work hard and live honestly. Log-cabin-to-White-House is not just an American dream. Other stable societies also share a similar vision. In the developing-country communities I examined, however, the fabric of society is getting frayed. Frustration and discontent are rising, especially among young people; their families' investments in education have failed to produce any rich benefit.

Current-day processes of economic growth have little use for semi-skilled people. Only the best-trained and well-fed can compete successfully. Below a certain threshold, people's life chances are drastically reduced. 'The ability of the poor to participate in economic growth depends on a variety of enabling social conditions,' asserts Amartya Sen. 'It is hard to participate in the expansionary process of the market mechanism (especially in a world of globalized trade) if one is illiterate and unschooled, or if one is weakened by undernourishment and ill-health.'[38]

Improving health care and enhancing the quality of public schools will have a cumulative effect, helping overcome several handicaps associated with an impoverished childhood. In addition, better career opportunities need to become more widely known and easier to access. Promoting social mobility is an urgent societal requirement. Otherwise, we might continue to face a situation in which inequality grows and polarization deepens, even as the economy advances in aggregate terms.

Connecting channels are needed in order to link poorer communities with the mainstreams of economic growth. Physical connections—roads, railways, etc.—are important. Cognitive connections are also necessary, as we saw in Chapter 6. Information institutions—such as employment offices, career counselors, and bureaus providing business advice—are largely lacking in poorer communities, so people remain unaware of diverse opportunities for personal advancement.

Information should be provided as a social service, together with higher quality education and better health care. Examples from countries where poverty has been substantially reduced in recent times show how information provision, better health care, and high quality education were centrally important parts of the policy package.

For instance, South Korea's post-war educational strategy broadened participation and helped foster equality of opportunity. Simultaneously, the Samuel
Undong program, which made up fully one-half of all government investments
during the 1970s, helped create physical and communication infrastructure,
linking rural residents with the urban centers of growth, and fostering a new
spirit of confidence and connectedness.[39] Simultaneously,

> there was major improvement in the health status of the population. Infant
> mortality decreased by 60 percent; the population per physician declined by
> 25 percent; the coverage of medical insurance increased dramatically; the
> death rate dropped; and average life expectancy reached the levels character-
> istic of more developed countries. Poverty decreased dramatically.[40]

In Hong Kong, similarly, 'government expenditures strongly favored low-
income groups, principally through the provision of housing, health, and educational benefits.' Government and corporate policies aimed to facilitate 'rapid
dissemination of information on employment and business opportunities.'[41]

Governments in other countries are beginning to take note of these examples. A recent statement by a high-level Chinese government official recognizes
'that the market cannot benefit all people automatically, while economic growth
cannot solve all poverty-related problems.' Three objectives have been framed
for guiding development programs of the future: 'First, to provide access to
television, access to highways, and access to electricity; second, to improve
medical care systems, specifically, building apace a new rural cooperative
medical insurance scheme; and third, to provide free textbooks and exempt
other charges for school education for students from poor rural families.'[42]

The Chinese government is reacting faster than many others to events and
trends that have wider effects. Other governments would also do well to develop
a two-pronged anti-poverty strategy, combining elements of protection and
opportunity.

And in the End...

Definitions of what it means to be poor vary, but experiences of poverty are
similar across countries and regions. Everywhere, people face two sets of events,
and it is the balance of negative and positive events they experience that determines which direction they will take.

Many people move out of poverty every year. Many others simultaneously fall into poverty. No universal solvent exists that can 'fix' poverty. There is no holy grail in the poverty domain. Falling and rising tides need to be dealt with simultaneously. Reasons associated with both tides need to be ascertained and addressed.

A great deal of hard work is required. More attention needs to be given to everyday lives and ordinary events. Certainly, calamitous events can make a big difference. Failed states matter. Natural disasters, military coups, and other epic events can have very serious consequences. However, focusing exclusively on such headline-making events results in ignoring the everyday struggles waged by ordinary people. Micro-level investigations, viewing smaller things, are important because they can help identify the nature of events—large or small, ordinary or calamitous—that make the biggest difference for escapes and descents within each particular region.

Economic growth needs to be pursued with vigor. Poverty reduction is a parallel and equally important policy goal, which requires specific research attention and dedicated resource support. We need to learn more about accelerating growth, but we also need to learn more about macro–micro links and about grassroots-level opportunities and threats. More must be learned in each particular context about how people escape poverty in practice. In parallel, we need to learn more—much more—about how people become poor in the first place.

Experiences of descent—such as Heera Gujar's and Kadijja Nantoga's and Marcos Honorio's, recounted in the previous chapters—must become rarer. Preventive assistance should become the norm. In parallel, opportunity must become more widely available. Attending more carefully in the future to prevention and opportunity will help make the world a better place for all.

APPENDIX

Measuring Poverty: Testing
Stages-of-Progress

Poverty has a complex, multi-faceted reality, and it is not feasible to examine all of these facets within any single study. Depending upon its specific purpose, each study focuses upon some particular facet or facets and neglects to attend to other important facets. The choice of methodology and measurement tool depends upon this prior selection of study objectives: What part of poverty one selects to study helps determine what should be measured and how.

No single measure of poverty can be universally useful nor indeed is any such measure universally utilized. Diverse measures of poverty co-exist, serving different objectives. The best known of these measures, the World Bank's dollar-a-day index, helps make comparisons of consumption poverty among countries. However, this possibility is gained at the cost of neglecting other important facets of poverty. The United Nation's Human Development Index (HDI) takes account of a broader concern by looking, in addition to income, at aspects related to education and health. By taking account as well of these additional facets, HDI scores can better reflect the overall living conditions of poorer people. Since these calculations do not address equity and distributional concerns, a third set of measures has been developed to examine these particular facets. A fourth set of measures has been developed to investigate gender-based differences in well-being. Social and political correlates of poverty are examined using yet another set of measures.

This ever-expanding set of poverty measures should come as no surprise. Poverty is not like blood pressure or height, for which some single definition or measure can be established by convention.

Methodological disputes are common. The apparent precision and simplicity of dollar-a-day sit atop a number of procedural disagreements. Which items of consumption should be included within these calculations, and which ones are better left out? Should one include only what each individual purchases directly for herself? Or should public goods—such as higher-quality public education, better-maintained public gardens, cleaner air, and fairer governance—also be counted within these calculations of individual well-being? Should expenditures on health care be included, or should they be excluded, being seen as indicators of pathology rather than components of well-being? Over how many days or weeks should people's consumption be averaged? Which seasons of the year should be considered? How should differences in the cost of living be harmonized across countries? Which particular basket of goods and services—those typically consumed in richer countries or in poorer ones—should be considered while making cross-country comparisons?[1]

No universally accepted or clear-cut answers are available for these questions. 'Poverty lines unavoidably retain an element of arbitrariness and inevitably embody some implicit or explicit normative judgments.'[2] The kinds of thumb rules that are adopted critically affect the results that are obtained. In India, for example, changing the period of recall—considering people's consumption expenditures over one week instead of one month—resulted in sharply lowering the calculation of the national poverty rate.[3] Because they are 'very sensitive to both survey design and post-survey analysis,'[4] seemingly precise quantitative poverty rates can be imperfect and capricious. Analysts are aware that estimates of 'the magnitude of the increase or decrease in the extent of world poverty since 1990 are crucially dependent on the assumptions made.'[5]

International comparisons are particularly error-prone. 'Finding a poverty line that is representative and comparable across countries and regions is an impossible task,' according to T. N. Srinivasan, a leading expert.[6] Understandings of poverty are inherently related to specific societal contexts. 'Poverty is not a certain small amount of goods, nor is it just a relation between means and ends; above all, it is a relation between people. Poverty is a social status. As such, it is the invention of civilizations.'[7] Thus, people's understandings of poverty are related to the context in which they live. A person who considers herself relatively poor in one context can suddenly discover that in another context she is relatively rich.

No particular measure or method helps overcome all of these different pitfalls. Depending upon the specific context that is studied and the particular facets of poverty that are explored, particular methods and measures will be useful. Instead of pushing ahead in every case with the same methodology, one should prefer to use the method and measure that help make a particular set of questions tractable.

The *Stages-of-Progress* methodology is a useful tool to employ in situations when one is interested in examining changes in households' circumstances over time and to ascertain context-specific reasons for escape and descent. It is especially good for examining these facets of poverty. It is less helpful for looking at some other facets.

Two Judgment Calls

Two methodological choices that were made while developing *Stages-of-Progress* are important to discuss in some detail. First, *Stages* utilizes a place-bound or local understanding of poverty that is different from the usual consumption- or income-based measures. Second, it employs a retrospective design and considers present-day households as its units of analysis. The rationale for each of these choices is explained in more detail below, starting with the selection of the scale of measurement.

A common procedure for measuring household poverty, including the well-known dollar-a-day calculations, relies upon calculating households' consumption expenses. A list of items commonly consumed in the area is drawn up, and household members are asked to recall how much of each item they have consumed over the previous 15 days or one month. Multiplying the quantities reported by a particular household with the set of prices prevailing in the particular region results in generating an estimate for this household's consumption expenditure. Households who fall below a certain threshold of consumption expenditure (e.g., US$1/day) are classified as poor. Others, who have higher consumption expenditures, are classified as non-poor.

This procedure seems relatively straightforward, and I could have adopted such a technique for assessing households' poverty status at the time of inquiry. But I was also interested in assessing their poverty status at some point in the past, and it would have been foolish to ask people to recall their consumption patterns—the precise quantities of cabbage and wheat flour and cooking oil that they had purchased—at some previous point of time, ten years (or, especially, 25 years) ago. Assets, being lumpy and limited in number, are easier to recollect with more precision. Instead of working with a consumption-based measure of poverty, I selected to work with an assets- and capacities-based measure.

My preference for working with such a measure gained strength after I examined the results of participatory poverty assessments and ethnographic studies. These initiatives have worked more closely with people's own understandings and assessments of poverty which, far from being standardized or uniform, vary considerably across different cultural contexts.[8] Researchers conducting such studies have found that local understandings of poverty are most often expressed in terms of discrete assets or capabilities, which are 'intrinsically important for people while low income is only instrumentally significant.'[9] The scales that I developed initially in Rajasthan were also phrased by the people in these villages in terms of assets and capabilities. Thus, an assets- and capabilities-based scale is advantageous in that it corresponds better with people's own understandings of poverty.

Further, working with assets and capabilities provides a more stable and reliable index for assessing longer term changes in material well-being. Incomes and consumption expenditures tend to fluctuate substantially from month to month and year to year, especially for poorer people, hardly any among whom get fixed monthly salaries.[10] Seasonality plays a large part in the lives of the rural poor,[11] resulting in 'damaging fluctuations' that limit the extent to which consumption (averaged over any particular fortnight or month) can serve as a stable or reliable measure of well-being.[12]

Observing these aspects, scholars have drawn an important distinction between *structural* and *stochastic* poverty.[13] The structural poor are those who lack assets. On average, their income and consumption levels fall below the poverty line. The stochastic poor, on the other hand, have sufficient asset endowments, so on average their incomes are above the poverty line. In some particular month or year, their incomes can dip, occasionally falling below the poverty line. However, measuring such temporarily lowered incomes does not give an accurate indication of this household's usual (or structural) conditions. Considering assets and capabilities is more reliable.[14]

For all these reasons, including both practical and theoretical ones, I selected to forego the usual consumption-based measure. Instead, I utilized measures, developed with the participation of the people concerned, which draw upon context-specific assets and capabilities.

A second methodological choice resulted in adopting a retrospective design. Households existing at the time of inquiry constituted the units of analysis for *Stages-of-Progress*. Pathways traveled by present-day households were traced backward in time. Events, processes, and household characteristics associated with different households' experiences were identified through extensive interviews. Comparing the trajectories of households with different experiences helped to recognize commonly occurring reasons for escape and descent. Policies and programs of assistance appropriate to particular contexts can be designed on the basis of this knowledge.

The robustness of these results can be compromised in situations where households migrate in or migrate out on a large scale. In the regions studied, relatively few households had, in fact, migrated into or out of their home communities. Individual members of households, particularly younger males, had left rural communities in significant numbers, but relatively few individuals had left permanently, leaving no trace behind, and fewer still had taken along their entire household.

When considered in terms of individuals, the proportions involved in migration can be quite large, but when calculated in relation to entire households these proportions are much smaller. The Dutch scholar, Jan Breman, who has followed developments over a long period of time in the Indian state of Gujarat, observed that he had 'seldom come across cases of households who left in their entirety to seek a new life elsewhere.'[15]

Such trends are not peculiar to the regions selected for this study. Similar results— showing a clear difference between individuals' and households' migration patterns— have been reported as well for other communities and other countries. Household surveys undertaken in 13 developing countries found that most people do not leave their home villages for very long, and those who migrate do not usually take along their dependents.[16] In 1979, scholars studied a group of 240 households in one village of the Indian state of Tamil Nadu. Returning 25 years later to the same village, they found '233 households out of the originally selected 240. Of the 233 households traced, some still remain under the same head. Others remain in the village but have a new head. Yet others have migrated but left enough traces in the village to enable us to find out to where they went.'[17]

Clearly, one can never expect to run a fully controlled experiment in which no one moves out, or dies, or is born during the period of study. Some level of flux is inevitable, and any longitudinal study, particularly one that considers longer periods of time, will have to find suitable ways of dealing with this risk. Considering households, rather than individuals, as the units of analysis helps render migration a less important source of risk. I will discuss some other aspects of this issue later in this chapter. Meanwhile, let me detail how some other potential biases were addressed.

Triangulation and Verification

Initially, while developing a new methodology, it is natural to experience some anxiety. Several adjustments and revisions were incorporated before I became easier in my mind that *Stages-of-Progress* worked reasonably well.

It helped to raise my faith that common stages of progress—at least, common initial stages—were consistently reported by different community groups. The small differences that arose were related to higher level stages of progress, which are reached long after poverty is overcome. People's needs are more varied and expenses are discretionary at these higher levels, because culture and human biology are less prescriptive.

I continued to be concerned about the reliability of recall. We were working with fairly long periods of time. Oral evidence can be faulty, incomplete, or deliberately skewed. Further, fear of stigma or elite domination of community groups could skew these results. A number of precautions were incorporated that helped deal reasonably effectively with each of these risks. In addition, I looked for sources of verification, seeking out objective evidence recorded in the past. These precautions and verification procedures are recounted briefly below.[18]

Intentionally, the *Stages-of-Progress* methodology has been designed to retrace *large* steps that are better remembered rather than finer distinctions that are more easily forgotten. Each movement upward along the *Stages-of-Progress* represents a significant improvement in material and social status. People in Kenya remembered quite easily, for instance, whether they lived in a mud or a brick house while growing up, whether their parents were in a position to send children to school, and so on.

Considering one's own case will help make clear what I mean about larger steps resulting in easier recall. Casting my mind back to 25 years ago, I can clearly locate my household's position on the Rajasthan communities' stages of progress. I remember, as I suppose each of us can, where my household was situated in terms of these clear referents. Did we: have the capacity to regularly eat enough food (yes); clothing (yes); could send children to school (yes); own a television set (yes); own the house in which we lived (no).

By seeking recall data in terms of clear, conspicuous, and sizeable referents, the *Stages-of-Progress* method helps add reliability to recall. The downside is that one misses out on smaller changes. Such smaller changes are better measured when consumption- or income-based measures are used. Since *Stages-of-Progress* works with a discrete number of levels of well-being, finer improvements in households' well-being cannot be captured using this methodology, although larger increments are reliably recorded.

Members of particular households remembered quite well where they were located along this hierarchy of stages, and these recollections were verified by others of the same community. It was rarely hard or controversial to locate any household's position, either at the present time or in the past.

Still, people's judgments, even though they were spontaneously given and corroborated by others, may be colored by the presence of some collective myth, for example, people might feel that 'everything was better in the past.' The risk of glorifying the past was limited by the design of these exercises, because communities were not asked to think in terms of better or worse. Distinct stages of progress were put up publicly on large charts, and community members were asked to locate where along these well-specified stages each particular household was located in the previous time period. Study team members could verify hard facts: 'Did they have a brick house at that time? Did they own cattle or only small animals?' Considerations of 'better or worse' were entirely avoided. Indeed, the terms 'poverty' and 'poor and rich' were hardly ever used.[19]

Triangulating all data by consulting multiple independent sources helped to guard against the risk of partial or biased data. Information about each household was obtained separately at both the community and the household levels.

Corroborating what we found with other available forms of evidence helped further verify the results that we obtained. As part of these verification exercises, I compared the stages recorded for particular households with the physical assets that these households possessed. Table A1 presents evidence in this regard from the study conducted in communities of Central and Western Uganda. Interviewed households were asked to provide information about ten different types of assets, including animals, radios, household furniture, and so on.

Not surprisingly—since *Stages* is an assets- and capabilities-based measure—a consistent relationship exists between a household's asset holdings and its stage reported by the community group. Other visible characteristics of a household's economic status—for example, its livestock ownership and the kind of house in which it lived—also align closely with its reported stage of progress. How well any household is doing

Table A1 *Stages-of-Progress* and Asset Ownership (36 Communities in Uganda)

Household's Stage at the Present Time	Average Number of Household Assets (Out of 10)
1	2.46
2	3.08
3	3.58
4	4.08
5	4.94
6	5.24
7	5.55
8	5.71
9	6.42
10	6.72
11	7.31
12	8.01

in terms of material achievement at the present time is thus quite well reflected by the stage recorded for the current period.

But what about the stage recorded for a previous period? Does it also align equally well with asset holdings in existence at that time?

In order to convert from this hypothetical question to one that could actually be addressed I conducted a study in 2004 within a group of 61 villages in Rajasthan, India where I had conducted a previous study seven years ago (that is, in 1997). This previous study was intended to examine social capital, economic development, and some other outcomes.[20] A random sample of individuals in each of these villages was interviewed, and information related to a number of different items, including asset ownership, was collected in 1997. The second study, undertaken in 2004, implemented *Stages-of-Progress*. A seven-year recall period was selected for this study. Each household's stage for the present time (that is, for 2004) and for seven years ago (that is, for 1997) was recorded. These recalled stages were compared with the results of the 1997 survey. Table A2 presents what we found.

There is a close match between the recall data and the data recorded seven years previously. Households' stages of progress for 1997 (as recalled in the community meetings of 2004) are closely correlated with asset holdings recorded by the 1997 survey. Whether considered in terms of agricultural land, large or small animals, or home construction quality, households who were recalled to have a lower stage of progress actually possessed fewer assets at that time.

Objective data from a more distant past are not readily available—and if they were, there would be no need for a recall-based methodology! I could think of only one

Table A2 Stages (as Recalled) v. Assets Possessed Seven Years Ago (61 Communities of Rajasthan, India)

Stage for 1997 (as Recalled in 2004)	Assets Possessed in 1997			
	Land (bighas)	Large Animals	Small Animals	Kaccha (mud) house
Very Poor (Stage 1–3)	3.6	1.8	2.8	86%
Poor (Stage 4–5)	5.5	2.5	3.7	77%
Middle (Stage 6–8)	8.1	3.1	5.1	51%
Better Off (Stage 9+)	10.6	4.3	3.1	22%

possibility of locating reliable written records for 25 years in the past. These are the official land registers that have existed unbroken for several decades in Rajasthan and in many other parts of India. Each register relates to a particular village, and it records the amount of land owned by each household. Land registers are handwritten in black or blue ink, with changes ('mutations') being inserted in red ink. Because paper tends to wear down with constant use, a new register is written up every four years, with the old registers being preserved, as carefully as possible, in government records rooms that have their own specialized staffs and procedures.[21]

By checking the official land registers for an earlier period it is theoretically possible to map stages (as recalled) against landholdings actually possessed 25 years ago. In practice, however, this task is both complicated and arduous. It can also be extremely expensive. Backtracking land ownership requires manually collating diverse hand-written registers, not all of which are available at a single location. It also requires matching present-day households with the households or individuals whose names were recorded in land registers of the past. Because households and their landholdings tend to get sub-divided over time, it becomes necessary as well to calculate the present-day household's notional share in the original household's landholding.

Finding a match with the historical land record for all 61 villages studied in Rajasthan was simply not possible given the resources available. Instead I selected a random sample of feasible size, picking 25 households at random from among all those who have fallen into poverty in five villages, which were also randomly selected from two districts of Rajasthan. I also selected 25 other households at random belonging to the other three categories (escaped poverty, remained poor, and remained not poor). With generous assistance provided by concerned government departments, landownership for all of these households was tracked backward over 25 years. Table A3 provides these results.

Notice that of these 25 households, all of which suffered descents into poverty, 22 households (88 percent) lost all or part of the land that they had owned 25 years ago. About half of these households lost all the land they had owned. The rest had to part with significant chunks of their landholdings. Hardly any other household in these villages has lost anywhere close to the same proportion of its prior-period land.

Observing this close match between land records and *Stages* data helped justify the enormous effort that went into obtaining this information. But I was not surprised to learn of these facts. The community members whom I met had given generously of their knowledge, and I had not detected any widely shared impulse to dissemble, distort, or fabricate.

Table A3 Impoverishment and Reduced Land Holdings

Village	Household Head	Stage 25 Years Ago	Stage in 2004	Land Owned in 1980 (Hectares)	Land Owned in 2004 (Hectares)	Change in Land Holding (Hectares)
Aamliya	Detali Beeram Das	4	1	0.65	0.00	-0.65
Aamliya	Hakri Vala	4	1	2.33	0.00	-2.33
Aamliya	Harda Pratha	4	1	0.66	0.00	-0.66
Aamliya	Kakudi Bai Lalu Ji	4	1	0.29	0.00	-0.29
Aamliya	Lalu Limba	4	1	0.38	0.00	-0.38
Aamliya	Laluji Nanka	4	1	0.75	0.75	0.00
Aamliya	Nukki Jala	4	1	0.32	0.00	-0.32
Aamliya	Phoola Bhima Ji	4	1	3.25	2.33	-0.92
Cheerwa	Ram Lal Bheru Lal	6	4	5.12	4.68	-0.44
Cheerwa	Hamira Geva	7	5	1.20	1.20	0.00
Cheerwa	Keshar Hemer Singh	7	5	0.75	0.00	-0.75
Cheerwa	Devoo Kalyan	4	1	2.20	0.00	-2.20
Khempur	Deva Lakhma	5	3	1.37	0.75	-0.62
Khempur	Ramji Kannaji	4	2	1.10	0.57	-0.53
Khempur	Logerlal Pemaji	8	4	2.20	1.00	-1.20
Khempur	Laluram Pema	8	4	2.10	0.90	-1.20
Namri	Mangni Ukarlal	9	3	3.69	2.56	-1.13
Namri	Heera Bai Roopa Ji	7	4	0.66	0.00	-0.66
Namri	Logari Bai Bhaga Ji	7	4	1.25	0.25	-1.00
Namri	Balu Kalu Ji	7	4	0.75	0.75	0.00
Shyampura	Mool Chand Kalu Ram	11	4	2.55	0.81	-1.74
Shyampura	Mava Ji Vaja	7	2	1.01	0.00	-1.01
Shyampura	Ratni Bai Kush	7	4	0.00	0.00	0.00
Shyampura	Balki Bai Dharmi Lal	6	2	0.35	0.00	-0.35
Shyampura	Mangla Chamna	4	1	2.92	0.70	-2.22

It helped to have local area residents working as the interviewers for these studies. Many questions cannot reasonably be asked by outsiders. People are more comfortable discussing important events in their lives with others who have a similar cultural and socioeconomic background; there is more empathy and sensitivity, and less embarrassment, on both sides. The interface between researcher and respondent is critical for this method to work well, which is why intensive training is built in at the start of every *Stages-of-Progress* exercise.

On occasion, it was heart-rending for both the interviewee and the interviewer to discuss particular events, particularly those involving the sickness and ultimate death of loved ones. Often, the interviewers had to stop and comfort their interviewees. In a small number of cases, these interviews had to be adjourned to the next day.

Risks and Remedies

Some of the risks involved were addressed reasonably successfully. Some other risks and limitations will not be as easily overcome. First, the methodology needs to deal better with intra-household, particularly gender-based, differences. Research has shown that females within households as well as female-headed households are likely to be poorer on average than their male counterparts.[22] It is important, therefore, to probe these differences further.

Using *Stages-of-Progress*, I was able to uncover the differences between male- and female-headed households, finding the latter group of households to be considerably worse off than the former group. However, considering entire households as the units of analysis made it difficult to drill further down. Differences within households, between male and female members, are not easily detected using this process. Further improvements are necessary that will make possible such intra-household comparisons. I continue to seek a viable means for incorporating these additional steps within *Stage-of-Progress*.

Another set of refinements were made necessary when newly formed and urban communities were selected for investigation. The North Carolina study was the first one of this type. Because poverty is less easily and less self-consciously discussed publicly in communities of the United States than in communities of the other countries studied, and because community composition also tends to be less stable in this part of the world, the *Stages-of-Progress* methodology was modified in a few respects when we conducted the study in North Carolina. First, we worked with a shorter time period, considering no more than ten years in all. Second, we relied more than we had in other contexts upon household interviews. Reasons for escape and descent were ascertained entirely through interviews with multiple household members; community groups did not provide this information. Thus, one element of triangulation was not available to us in North Carolina. Another set of improvements is required on this account.

Applying *Stages* within community settings helped abate to a considerable extent the danger of stigmatization. By categorizing people as occupying a particular stage (1–13) or a particular category (A–D), we had no need to refer to particular individuals as 'poor' or 'rich.' Tracy Rhoney, an enthusiastic and well-regarded community organizer in Burke County, North Carolina, explained to me in her unforgettable accent: 'It's almost like asking a woman about her dress size: Are you a five or a four? Are you Stage 5, or are you Stage 4? It's that simple. People don't mind talking about these things.' She was right in this regard: People who attended these North Carolina community meetings spoke freely about their own positions along the stages of progress. They were more wary and close-mouthed, however, when someone else's situation was being discussed. It was quite different in communities of the other regions studied, where people spoke more freely and openly about each others' situations, perhaps because in these contexts poverty is less often considered as an indicator of personal failure.

I referred earlier to the possibility of elite domination. In the *Stages* process, it is made clear at the start of every community meeting that no tangible benefits will be given out to anyone. This reduces the incentives that people might have to distort the facts, but the danger of elite domination is still present. We have maintained some balance in the composition of the community groups. In India, for instance, we did not commence discussions until lower and upper caste people were both present at the community meeting. We have also learned techniques for rotating community respondents and isolating domineering speakers by taking them aside for separate interviews. One other part of the *Stages* process helped to reduce the possibility of elite domination. All facts ascertained in the community meeting were separately verified in privately held household interviews. To the extent that the fear of elites does not also extend into private spaces, imbalances arising in the community group were ironed out at this point. I welcome suggestions about other safeguards that can be employed to deal better with this source of risk.

Another likely pitfall, common to all longitudinal studies, arises on account of the changing compositions of communities and households. Migration is one reason why the composition of households and communities can change over time, but there are also some other reasons, having to do with natural processes of birth, death, and aging.

Such effects will be more pronounced the longer is the period that is studied. Over a period of 25 years, new households will be inevitably set up and some old households will cease to exist.

Because households do not retain their original composition, some simplifying assumptions are made by all longitudinal studies. The objective of the study guides the assumptions that are made. Prospective studies consider households in the starting year of the study. They compare this original set of households over time, usually neglecting to study other households that get established in subsequent years. This assumption about the appropriate units of analysis (and the consequent neglect of newly established households) does not, however, detract from the basic objective of these studies, which is to understand what happened to the original households at later times.

Retrospective studies, such as those that use *Stages-of-Progress*, risk incurring the opposite neglect. Because they regard present-day households as their units of analysis, such studies can fail to take account of households that existed in the past but faded away. We found in a few locations where we inquired about this disappearance that it was undergone by roughly equal numbers of very rich and very poor households. On average, around 2 percent of households had vanished from both tails of the asset distribution. Once again, the assumptions that we made did not compromise the basic objective of these studies. They were primarily intended to answer the two *why* questions, that is, to identify the natures of reasons involved in escapes and descents, and this objective has been adequately served by these studies.

To conclude this relatively brief discussion of methodological issues, I will mention one last cause for concern, which is also the hardest one to address. Understandings of poverty can change over time. As the world around them advances, people's conceptions of what it means to be poor are commensurately revised. Can comparisons be validly made between two periods of time that are characterized by different poverty definitions?

For the sake of comparability, analysts generally evade this question, preferring to work with one fixed measure of poverty. Usually, they adopt the measure that is prevalent at the time when the study is commenced. Valid concerns can be raised about how much relevance any such measure has for some period in the past (or some period in the future). Practically, some such (admittedly arbitrary) selection has to be made. For if we worked with separate definitions (and different measures) for the previous period and the present time, then what exactly would we end up comparing?

The methodological complications associated with studying change over time are many. Nevertheless, such analyses have to be undertaken. In order to design more effective policies, it is essential to identify the factors that propel change over time. While remaining aware of all that can go wrong in longitudinal investigations, one must try to uncover as much as possible that is reliable and useful. Different methodologies can help fill this knowledge gap in some part. *Stages-of-Progress* is important among these methods.

NOTES

Chapter I

1. Hacker (2006: 12–13).
2. Zhao (2006: 475).
3. Labonte and Schrecker (2007: 11).
4. Deaton (1997: 37) comments on the 'rarity of such data from developing countries.' In their review of panel studies available at the start of the current millennium, Baulch and Hoddinott (2000: 18) lament the 'continuing paucity of longitudinal household studies.' In OECD countries, such data are more abundant. In the United States, the Panel Study of Income Dynamics (PSID) contains data on roughly 8,000 families and 18,000 family members, selected initially to be statistically representative of the entire nation. These family members have been tracked regularly from 1968 through 1997. (See <psidonline.isr.umich.edu>.) McKernan and Ratcliffe (2002) provide a partial review of studies that draw upon these data. The European Community Household Panel (ECHP) involves annual interviewing of a panel of roughly 60,500 nationally representative households in 12 European Union countries, covering a wide range of topics, with data collected from 1994 to 2001 (see <circa.europa.eu/irc/dsis/echpanel/info/data/information. html>). Other data sets, covering different topics and smaller numbers of OECD countries, are also available (see OECD 2001).
5. For example, 'In Ghana, between 1987 and 1991, the fall in national poverty was composed of a fall in rural areas and a rise in urban areas. [In contrast] in Mexico between 1990 and 1994, the fall in national poverty was composed of a fall in urban areas but an increase in some rural regions' (Kanbur 2001: 7–8).
6. For example, see Wiggins (2000); Christiaensen, et al. (2002); Jayne, et al. (2003); and Elbers, et al. (2004).
7. Ravallion (2001: 1811).
8. Ellis (2000: 184).
9. These results—the first ones from the *Stages-of-Progress* inquiries—are presented in Krishna (2003).
10. See, for example, Landes (1999); Diamond (2000); Acemoglu, et al. (2001); and Collier (2007).

11. Sen (2003: 522).

12. Morduch (2005). These calculations show that micro-level factors, observed at the household and individual levels, account for between 75 to 96 percent of the total variance in household incomes.

13. See, for example, Carter (1991); Townsend (1995); Deaton (1997); and Kenjiro (2005). An earlier discussion, provided by Chayanov (1966), focuses on demographic and life-cycle events.

14. I use the terms 'we' and 'they' in the sense implied by Robert Chambers (1997), with the former term referring to experts and outsiders, and the latter to poorer and more powerless people.

15. For the structure–agency distinction, see Sewell (1992). For an application in the context of poverty and development, see Amartya Sen (1999).

16. See Krishna (2004: 128).

17. These findings are reported in Krishna (2006: 280), (2007b: 65–7), (2007d: 182–3); and in Krishna, et al. (2004: 222) and (2005: 1180).

18. As reported in Narayan, et al. (2009).

19. The numbers of people living below the US$1.25 poverty line fell from 1.9 billion in 1981 to 1.4 billion in 2005, while the numbers of people living between US$1.25 and US$2 increased from less than 600 million in 1981 to 1.2 billion in 2005.

20. For a more detailed discussion on individuals' differential 'capacities to aspire,' see Appadurai (2004) and Ray (2006).

21. See, for instance, Wade (2002, 2004); Milanovic (2005); and United Nations (2005).

22. Collier (2007). Also see, for example, North (1990); Evans (1995); Olson (2000); Rodrik (2000, 2007); Chang (2002); and Kohli (2004).

Chapter 2

1. These numbers, like many others related to poverty measurement, are the subject of considerable dispute. Controversies abound concerning the 'right' way to measure poverty. For discussions of these controversies in the context of India, see Gaiha (1989); Visaria (1999); Deaton (2000); Palmer-Jones and Sen (2001); Vaidyanathan (2001); Datt and Ravallion (2002); Sen and Himanshu (2004); and Saith (2005).

2. The first published works—Krishna (2003, 2004); Krishna, et al. (2004)—were followed by a string of others that are listed in the bibliography. Workshop presentations were made at the Chronic Poverty Research Center (in 2003), at the World Bank (in 2003 and 2004), and in several other academic and policy settings.

3. For examples of participatory poverty assessments, see Salmen (1987); Chambers (1995); Narayan, Chambers, et al. (2000); and Narayan, Patel, et al. (2000). For examples of ethnographic studies, see Attwood (1979); Van Schendel (1981); Jodha

(1988); Wadley (1994); Eder (1999); Davis (2006); Moser and Felton (2007); and Perlman (2007). Several examples of panel data studies are presented in the following chapter.

4. As discussed below, panel data studies have not usually recorded event histories, instead comparing consumption or income data at two points of time, so they have been unable to uncover the reasons associated, respectively, with escapes and descents. Participatory poverty assessments, which have more often worked with people's own ideas and understandings of poverty, have typically not constructed prospectively (nor reconstructed retrospectively) the pathways taken by different households over time, so they have also been unable to account for the processes that drive change. Ethnographic studies have undertaken much more process tracing, so they have produced a better sense of households' pathways over time, but the usually tiny scale of such studies, which are very intensive and rich in detail, makes it hard to pick out special effects from more widely experienced poverty dynamics.

5. In the few areas where sample surveys have been conducted in the past it might be possible to identify who was poor previously. However, useful data from the past are available for only a handful of places. Baulch and Hoddinott (2000) report how the available data cover small parts of only 12 out of more than 100 middle- or low-income countries. Analyses of poverty flows are consequently focused on only 'a handful of data sets, with most stylized facts entering into textbooks based on data from three villages in South India' (Dercon 2005: 25).

6. Sawhill (1988: 1085). See also Bane and Ellwood (1986); and Baulch and Hoddinott (2000).

7. Bane and Ellwood (1986: 4).

8. Walker and Ryan (1990: 99).

9. Addison, et al. (2009: 11–12).

10. See, for example, Barrett, et al. (2006); Baulch and Davis (2007); Davis (2007); and Quisumbing (2007).

11. Krishna (2003) describes these difficulties in greater detail.

12. This term has been made popular in the development literature by various works of Nobel Laureate Amartya Sen, in whose very broad understanding capabilities are regarded as the substantive freedoms people enjoy for leading the lives *they* have reason to value. See Sen (1981, 1984).

13. Respectively, Krishna (2003, 2004); Krishna, et al. (2005); Krishna (2006).

14. Ahluwalia (2000) provides these comparisons.

15. See Krishna, et al. (2004); and Kristjanson, et al. (2009).

16. These districts are Mukono, Ssembabule, and Luwero (in the Central Region) and Bushenyi, Kabale, and Ntungamo district (in the Western region). See Krishna, Lumonya, et al. (2006) for further details.

17. See Krishna, Kristjanson, et al. (2006) and Kristjanson, et al. (2007).

18. This study was undertaken within selected communities of Beaufort, Burke, Gates, and Vance Counties. See Krishna, Gibson-Davis, et al. (2006) for more details.

19. Households were defined consistently as people related by blood or marriage who share the same kitchen.

20. Q2 analyses, combining both kinds of information, are now widely regarded as being more informative and insightful. See Kanbur (2003).

21. Individuals associated with the following institutions had adapted and utilized this methodology at the time of writing: BRAC, CARE, CIP, the World Agro-forestry Center, the Government of Kenya, the International Food Poverty Research Center, the Food and Agriculture Organization of the United Nations, the International Livestock Research Institute, SEWA, Uppsala University (Sweden), University of Edinburgh (UK), Humboldt University (Germany), and the World Bank.

22. BRAC, the Bangladeshi NGO, now also working internationally, is using *Stages-of-Progress* for evaluating components of its Ultra-Poor Program. SEWA, another well-known and well-regarded NGO, has used this methodology for program development in areas of Gujarat, India (see Chapter 5).

23. Multiple journal articles describing the *Stages-of-Progress* methodology had appeared well before the World Bank began developing its methodology (e.g., Krishna 2003, 2004; Krishna, et al. 2004). I had also presented this work at conferences and workshops starting in 2002. The World Bank's Moving Out of Poverty study team invited me to present my methodology at one of their first planning workshops, held in Washington, DC, on July 15–17, 2003. The World Bank team continued to solicit, and I made available to them, further details about the *Stages-of-Progress* methodology and my research findings. A second presentation at the World Bank followed on November 14, 2004, and I contributed an essay to the first volume of the World Bank's thematic series on Moving Out of Poverty (Krishna 2007d), which included a detailed description of *Stages-of-Progress*. The second volume in this series unveiled Ladder of Life, and it makes no mention of *Stages-of-Progress*, instead claiming to have developed a 'new method' (Narayan, et al. 2009: 100). The sequence of steps adopted by Ladder of Life is very similar to *Stages-of-Progress*. The core insight is identical (although triangulation and verification procedures appear to be missing): Work with a close-knit community group to develop a scale on which people rank their own and other people's economic status at the present time and in the past, and follow-up by asking households about reasons associated with their particular experience. Clearly, I did not borrow this logic from Ladder of Life (which did not exist when *Stages-of-Progress* was developed).

Chapter 3

1. I follow the local custom in referring to an entire household by invoking the name of its oldest male member. Clearly, the women of these families have also played very important roles.

2. A note of caution is in order here. Because the *Stages-of-Progress* methodology results in producing a somewhat different construction of poverty across culturally dissimilar regions—even though similar definitions and measures of poverty were provided by communities *within* each particular region—the numbers reported in Table 3.1 are not strictly comparable across regions and countries.

3. Krishna (2006) provides additional details.

4. For more details about geographic poverty traps, see Jalan and Ravallion (1998); and Carter and Barrett (2006).

5. See, for example, Gaiha (1989); Grootaert and Kanbur (1995); Gaiha and Kulkarni (1998); Glewwe and Hall (1998); Baulch and Hoddinott (2000); Dercon and Krishnan (2000); Scott (2000); Devereaux and Sharp (2003); Mehta and Shah (2003); CPRC (2005); Barrett, et al. (2006); and Narayan, et al. (2009).

6. On the distinction between chronic and transitory poverty, discussed in more detail below, see, in particular, Hulme and Shepherd (2003) and CPRC (2005).

7. Aliber (2003).

8. Walker and Ryan (1990: 65).

9. Attwood (1979: 500).

10. Counting the number of stages by which a household's situation has changed over the period of study gives an idea of how far this household has moved up or fallen down. Three percent of all households who fell into poverty in the 36 communities examined in Gujarat descended by just one stage, and another 11 percent of households fell by two stages. However, 74 percent of all descending households fell by between three and five stages, and the other 12 percent fell even further, by six or more stages, that is, they moved down all the way from relative prosperity in the previous period to acute poverty at the current time. Similarly, in Andhra Pradesh, 34 percent of all households who suffered descents fell by only one or two stages. The remaining 66 percent of descending households fell by three or more stages.

11. For more on the concept of poverty traps, see Carter and May (2001); Bowles, et al. (2006); Carter and Barrett (2006); and Collier (2007).

12. 'A plausible common sequence involves the progressive liquidation of small stock, livestock, consumer goods, and eventually the failure to protect from the sale the key productive assets, female assets (gold and other moveable collateral) before male assets (land)' (Harriss-White 2007: 199).

13. OECD (2001: 39, 48).

14. For example, see Duncan (1984); Bane and Ellwood (1986); Newman (1988); Sawhill (1988); Corcoran (1995); Stevens (1999); Rodgers (2000); and Hacker (2006).

15. McKernan and Ratcliffe (2002: viii).

16. Hacker (2006: 12–13; emphasis original).

17. Appleton (2001); Pender, et al. (2004).

18. Kappel, et al. (2005).

19. Results from participatory poverty assessments suggest that this might have been the case (McGee 2004).

20. See Kristjanson, et al. (2009).

21. Kozel and Parker (2007: 16).

22. In previous publications (Krishna 2007e, g), I have presented in greater detail the argument that because 'the poor' is not a stable, consistent, or homogeneous category, analyses should focus instead upon specific subgroups. A subsequent World Bank volume (Narayan, et al. 2009) picked up on and amplified the same message, but without acknowledging the prior work.

23. Toye (1999: 10).

24. An early statement to this effect was provided by Matin and Halder (2002: 4), who stated that 'it is now clear how effective poverty reduction requires both a promotional component (that increases the incomes, productivity, or employment prospects of poor people) and a protection component (that reduces vulnerability).'

25. See endnote 6 in Chapter 3 for some key references to the literature on chronic and transitory poverty. Jalan and Ravallion (2000) and Krishna (2009) demonstrate how people in each of these categories can have very different needs. Gaiha (1989) shows how the chronically poor may not always be the poorest among the poor.

Chapter 4

1. Bane and Ellwood (1986).

2. See, for example, Baulch and McCulloch (2002); McKernan and Ratcliffe (2002); Sen (2003); Barrett and McPeak (2005); and Barrett, et al. (2006).

3. Sinha and Lipton (1999: 39) contend that *four* different kinds of costs are involved, including '(a) utility cost—the unpleasantness of being ill: pain, discomfort, lack of information and foreknowledge, at worst death; family distress; (b) direct cost of prevention, care, or cure; (c) opportunity cost—of lost labor income, education, etc., and (d) aversion cost to the well, from lost income due to reluctance to work in places thought to be [unhealthy], to adoption of low-risk/low-return portfolios due to fear of illness.'

4. Readers interested to look at these results of multiple regression analyses should consult Krishna (2006); Krishna, Kristjanson, et al. (2006); Krishna, Lumonya, et al. (2006); Kristjanson, et al. (2007, 2009); and Krishna and Lecy (2008).

5. For more details on this particular study, see Krishna, et al. (2005).

6. Other analyses, undertaken in different parts of Uganda, have also pointed to the critical importance for poverty of health-related factors. See, for example, Lwanga-Ntale and McClean (2003); Lawson (2004); and Yates, et al. (2006).

7. Because multiple negative events—and not any single event—were associated with most cases of descent, the totality of events adds up to more than 100 percent.

8. Fabricant, et al. (1999).

9. Chaudhury, et al. (2006).

10. See, for example, Noponen (1991); Kochar (1995); Behrman (1996); Jacoby and Skoufias (1997); Strauss and Thomas (1998); Fabricant, et al. (1999); Farmer (1999); Barrett, Bezuneh, and Aboud (2001); Deolalikar (2002); Asfaw (2003); Deininger and Okidi (2003); Pryer, et al. (2003); Asfaw and von Braun (2005); and Narayan, et al. (2009).

11. Kenjiro (2005: 779).

12. De Waal (1989).

13. Deaton (2006: 22).

14. *Christian Science Monitor*, January 22, 2004.

15. Case, et al. (2008).

16. Oldenburg (2002).

17. See, for example, Iliffe (1987).

18. See Krishna (2006) for these results.

19. Ensor and San (1996); Dilip and Duggal (2002).

20. Breman (1993: 330).

21. Even higher rates of interest are charged to poorer people by private moneylenders in different countries. A compilation of such rates is provided in Robinson (2001). See, especially, her table 6.1. For a more sympathetic view, see Collins, et al. (2009).

22. For an interesting examination of 'laziness' as a factor that is uncritically associated by some analysts with abiding poverty in rural Africa, see Whitehead (2000).

23. See Krishna (2004: 128), (2006: 280), (2007b: 65–7), (2007d: 182–3); and Krishna, et al. (2004: 222) and (2005: 1180). A subsequent World Bank study (Narayan, et al. 2009), following up on these results, similarly found little evidence in support of the view that alcoholism, drug use, and laziness are responsible for descents into poverty.

24. McIntyre, et al. (2006: 858).

25. Xu, et al. (2003: 115).

26. See, for example, Russell (2004); Christiaensen and Subbarao (2005); and Chuma, et al. (2006).

27. The exact nature of these ailments was hard to pin down in particular cases. Members of investigating teams had little or no specialized epidemiological training. Often, interviewees were reluctant to speak of particular diseases, especially HIV/AIDS, which continues to be stigmatized and hidden away in some of the communities studied. Additional work is required in order to assess the poverty-inducing effects of different kinds of health episodes in different regions of the world.

28. Xu, et al. (2003).

29. I thank Robert Chambers for suggesting this formulation.

30. Fabricant, et al. (1999: 181–2).

31. Moser (1998: 10).

32. Zhao (2006: 473, 475).

33. Labonte and Schrecker (2007: 11).

34. Zhao (2006: 475–7).

35. Sen, et al. (2002).

36. Himmelstein, et al. (2005).

37. Hacker (2006: 138).

38. UNDP (2005: 29–30).

39. EQUITAP (2005).

40. Whitehead, et al. (2001: 833).

41. I thank an anonymous reviewer for drawing my attention to these innovations.

42. See, for example, Preker, et al. (2002) and Ekman (2004). For an insightful examination of some key issues involved in designing micro insurance schemes, see Morduch (2006).

43. Whitehead, et al. (2001: 833–5).

44. Farmer (2003: 152).

45. Wang, et al. (2007: 3).

46. For examples of such programs and analyses of how they have worked, see, for example, Das, et al. (2005); Handa and Davis (2006); Schubert and Slater (2006); and Adato and Hoddinott (2007).

47. Email message from Ira Weiss to the author.

48. As mentioned earlier, 'scheduled tribe' is the official terminology in India for communities of indigenous people. Historically disadvantaged and geographically marginalized, these communities demonstrate some of the highest poverty rates in India.

49. Despite the lower significance of these social expenditures, poverty remains larger by far in Dungarpur compared to most other districts of Rajasthan. More than 85 percent of all village households in Dungarpur belong to scheduled tribe communities, and their health care and employment status give cause for concern.

50. I thank Norman Uphoff for bringing these important examples to my attention.

51. Dercon, et al. (2004).

52. Bhattamishra (2008) shows how in rural Orissa, India, inhabited predominantly by poorer scheduled tribe populations, grain banks established during the 1980s and 1990s by a local NGO helped reduce the incidence and amount of borrowing from predatory moneylenders.

53. Bhattamishra and Barrett (2008) examine various experiences of this kind. While exploring the potential for effective risk-pooling by community groups, they also indicate how the process and the benefits may be captured by elites, resulting in exclusion of minority members and others.

54. According to a survey of national health care systems put together by experts at the World Health Organization (see <www.who.int/whr/2000/en>), Colombia and Costa Rica rank ahead of the United States, and Cuba ranks ahead of New Zealand.
55. Barrientos and Hulme (2008: 13).

Chapter 5

1. Castells (2004: 3).
2. Friedman (2005) introduced the term, 'flat world.' It has been misapplied, for example, in the context of India, where, as I argue, a hierarchically related dollar economy and rupee economy are evolving in parallel. See Krishna and Pieterse (2008).
3. Ellis (1998: 2).
4. Lipton and Ravallion (1995: 2601).
5. Chen (2006) provides an insightful typology of the array of institutions and working arrangements involved in the informal sector.
6. ILO (2002a: 1).
7. ILO (2002b).
8. ILO (2002a: 25–32).
9. De Soto (1989, 2000).
10. This high proportion of escapes from poverty due to jobs in the government sector (39 percent) in Gujarat is accounted for by a one-time expansion of school teachers. It is not a replicable or recommended strategy. See Krishna, et al. 2005.
11. See Hirway (2000) and Kundu (2000) for more detailed discussions of industrial growth, employment generation, and poverty reduction in Gujarat. The ILO (2002a, b) provides a more general discussion of trends in formal sector employment.
12. Khan and Riskin (2001: 110–12).
13. See <indiabudget.nic.in/es2005-06/chapt2006/tab33.pdf>.
14. Rajasekhar (2008: 125).
15. In the context of remittances, see also Valdivia and Escobal (2004).
16. Deininger and Okidi (2003).
17. Bhide and Mehta (2003).
18. See Munshi and Rosenzweig (2005); and Jeffrey, et al. (2008).
19. Examinations of household budgets, assessing both inflows and outflows over longer periods of time, show similarly that threats and opportunities which are unrelated to life-cycle events have accounted for a larger part of households' financial transactions. See Collins, et al. (2009: 95–109).
20. Krishna (2002).

21. This result, which I reported from my first study, in Rajasthan, India (Krishna 2003: 538, 2004: 130), I found to be valid as well in the other developing country regions that I studied. See Krishna (2006: 283–4, 2007d: 186); Krishna, et al. (2005: 1175); and Krishna, Kristjanson, et al. (2006: 1015–16). Subsequently, a World Bank team reproduced this finding for another group of regions, extending its general validity (Narayan, et al. 2009).

22. See Sachs (2005).

23. A more detailed discussion of this study and its results is provided in Krishna and Lecy (2008).

24. The full statistical analysis can be seen in Krishna, Lumonya, et al. (2006).

25. Chen and Ravallion (2007: 3).

26. See World Bank (2008: 6). This report goes on to add that 'For China, aggregate growth originating in agriculture is estimated to have been 3.5 times more effective in reducing poverty than growth outside agriculture—and for Latin America 2.7 times more. Rapid agricultural growth in India and in China was accompanied by major declines in rural poverty. More recently, in Ghana, rural households accounted for a large share of a steep decline in poverty induced in part by agricultural growth…Many [other] countries that had fairly high agricultural growth rates saw substantial reductions in rural poverty,' including Bangladesh, Moldova, Uganda, and Vietnam (World Bank 2008: 45).

27. Ravallion and Datt (1996).

28. Ravallion and Chen (2004: 21).

29. Khan and Riskin (2001: 8). An official report of the Chinese government largely agrees with this conclusion, considering the period of agricultural growth, from 1978 to 1985, as 'the stage of large-scale poverty mitigation' (Xiaojian 2007).

30. Across 27 countries, agricultural growth was found to be a central force for lowering poverty and unemployment (Timmer 1997). Another analysis found that across a wide group of developing countries more than three-quarters of all employment growth originated within the agriculture sector (Mellor 1999).

31. Livelihood zones were described in Chapter 3 as contiguous areas with common agro-ecological conditions and similar livelihood options.

32. GOI (2007).

33. Davis (2006: 19).

34. Dasgupta (2003: 75).

35. Appadurai (2002: 26–7).

36. Bearak (2001).

37. ILO (2002a: 12).

38. Barrett, et al. (2001).

39. Klitgaard (1997: 1968).

40. For a more detailed discussion on why program replication can have indifferent results, see Uphoff, et al. (1998: 66, 202–5).

Chapter 6

1. See, for example, Roemer (1998, 2000); Benabou (2000); Birdsall and Graham (2000); Bowles and Gintis (2002); Dardanoni, et al. (2004); Jencks and Tach (2005); Hout and DiPrete (2006); Birkelund (2006); and Morgan (2006).

2. Roemer (2000: 21).

3. World Bank (2006: 136).

4. For some initial examinations in particular developing country contexts, see Castaneda and Aldaz-Carroll (1999); Behrman, et al. (2000); Graham (2000); Christiaensen and Alderman (2004); Grawe (2004); Quisumbing (2006); Moser and Felton (2007); and Perlman (2007). A review of studies in China, presented in Bian (2002), shows that context and history are important to examine: Communist party membership is an important factor explaining upward mobility.

5. See, for instance, Ganzeboom, Treiman and Ultee (1991); Solon (2002); Corak (2004); Jantti, et al. (2005); Mazumdar (2005); and Smeeding (2005).

6. Hout and DiPrete (2006: 5).

7. Jantti, et al. (2005: i). Other calculations also show that 'in the United States and the United Kingdom at least 40 percent of the economic advantage high-income parents have over low-income parents is passed on to the next generation. The Nordic countries and Canada seem to be the most mobile societies, with less than 20 percent of an income advantage being passed on between parent and child' (Corak 2004: 9). Within-country changes in income and class mobility are generally slow, supporting Erikson and Goldthorpe's (1992) notion of a 'constant flux.' See, however, Shavit and Blossfeld (1993); and Hout (2006).

8. See Grawe (2004).

9. Breen and Jonsson (2005: 236).

10. Esping-Andersen (2005: 149).

11. Erikson and Goldthorpe (2002: 37–8).

12. Esping-Andersen (2005).

13. See, for example, Trzcinski and Randolph (1991); Scott and Litchfield (1994); Griffin and Ickowitz (1997); Behrman, Birdsall, and Szekely (2001); Bhide and Mehta (2003); Deininger and Okidi (2003); Paxson and Schady (2005); and ECLAC (2007).

14. See, for example, DiMaggio (1982); Bourdieu (1986); Mayer (1997); Currie (2001); Danziger and Waldvogel (2005); Esping-Andersen (2005); and Hannum and Buchmann (2005).

15. Bowles, et al. (2005: 20).

16. Ibid. 3.

17. Work commenced relatively recently, comparing *intra*-generational inequality in different OECD countries, should help add new knowledge about factors associated with differential success. See, for example, Gangl (2005); and Gangl, et al. (2007).

18. I thank Ramesh Ramanathan and Subroto Bagchi for helping make these connections.

19. Cook, et al. (2000) report the average response rate for internet surveys to be around 34 percent. For more details regarding the survey and the results, see Krishna and Brihmadesam (2006).

20. These figures are taken from Census of India 2001 (see table C8: Educational Levels by Age and Sex for Population aged 7 and above, India 2001).

21. For example, in his otherwise upbeat account of recent developments in India, *New York Times* columnist, Thomas Friedman (2005: 382–3) is careful to note that: 'As exciting and as visible as the flat Indian high-tech sector is, have no illusions. It accounts for 0.2 percent of employment in India. Add those Indians involved in manufacturing for export, and you get a total of 2 percent of employment for India.'

22. For an examination of the different ways in which mothers with higher education can affect their children's educational outcomes, see Attewell and Lavin (2007), especially Chapter 5. Because parents' influence on children can follow diverse pathways, Roemer (2004) suggests using parents' education levels, rather than their incomes, as the measure of choice for examining intergenerational mobility.

23. In rural India, as in many other places, male children are better provided with nourishment and education compared to their female siblings. See, for example, Behrman (1997); Garg and Morduch (1998); Morduch (2000); and Estudillo, et al. (2001).

24. Apart from emphasizing 'any walk of life,' we did not further specify any particular positions. We let the villagers define these highest achievements by themselves. In one case, people mentioned 'smuggler' among the highest achieved positions. In general, however, there was very little confusion—and very little dissimilarity across communities.

25. Surveys conducted in six Indian states by the Mumbai-based International Institute of Population Sciences (IIPS), in collaboration with the Population Council, have documented high and rising joblessness among educated youth. The unemployment rate among youth (15–24 years) with 12 years of schooling was found to be as high as 77 percent in Rajasthan and 72 percent in Andhra Pradesh (see <www.popcouncil.org/pdfs/India_FactsheetRajasthan.pdf> and <www. popcouncil.org/pdfs/India_FactsheetAndhraPradesh.pdf>). These numbers are probably overestimates, perhaps because people not actively seeking jobs have also been counted among the unemployed. However, it has become common to see in village squares, across both these Indian states and several others, large and growing knots of educated and unemployed young men. The situation is not dissimilar in many other developing countries. In a speech that he gave in 1995 to the World Commission on Social Development, former President of Kenya, Daniel

Arap Moi, stated how 'we in Kenya are now faced with a big pool of trained, educated but unemployed youth,' who are largely being absorbed within the *Juakali* sector (see <www.un.org/documents/ga/conf166/gov/950312110352.htm>). More recently, in August 2009, Uganda's President, Yoweri Museveni, made reference to the growing problem of the educated unemployed in his country (see <www.statehouse.go.ug/news.php?catId=1&item=610>).

26. ECLAC (2000: 61), emphasis added.

27. Ibid. 68.

28. Berner (1997: 170).

29. World Bank (2006: 45).

30. Berry (1997); Ranis and Stewart (2001).

31. United Nations (2005: 50).

32. 'Persistent inequalities within both India and China ... are impeding the prospects for poor people. In the future, high and rising inequality will make it harder for either country to maintain its past rate of progress against poverty' (Chaudhuri and Ravallion 2007: 209).

33. On this point, see, for example, Bollen and Jackman (1985); Muller (1988); Rueschmeyer, Stephens, and Stephens (1992); Acemoglu and Robinson (2000, 2006); Boix (2003); and Booth and Seligson (2008).

34. United Nations (2005: 81).

35. The parents of these young adults, interviewed separately, reported a very similar pattern of aspirations for their wards.

36. Ray (2006: 409).

37. Easterly (2001: 73).

38. Appadurai (2004: 68–70). Empirical support for these assertions was found, for example, by an examination undertaken in 18 Latin American countries which revealed 'how widely separated the various socioeconomic strata are in terms of their expectations of social mobility. People living in the more vulnerable households have lower expectations regarding their children's future well-being than members of households that are in a better economic position' (ECLAC 2007: 20). See also Barr and Clark (2007).

39. See, for example, Bigsten (2007).

40. Stiglitz (2001: 488).

41. See, for example, Akerlof (1970); Rothschild and Stiglitz (1976); and Stiglitz (2000, 2001).

42. David Leonard (1991: 35), who has studied social mobility in Kenya, notes how even 'a casual informal survey of Kenya's senior civil servants will reveal that a surprisingly large minority have parents of similar background. Surveys of university students in East Africa have shown that the children of schoolteachers are over-represented by 20 times their proportion in the population.' Similarly, in post-reform China, Bian (2002: 95) has observed that rural cadres of the Communist

party have 'capitalized on information and influence networks' in order to advance their own economic positions.

43. Ahuja, et al. (1997: 49).

44. See Whang (1981); and Kwon (1998).

45. Personal communication from Blagsvedt.

46. Giridhardas (2007).

47. The management specialist, C. K. Prahalad, has identified some notable innovations of this kind, including the e-choupal program run by ITC, a for-profit company, in India. See Prahalad (2005).

48. In India, for example, where government-run schools are more often attended by poorer children, 25 percent of government school teachers were found to be regularly and unaccountably absent from the classroom. See Kremer, et al. (2004).

49. Durlauf (2006). Also see Macleod (1995) for an insightful, case-study-based examination of how structural impediments, importantly including lack of information and role models, resulted in depressed aspirations and diminished attainments in a low-income American neighborhood.

50. See <www.shantibhavanonline.org>.

51. In collaboration with Microsoft Research (Bangalore), Babajob.com, and some other entities, I am undertaking a separate research project intended both to ascertain the relative importance of different factors and to identify key policy interventions.

52. Dreze and Sen (1995: 181).

Chapter 7

1. Analysts have critically characterized these practices as 'solutions looking for problems.' See Pritchett and Woolcock (2004).

2. Easterly (2006: 369).

3. See Amartya Sen (1999).

4. Jawaharlal Nehru, Letter to Chief Ministers, June 27, 1961, cited in Shourie (2006: x).

5. For reports about program performance, see, for example, Lipton and Ravallion (1995); Chambers (1997); UNDP (2000); Easterly (2001); Gelbach and Pritchett (2002); Dichter (2003); and Coady, et al. (2004).

6. See, for example Moore, et al. (1998); and O'Connor (2001).

7. For example, implementing *Stages-of-Progress* in 72 communities of two Indian states, Gujarat and Andhra Pradesh, entailed total costs equal to about US$45,000, which is hardly a large amount, given the scope of these studies. Information was gained that is relevant to the conditions of nearly five million people within each of these states. Further reductions in costs are possible in the future. Especially when community members become capable of running these exercises by themselves, and the need for outside experts is reduced, costs can be brought down substantially.

8. A more comprehensive version of this argument is presented by Krishna (2007a).

9. These debates are longstanding ones and have generated a copious literature. See, for example, Cheema and Rondinelli (1983); Smith (1985); Rondinelli, et al. (1989); Samoff (1990); Smoke and Lewis (1996); Schönwälder (1997); Tendler (1997); Bird and Vaillancourt (1998); Crook and Manor (1998); Litvack, et al. (1998); Cohen and Peterson (1999); Manor (1999); Blair (2000); and USAID (2000).

10. For a more detailed examination of polycentricity, see Ostrom, et al. (1993); Ostrom (1996, 2001); and Therkildsen (2000).

11. See Yunus (1997).

12. See Lecomte and Krishna (1997).

13. Chambers (2008) presents some examples of relatively low-cost methodologies that are useful for studying different facets of poverty.

14. For the state of Rajasthan in India, with a population of 56 million people, I estimate that no more than seven poverty monitoring stations will be required in all, each with a permanent staff of ten individuals and an annual budget—based on back-of-the-envelope calculations—of no more than US$75,000. These amounts are puny compared to the annual expenditure on poverty reduction in Rajasthan. For one program alone, the rural employment guarantee scheme, upward of US$350 million are spent each year.

15. A cross-country examination, showing a robust negative correlation between growth rates and national stocks of poverty, is provided by, for instance, Dollar and Kraay (2000). These results have been challenged, however, on grounds of statistical validity, econometric method, and causal logic. See, for instance, Lipton (1997); Rodrik and Rodríguez (2001); Reddy and Pogge (2002); Rodrik (2002); Srinivasan (2004); and Wade (2004).

16. Ravallion (2007: 2).

17. On this point, see, for example, Evans (1995); Hall and Soskice (2001); Chang (2002); Sahn and Stifel (2003); Root (2006); Brady, et al. (2007); Rodrik (2007); Sandbrook, et al. (2007); and Brady (2009).

18. Milly (1999: 219, 222).

19. See Milly (1999); and Kasza (2006).

20. As a recent United Nations report points out, 'the impact on land, water, energy and other natural resources would be devastating' if the consumption practices of today's affluent countries were to be replicated by even half of the projected global population of 2050 (United Nations 2005: 85).

21. The 'pervasive illusion,' Sachs (2005: 326) points out, 'is that the remaining problems of extreme poverty will take care of themselves because economic development will spread everywhere: A rising tide lifts all boats, as the old expression puts it.'

22. Kanbur (2001: 13).

23. Scruggs and Allan (2006: 901). Also see Macinko, et al. (2004).

24. Salonen (2001: 144).

25. Kangas and Palme (2005: 27).

26. Health care systems of these countries are ranked among the top 50 out of 190 different countries assessed by experts at the World Health Organization. See <www.who.int/whr/2000/en>.

27. Pei (2006).

28. Zhao (2006: 475).

29. Gan, et al. (2005).

30. Garg and Karan (2005: 11–12). The authors derive these numbers by recalculating the official consumption poverty statistics after subtracting from each sample household's consumption expenses the amount that it spent on health care services. Such a correction is necessary in the authors' views (and in the view of many others), because spending larger sums of money on medical treatment can hardly be regarded as an indication of superior well-being.

31. Gupta and Mitra (2004).

32. French (2006).

33. See Fabricant, et al. (1999); Whitehead, et al. (2001); and EQUITAP (2005). According to the United Nations, across the entire group of developing countries, 'over half of all mortality...is avoidable' (UNDP 2005: 25).

34. See, for example, Asgary, et al. (2004); Asfaw and von Braun (2005); Bärninghausen, et al. (2007); Dror, et al. (2007).

35. A comprehensive health insurance scheme introduced in the early 1980s has two regimes that operate in parallel. A contributory regime is intended for workers with monthly incomes higher than US$170. Separately, there is a subsidized regime for those who earn lower amounts. See Van der Gaag (2007).

36. Obama (2006: 184).

37. A common theme that I detected among the five 'successful' national health care systems reviewed by Reid (2009)—including those operated in France, Germany, Japan, the UK, and Canada—relates to this co-occurrence of affordable (and universal) health care coverage, effective regulation, and consumers empowered by information and the right to seek redress.

38. Sen (2002: 13–14).

39. Whang (1981).

40. Adelman (n.d.).

41. Findlay and Wellisz (1993: 53, 77).

42. Xiaojian (2007).

Appendix

1. For a discussion of these and other issues that tend to complicate the tasks of poverty measurement, see, for example, Chaudhuri and Ravallion (1994); Lanjouw (1998); Lok-Desallien (1999); Schelzig (2001); Johnson (2002); Reddy and Pogge

(2002); Karshenas (2003); Krishna (2003); Kakwani and Son (2006); Reddy and Minoiu (2007); Wade (2004); and Reddy (2008).

2. Lanjouw (1998: 4).

3. See Visaria (1999); and Sen and Himanshu (2004).

4. Sen and Himanshu (2004: 4247).

5. Reddy and Minoiu (2007: 500).

6. Srinivasan (2004: 4).

7. Sahlins (1972: 37).

8. See Jodha (1988); Clark and Sisson (2003); Franco and Saith (2003); Karshenas (2003); Laderchi, et al. (2003); and McGee (2004).

9. Kanbur and Squire (1999: 10).

10. See, for instance, Dercon and Krishnan (2000); Jalan and Ravallion (2000); Baulch and McCulloch (2002); and Naschold and Barrett (2007).

11. Chambers, et al. (1981).

12. Sinha and Lipton (1999).

13. Carter and May (2001).

14. Sherraden (1991, 2001); Carter and Barrett (2006).

15. Breman (1996: 37).

16. Banerjee and Duflo (2006).

17. Djurfeldt, et al. (2008: 7).

18. A more detailed methodology manual, which also provides guidance on training procedures, can be downloaded from the author's web site.

19. I thank Patti Kristjanson for drawing my attention to this important point.

20. See Krishna (2002).

21. Sporadic experiments to computerize land records have been ongoing since the late 1980s.

22. See, for example, Haddad and Kanbur (1990); Haddad, et al. (1996); Ravnborg, et al. (2004); Kabeer (2005); Molyneux and Razavi (2005); and Iyer, et al. (2007).

REFERENCES

Acemoglu, Daren, and James A. Robinson. (2000). "Why did the West Extend the Franchise? Democracy, Inequality, and Growth in Historical Perspective." *Quarterly Journal of Economics*, 115 (4): 1167–99.

————(2006). *Economic Origins of Dictatorship and Democracy*. New York: Cambridge University Press.

——Simon Johnson, and James A. Robinson. (2001). "The Colonial Origins of Comparative Development: An Empirical Investigation." *American Economic Review*, December, 1369–401.

Adato, Michelle, and John Hoddinott. (2007). "Conditional Cash Transfer Programs: A 'Magic Bullet' for Reducing Poverty?" *2020 Focus Brief on the World's Poor and Hungry People*. Washington, DC: IFPRI. Accessed at <www.ifpri.org/2020 Chinaconference/pdf/beijingbrief_adato.pdf>.

Addison, Tony, David Hulme, and Ravi Kanbur. eds. (2009). "Poverty Dynamics: Measurement and Understanding from an Interdisciplinary Perspective." *Poverty Dynamics: Interdisciplinary Perspectives*, pp. 3–26. Oxford: Oxford University Press.

Adelman, Irma. (n.d.). "Social Development in South Korea, 1953–1993." Available at <http://are.berkeley.edu/~adelman/KOREA.html>.

Ahluwalia, M. S. (2000). "Economic Performance of States in Post-Reforms Period." *Economic and Political Weekly*, Bombay, May 6, 1637–48.

Ahuja, Vinod, Benu Bidani, Francisco Ferreira, and Michael Walton. (1997). *Everyone's Miracle? Revisiting Poverty and Inequality in East Asia*. Washington, DC: World Bank.

Akerlof, George A. (1970). "The Market for 'Lemons': Quality Uncertainty and the Market Mechanism." *Quarterly Journal of Economics*, 84 (3): 488–500.

Aliber, Michael. (2003). "Chronic Poverty in South Africa: Incidence, Causes and Policies." *World Development*, 31 (3): 473–90.

Appadurai, Arjun. (2002). "Deep Democracy: Urban Governmentality and the Horizon of Politics." *Public Culture*, 14 (1): 21–47.

——(2004). "The Capacity to Aspire: Culture and the Terms of Recognition." In Vijayendra Rao and Michael Walton, eds., *Culture and Public Action: A Cross-Disciplinary Dialogue on Development Policy*, pp. 59–84. Palo Alto, CA: Stanford University Press.

Appleton, Simon. (2001). "Poverty in Uganda, 1999/2000: Preliminary Estimates from the UNHS." Working paper, University of Nottingham, UK.

Asfaw, Abay. (2003). "How Poverty Affects the Health Status and the Healthcare Demand Behavior of Households: The Case of Rural Ethiopia." Paper presented at the International Conference on Staying Poor: Chronic Poverty and Development Policy, Manchester, UK, April 7–9, 2003. Available at <http://idpm.man.ac.uk/cprc/Conference/conferencepapers/Abay%20Asfaw%2007.03.03.pdf>.

——Joachim von Braun. (2005). "Innovations in Health Care Financing: New Evidence on the Prospect of Community Health Insurance Systems in Rural Areas of Ethiopia." *International Journal of Health Care Finance and Economics*, 5 (3): 241–53.

Asgary, Ali, Ken Willis, Ali Taghvaei, and Mojtaba Rafeian. (2004). "Estimating Rural Households' Willingness to Pay for Health Insurance." *European Journal of Health Economics*, 5 (3): 209–15.

Attewell, Paul, and David E. Lavin. (2007). *Passing the Torch: Does Higher Education for the Disadvantaged Pay Off across Generations?* New York: Russell Sage Foundation.

Attwood, Donald W. (1979). "Why Some of the Poor Get Richer: Economic Change and Mobility in Rural West India." *Current Anthropology*, 20 (3): 495–516.

Bane, M. J., and D. T. Ellwood. (1986). "Slipping Into and Out of Poverty: The Dynamics of Spells." *Journal of Human Resources*, 21 (1): 1–23.

Banerjee, Abhijit, and Esther Duflo. (2006). "The Economic Lives of the Poor." Bureau for Research and Economic Analysis of Development (BREAD) Working Paper No. 135, BREAD.

Bärninghausen, Till, Yuanli Liu, Xinping Zhang, and Rainer Sauerborn. (2007). "Willing to Pay for Social Health Insurance among Informal Workers in Wuhan, China: A Contingent Valuation Study." *BMC Health Services Research*, 7: 114–25.

Barr, Abigail, and David A. Clark. (2007). "A Multidimensional Analysis of Adaptation in a Developing Country Context." CSAE Working Paper WPS 2007–19, Centre for the Study of African Economies, University of Oxford, UK.

Barrett, Christopher. (2001). "Nonfarm Diversification and Household Livelihood Strategies in Rural Africa: Concepts, Dynamics, and Policy Implications." *Food Policy*, 26: 315–31.

——John G. McPeak. (2005). "Poverty Traps and Safety Nets." In Alain de Janvry and Ravi Kanbur, eds., *Poverty, Inequality and Development: Essays in Honor of Erik Thorbecke*. Amsterdam: Springer.

——M. Bezuneh, and A. Aboud. (2001). "Income Diversification, Poverty Traps and Policy Shocks in Côte d'Ivoire and Kenya." *Food Policy*, 26: 367–84.

——Paswel Phiri Marenya, John G. McPeak, et al. (2006). "Welfare Dynamics in Rural Kenya and Madagascar." *Journal of Development Studies*, 42 (2): 248–77.

Barrientos, Armando, and David Hulme. eds. (2008). "Social Protection for the Poor and Poorest: An Introduction." *Social Protection for the Poor and Poorest: Concepts, Policies and Politics*, pp. 3–26. New York: Palgrave Macmillan.

Baulch, Bob, and Peter R. Davis. (2007). "Poverty Dynamics and Life Trajectories in Rural Bangladesh." Paper prepared for the Wellbeing in International Development Conference, University of Bath, UK, June 28–30.

——John Hoddinott. (2000). "Economic Mobility and Poverty Dynamics in Developing Countries." *Journal of Development Studies*, 36 (6): 1–24.

——Neil McCulloch. (2002). "Being Poor and Becoming Poor: Poverty Status and Poverty Transitions in Rural Pakistan." *Journal of Asian and African Studies*, 37 (2): 168–85.

Bearak, Barry. (2001). "Lives Held Cheap in Bangladesh Sweatshops." *New York Times*, April 15.

Behrman, Jere. (1996). "The Impact of Health and Nutrition on Education." *World Bank Research Observer*, 11 (1): 23–37.

——(1997). "Intra-household Distribution and the Family." In Mark Rozensweig and Oded Stark, eds., *Handbook of Population and Family Economics*, pp. 107–68. Amsterdam: North-Holland Publishing.

——Nancy Birdsall, and Miguel Szekely. (2001). "Intergenerational Mobility in Latin America: Deeper Markets and Better Schools Make a Difference." In Nancy Birdsall and Carol Graham, eds., *New Markets, New Opportunities: Economic and Social Mobility in a Changing World*, pp. 135–67. Washington, DC: Brookings.

Benabou, Roland. (2000). "Meritocracy, Redistribution, and the Size of the Pie." In Kenneth Arrow, Samuel Bowles, and Steven Durlauf, eds., *Meritocracy and Economic Inequality*, pp. 317–39. Princeton: Princeton University Press.

——and Efe A. Ok. (2001). "Social Mobility and the Demand for Redistribution: The POUM Hypothesis." *Quarterly Journal of Economics*, 116 (2): 447–87.

Berner, Erhard. (1997). "Opportunities and Insecurities: Globalisation, Localities and the Struggle for Urban Land in Manila." *European Journal of Development Research*, 9 (1): 167–82.

Berry, Albert. (1997). "The Income Distribution Threat in Latin America." *Latin American Research Review*, 32 (2): 3–38.

Bhattamishra, Ruchira. (2008). "Do Grain Banks Displace Moneylenders? Matching-based Evidence from Rural India." Available at <www.bu.edu/econ/neudc/papers/ Section 3/Session 12/256.pdf>.

——Christopher B. Barrett. (2008). "Community-based Risk Management Arrangements: An Overview and Implications for Social Fund Programs." SP Discussion Paper Number 0830, Social Protection and Labor, World Bank, Washington, DC. Available at <siteresources.worldbank.org/SOCIALPROTECTION/Resources/ SP-Discussion-papers/Social-Funds-DP/0830.pdf>.

Bhide, S. and A. K. Mehta. (2003). "Chronic Poverty in Rural India: An Analysis using Panel Data: Issues and Findings." Paper presented at the International Conference on Staying Poor: Chronic Poverty and Devleopment Policy, Manchester, UK, April 7–9. Available at <http://idpm.man.ac.uk/cprc/Conference/conferencepapers/Bhide%20&%20Mehta%2023.02.03.pdf>.

Bian, Yanjie. (2002). "Chinese Social Stratification and Social Mobility." *Annual Review of Sociology*, 28: 91–116.

Bigsten, Arne. (2007). "Can China Learn from Sweden?" *World Economics*, 8 (2): 1–24.

Bird, Richard M., and François Vaillancourt. (1998). *Fiscal Decentralization in Developing Countries*. Cambridge: Cambridge University Press.

Birdsall, Nancy, and Carol Graham. eds. (2000). "Mobility and Markets: Conceptual Issues and Policy Questions." *New Markets, New Opportunities: Economic and Social Mobility in a Changing World*, pp. 3–21. Washington, DC: Brookings.

Birkelund, Gunn E. (2006). "Welfare States and Social Inequality: Key Issues in Contemporary Cross-national Research in Social Stratification and Mobility." *Research in Social Stratification and Mobility*, 24: 333–51.

Blair, Harry. (2000). "Participation and Accountability at the Periphery: Democratic Local Governance in Six Countries." *World Development*, 28 (1): 21–39.

Boix, Carles. (2003). *Democracy and Redistribution*. Cambridge: Cambridge University Press.

Bollen, Kenneth, and Robert Jackman. (1985). "Political Democracy and the Size Distribution of Income." *American Sociological Review,* 50: 438–57.

Booth, John A., and Mitchell A. Seligson. (2008). "Inequality and Democracy in Latin America: Individual and Contextual Effects of Wealth on Political Participation." In Anirudh Krishna, ed., *Poverty, Participation, and Democracy: A Global Perspective*, pp. 94–124. Cambridge: Cambridge University Press.

Bourdieu, Pierre. (1984). *Distinction: A Social Critique of the Judgement of Taste*. London: Routledge.

—— (1986). "The Forms of Capital." In J. G. Richardson, ed., *The Handbook of Theory: Research for the Sociology of Education*, pp. 241–58. New York: Greenwood Press.

Bowles, Samuel, and Herbert Gintis. (2002). "The Inheritance of Inequality." *Journal of Economic Perspectives*, 16 (3): 3–30.

—————— Melissa Osborne Groves. (2005). "Introduction." In Samuel Bowles, Herbert Gintis, and Melissa Osborne Groves, eds., *Unequal Chances: Family Background and Economic Success*, pp. 1–22. Princeton: Princeton University Press.

—— Steven N. Durlauf, and Karla Hoff. (2006). "Introduction." In Samuel Bowles, Steven N. Durlauf, and Karla Hoff, eds., *Poverty Traps*, pp. 1–14. Princeton: Princeton University Press.

Brady, David. (2009). *Rich Democracies, Poor People: How Politics Explain Poverty*. Oxford: Oxford University Press.

——Yunus Kaya, and Jason Beckfield. (2007). "Reassessing the Effect of Economic Growth on Well-being in Less-developed Countries, 1980–2003." *Studies in Comparative International Development*, 42 (1): 1–35.

Breen, Richard, and Jan O. Jonsson. (2005). "Inequality of Opportunity in Comparative Perspective: Recent Research on Educational Attainment and Social Mobility." *Annual Review of Sociology*, 31: 223–43.

Breman, Jan. (1993). *Beyond Patronage and Exploitation: Changing Agrarian Relations in South Gujarat*. Delhi: Oxford University Press.

——(1996). *Footloose Labour: Working in India's Informal Economy*. Cambridge: Cambridge University Press.

Carter, Michael R. (1991). "Risk, Reciprocity, and Conditional Self-insurance in the Sahel: Measurement and Implications for the Trajectory of Agricultural Development in West Africa." Working Paper, Department of Agricultural Economics, University of Wisconsin, Wisconsin.

——Christopher B. Barrett. (2006). "The Economics of Poverty Traps and Persistent Poverty: An Asset-based Approach." *Journal of Development Studies*, 42 (2): 178–99.

——Julian May. (2001). "One Kind of Freedom: Poverty Dynamics in Post-apartheid South Africa." *World Development*, 29 (12): 1987–2006.

Case, Anne, Anu Garrib, Alicia Menendez, and Analia Olgiati. (2008). "Paying the Piper: The High Cost of Funerals in South Africa." NBER Working Paper 14456. Available at <www.nber.org/papers/w14456>.

Castaneda, Tarsicio, and Enrique Aldaz-Carroll. (1999). "The Intergenerational Transmission of Poverty: Some Causes and Policy Implications." Inter-American Development Bank Discussion Paper. Available at <www.iadb.org/sds/doc/1258eng.pdf>.

Castells, Manuel. ed. (2004). *The Network Society: A Cross-cultural Perspective*. Northampton, MA: Edward Elgar.

Chambers, Robert. (1995). "Poverty and Livelihoods: Whose Reality Counts." Discussion Paper 347, Institute of Development Studies, Brighton.

——(1997). *Whose Reality Counts? Putting the First Last*. London: Intermediary Technology Publications.

——(2008). *Revolutions in Development Inquiry*. London: Earthscan Publications.

——R. Longhurst, and A. Pacey. (1981). *Seasonal Dimensions to Rural Poverty*. London: Frances Pinter.

Chang, Ha-Joon. (2002). *Kicking Away the Ladder? Policies and Institutions for Development in Historical Perspective*. London: Anthem Press.

Chaudhuri, Shubham, and Martin Ravallion. (1994). "How Well do Static Indicators Identify the Chronic Poor?" *Journal of Public Economics*, 53: 367–94.

————(2007). "Partially Awakened Giants: Uneven Growth in India and China." In L. Alan Winters and Shahid Yusuf, eds., *Dancing with Giants: China, India, and the Global Economy*, pp. 175–210. Washington, DC: World Bank.

Chaudhury, Nazmul, Jeffrey Hammer, Michael Kremer, Karthik Muralidharan, and F. Halsey Rogers. (2006). "Missing in Action: Teacher and Health Worker Absence in Developing Countries." *Journal of Economic Perspectives*, 20 (1): 91–116.

Chayanov, Alexander V. (1966). *The Theory of the Peasant Economy*. Homewood: Irwin.

Cheema, G. Shabbir, and Dennis A. Rondinelli. (1983). *Decentralization and Development: Policy Implementation on Developing Countries*. New Delhi: Sage Publications.

Chen, Martha A. (2006). "Rethinking the Informal Economy: Linkages with the Formal Economy and the Formal Regulatory Environment." In Basudeb Guha-Khasnobis, Ravi Kanbur, and Elinor Ostrom, eds., *Linking the Formal and Informal Economy: Concepts and Practices*, pp. 75–92. Oxford: Oxford University Press.

Chen, Shaohua, and Martin Ravallion. (2007). "The Changing Profile of Poverty in the World." *2020 Focus Brief on the World's Poor and Hungry People*. Washington, DC: IFPRI.

Christiaensen, Luc, and Harold Alderman. (2004). "Child Malnutrition in Ethiopia: Can Maternal Knowledge Augment the Role of Income?" *Economic Development and Cultural Change*, 52 (2), 287–312.

——Kalanidhi Subbarao. (2005). "Towards an Understanding of Household Vulnerability in Rural Kenya." *Journal of African Economies*, 14 (4): 520–58.

——Lionel Demery, and Stefano Paternostro. (2002). *Growth, Distribution and Poverty in Africa: Messages from the 1990s*. Washington, DC: World Bank.

Chuma, Jane M., Michael Thiede, and Catherine S. Molyneux. (2006). "Rethinking the Economic Costs of Malaria at the Household Level: Evidence from Applying a New Analytical Framework in Rural Kenya." *Malaria Journal*, 5 (76).

Clark, Gerard, and Marites Sisson. (2003). "Voices from the Top of the Pile: Elite Perceptions of Poverty and the Poor in the Philippines." *Development and Change*, 34 (2): 215–42.

Coady, D., M. Grosh, and J. Hoddinott. (2004). "Targeting of Transfers in Developing Countries: Review of Lessons and Experience." World Bank Discussion Paper, Washington, DC.

Cohen, John M., and Stephen B. Peterson. (1999). *Administrative Decentralization: Strategies for Developing Countries*. West Hartford, CT: Kumarian Press.

Collier, Paul. (2007). *The Bottom Billion: Why the Poorest Countries are Failing and What Can Be Done About It*. Oxford: Oxford University Press.

Collins, Daryl, Jonathan Morduch, Stuart Rutherford, and Orlanda Ruthven. (2009). *Portfolios of the Poor: How the World's Poor Live on $2 a Day*. Princeton: Princeton University Press.

Cook, C., F. Heath, and R. Thompson. (2000). "A Meta-analysis of Response Rates in Web- or Internet-based Surveys." *Educational and Psychological Measurements*, 60 (6): 821–36.

Corak, Miles. ed. (2004). "Generational Income Mobility in North America and Europe: An Introduction." *Generational Income Mobility in North America and Europe*, pp. 1–37. Cambridge: Cambridge University Press.

Corcoran, Mary. (1995). "Rags to Riches: Poverty and Mobility in the United States." *Annual Review of Sociology*, 21: 237–67.

Cord, Louise J. (2007). "Overview." In Timothy Besley and Louise J. Cord, eds., *Delivering on the Promise of Pro-Poor Growth*, pp. 1–27. Washington, DC: World Bank.

CPRC (Chronic Poverty Research Centre). (2005). *The Chronic Poverty Report 2004–05*. Manchester: CPRC.

Crook, Richard, and James Manor. (1998). *Democracy and Decentralization in South Asia and West Africa: Participation, Accountability and Performance*. Cambridge: Cambridge University Press.

Currie, Janet. (2001). "Early Childhood Intervention Programs." *Journal of Economic Perspectives*, 15: 213–38.

Danziger, Sheldon, and Jane Waldvogel. (2005). *Securing the Future: Investing in Children from Birth to College*. New York: Russell Sage.

Dardanoni, Valentino, Gary Fields, John Roemer, and Maria Laura Sánchez Puerta. (2004). "How Demanding Should Equality of Opportunity Be, and How Much Have We Achieved?" Working Paper. Available at <pantheon.yale.edu/~jer39/Fields.12.2004.pdf>.

Das, Jishnu, Quy-Toan Do, and Berk Özler. (2005). "Reassessing Conditional Cash Transfer Programs." *World Bank Research Observer*, 20: 57 – 80.

Dasgupta, S. (2003). "Structural and Behavioural Characteristics of Informal Service Employment: Evidence from a Survey in New Delhi." *Journal of Development Studies*, 39 (3): 51–80.

Datt, Gaurav, and Martin Ravallion. (2002). "Is India's Economic Growth Leaving the Poor Behind?" *Journal of Economic Perspectives*, 16 (3): 89–108.

Davis, Mike. (2006). *Planet of Slums*. London: Verso.

Davis, Peter. (2006). "Poverty in Time: Exploring Poverty Dynamics from Life History Interviews in Bangladesh." CPRC Working Paper 69, Manchester, UK. Available at <www.chronicpoverty.org/pdfs/69Davis.pdf>.

—— (2007). "Discussions Among the Poor: Exploring Poverty Dynamics with Focus Groups in Bangladesh." CPRC Working Paper 84, Manchester, UK.

De Soto, Hernando. (1989). *The Other Path: The Invisible Revolution in the Third World*. New York: Harper and Row.

—— (2000). *The Mystery of Capital: Why Capitalism Triumphs in the West and Fails Everywhere Else*. New York: Basic Books.

De Waal, Alexander. (1989). *Famine that Kills: Darfur, Sudan, 1984–1985*. Oxford: Clarendon Press.

Deaton, Angus. (1997). *The Analysis of Household Surveys: A Microeconometric Approach to Development Policy*. Baltimore and London: Johns Hopkins University Press.

Deaton, Angus. (2000). "Counting the World's Poor: Problems and Possible Solutions." Available at <www.princeton.edu/~rpds/downloads/deaton_worlds_poor.pdf>.

——(2006). *Global Patterns of Income and Health: Facts, Interpretations, and Policies.* WIDER Annual Lecture 10. Available at <www.wider.unu.edu/publications/annual-lectures/annual-lecture-2006.pdf>.

Deininger, Klaus, and J. Okidi. (2003). "Growth and Poverty Reduction in Uganda, 1992–2000: Panel Data Evidence." *Development Policy Review*, 21 (4): 481–509.

Deolalikar, Anil. (2002). "Access to Health Services by the Poor and the Non-poor: The Case of Vietnam." *Journal of Asian and African Studies*, 37 (2): 244–61.

Dercon, Stefan. (2004). "Growth and Shocks: Evidence from Rural Ethiopia." *Journal of Development Economics*, 74 (2): 309–29.

——ed. (2005). "Risk, Insurance, and Poverty: A Review." *Insurance against Poverty*, pp. 9–37. Oxford: Oxford University Press.

——Pramila Krishnan. (2000). "Vulnerability, Seasonality and Poverty in Ethiopia." *Journal of Development Studies*, 36 (6): 25–53.

——Tessa Bold, Joachim De Weerdt, and Alula Pankhurst. (2004). "Extending Insurance? Funeral Associations in Ethiopia and Tanzania." Working Paper No. 240, OECD Development Centre, Paris.

Devereaux, S., and K. Sharp. (2003). "Is Poverty Really Falling in Rural Ethiopia?" Working Paper, Institute of Development Studies at the University of Sussex, Brighton, UK.

Diamond, Jared. (2000). *Guns, Germs and Steel: The Fates of Human Societies.* New York: Norton.

Dichter, Thomas W. (2003). *Despite Good Intentions: Why Development Assistance to the Third World Has Failed.* Boston, MA: University of Massachusetts Press.

Dilip, T. R., and Ravi Duggal. (2002). "Incidence of Non-fatal Health Outcomes and Debt in Urban India." Working Paper, Center for Enquiry into Health and Allied Themes (CEHAT), Mumbai, India.

DiMaggio, Paul. (1982). "Cultural Capital and School Success." *American Sociological Review*, 47 (2): 189–201.

Djurfeldt, Göran, Venkatesh Athreya, N. Jayakumar, et al. (2008). "Agrarian Change and Social Mobility in Tamil Nadu." Working Paper, Department of Sociology, Lund University, Sweden.

Dollar, David, and Aart Kraay. (2000). "Growth is Good for the Poor." *Journal of Economic Growth*, 7: 195–225.

Dreze, Jean and Amartya Sen. (1995). *India: Economic Development and Social Opportunity.* New Delhi: Oxford University Press.

Dror, David M., Ralf Radermacher, and Ruth Koren. (2007). "Willingness to Pay for Health Insurance among Rural and Poor Persons: Field Evidence from Seven Micro Insurance Units in India." *Health Policy*, 82 (1): 12–27.

Duncan, Greg J. (1984). *Years of Poverty, Years of Plenty.* Ann Arbor: University of Michigan, Institute for Social Research.

Durlauf, Steven N. (2006). "Groups, Social Influences, and Inequality." In Samuel Bowles, Steven N. Durlauf, and Karla Hoff, eds., *Poverty Traps,* pp. 141–75. Princeton: Princeton University Press.

Easterly, William. (2001). *The Elusive Quest for Growth: Economists' Adventures and Misadventures in the Tropics.* Cambridge, MA: MIT Press.

—— (2006). *The White Man's Burden: Why the West's Efforts to Aid the Rest Have Done So Much Ill and So Little Good.* New York: Penguin Press.

ECLAC (Economic Commission for Latin America and the Caribbean). (2000). *Social Panorama of Latin America, 1999–2000.* Santiago, Chile: United Nations ECLAC.

—— (2007). *Social Panorama of Latin America, 2006–2007.* Santiago, Chile: United Nations ECLAC.

Eder, J. (1999). *A Generation Later: Household Strategies and Economic Change in the Rural Philippines.* Honolulu: University of Hawaii Press.

Ekman, Björn. (2004). "Community-based Health Insurance in Low-income Countries: A Systematic Review of the Evidence." *Health Policy and Planning,* 19 (5): 249–70.

Elbers, C., P. Lanjouw, J. Mistiaen, and K. Simler. (2004). On the Unequal Inequality of Poor Communities. *World Bank Economic Review,* 18 (3): 401–21.

Ellis, Frank. (1998). "Household Strategies and Rural Livelihood Diversification." *Journal of Development Studies,* 35: 1–38.

—— (2000). *Rural Livelihoods and Diversity in Developing Countries.* New York: Oxford University Press.

Ensor, Tim, and Pham Bich San. (1996). "Access and Payment for Health Care: The Poor of Northern Vietnam." *International Journal of Health Planning and Management,* 11 (1): 69–83.

EQUITAP. (2005). "Paying Out-of-pocket for Health Care in Asia: Catastrophic and Poverty Impact." Equitap Project Working Paper No. 2. Available at <www.equitap.org>.

Erikson, Robert, and John H. Goldthorpe. (1992). *The Constant Flux: A Study of Class Mobility in Industrial Societies.* Oxford: Clarendon Press.

———— (2002). "Intergenerational Inequality: A Sociological Perspective." *Journal of Economic Perspectives,* 16 (3): 31–44.

Esman, M., and N. Uphoff. (1984). *Local Organizations: Intermediaries in Rural Development.* Ithaca, NY: Cornell University Press.

Esping-Andersen, Gosta. (2005). "Education and Equal Life-chances: Investing in Children." In Olli Kangas and Joakim Palme, eds., *Social Policy and Economic Development in the Nordic Countries,* pp. 147–63. New York: Palgrave Macmillan.

Estudillo, Jonna, Agnes Quisumbing, and Keijiro Otsuka. (2001). "Gender Differences in Land Inheritance, Schooling, and Lifetime Income: Evidence from the Rural Philippines." *Journal of Development Studies,* 37 (4): 23–48.

Evans, Peter. (1995). *Embedded Autonomy: States and Industrial Transformation.* Princeton: Princeton University Press.

Fabricant, S., C. Kamara, and A. Mills. (1999). "Why the Poor Pay More: Household Curative Expenditures in Rural Sierra Leone." *International Journal of Health Planning and Management,* 14: 179–99.

Farmer, Paul. (1999). *Infections and Inequalities: The Modern Plagues.* Berkeley: University of California Press.

—— (2003). *Pathologies of Power: Health, Human Rights, and the New War on the Poor.* Berkeley: University of California Press.

Fields, Gary. (2001). *Distribution and Development: A New Look at the Developing World.* New York: Russell Sage Foundation.

Findlay, Ronald, and Stanislaw Wellisz. eds. (1993). "Hong Kong." *Five Small Open Economies,* pp. 16–92. New York: Oxford University Press.

Franco, S., and R. Saith. (2003). "Different Conceptions of Poverty: An Empirical Investigation and Policy Implications." Available at <www.wider.unu.edu/conference/conference-2003-2/conference%202003-2-papers/papers-pdf/Franco%20270503.pdf>.

French, Howard W. (2006). "Wealth Grows, but Health Care Withers in China." *New York Times,* January 14.

Friedman, Thomas L. (2005). *The World is Flat: A Brief History of the Twenty-First Century.* New York: Farrar, Strauss, and Giroux.

Friedmann, John. (2005). "The World City Hypothesis." In Jan Lin and Christopher Mele, eds., *The Urban Sociology Reader,* pp. 223–9. London, UK: Routledge.

Gaiha, Raghav. (1989). "Are the Chronically Poor also the Poorest in Rural India?" *Development and Change,* 20: 295–322.

——Vani Kulkarni. (1998). "Is Growth Central to Poverty Alleviation in India?" *Journal of International Affairs,* 52 (1): 145–80.

Gan, Li, Lixin Colin Xu, and Yang Yao. (2005). "Health Shocks, Village Governance, and Farmers' Long-term Income Capabilities: Evidence from Rural China." FED Working Paper No. FE20050066. Available at <www.ded.org.cn>.

Gangl, Markus. (2005). "Income Inequality, Permanent Incomes, and Income Dynamics: Comparing Europe to the United States." *Work and Occupations,* 32 (2): 140–62.

——Joakim Palme, and Lane Kenworthy. (2007). "Is High Inequality Offset by Mobility?" Working Paper. Available at <www.u.arizona.edu/~lkenwor/ishighinequalityoffsetbymobility.pdf>.

Ganzeboom, Harry, Donald Treiman, and Wout Ultee. (1991). "Comparative Intergenerational Stratification: Three Generations and Beyond." *Annual Review of Sociology,* 17: 277–302.

Garg, Charu C., and Anup K. Karan. (2005). "Health and Millennium Development Goal 1: Reducing Out-of-pocket Expenditures to Reduce Income Poverty—Evidence from India." Equitap Project Working Paper No. 15. Available at <www.equitap.org>.

Garg, Ashish, and Jonathan Morduch. (1998). "Sibling Rivalry and the Gender Gap: Evidence from Child Health Outcomes in Ghana." *Journal of Population Economics,* 11 (4): 471–93.

Gelbach, J., and L. Pritchett. (2002). "Is More for the Poor Less for the Poor? The Politics of Means-tested Targeting." *Topics in Economic Analysis and Policy,* 2 (1).

Giridhardask, Anand. (2007). "In India, Poverty Inspires Technology Workers to Altruism." *New York Times,* October 30.

Glewwe, P., and J. Van der Gaag. (1990). "Identifying the Poor in Developing Countries: Do Different Definitions Matter?" *World Development,* 18 (6): 803–14.

—— and G. Hall. (1998). *Who is Most Vulnerable to Macroeconomic Shocks? Hypothesis Tests Using Panel Data from Peru.* Washington, DC: World Bank.

GOI (Government of India) (2007). *Report of the Expert Group on Agricultural Indebtedness.* New Delhi: Department of Economic Affairs, Ministry of Finance, GOI.

Graham, Carol. (2000). "The Political Economy of Mobility: Perceptions and Objective Trends in Latin America." In Nancy Birdsall and Carol Graham, eds., *New Markets, New Opportunities: Economic and Social Mobility in a Changing World,* pp. 225–66. Washington, DC: Brookings.

Grawe, Nathan D. (2004). "Intergenerational Mobility for Whom? The Experience of High- and Low-earning Sons in International Perspective." In M. Corak, ed., *Generational Income Mobility in North America and Europe,* pp. 58–89. Cambridge: Cambridge University Press.

Griffin, Keith, and Amy Ickowitz. (1997). "The Distribution of Wealth and the Pace of Development." Working Paper No. 3, Social Development and Poverty Elimination Division, United Nations Development Programme, New York.

Grootaert, C., and R. Kanbur (1995). "The Lucky Few Amidst Economic Decline: Distributional Change in Cote d'Ivoire as seen through Panel Data Sets, 1985–88." *Journal of Development Studies,* 31 (4): 603–19.

Gupta, Indrani, and Arup Mitra. (2004). "Economic Growth, Health and Poverty: An Exploratory Study for India." *Development Policy Review,* 22 (2): 193–206.

Hacker, Jacob. (2006). *The Great Risk Shift.* New York: Oxford University Press.

Haddad, Lawrence, and Akhter Ahmed. (2003). "Chronic and Transitory Poverty: Evidence from Egypt, 1997–99." *World Development,* 31 (1): 71–85.

—— Ravi Kanbur. (1990). "How Serious is the Neglect of Intra-household Inequality?" Working Paper No. 296, Policy, Planning, and Research, World Bank, Washington, DC.

—— Christine Pena, Chizuru Nishida, Agnes Quisumbing, and Alison Slack. (1996). "Food Security and Nutrition Implications of Intrahousehold Bias: A Review of the Literature." Discussion Paper 19, Food Consumption and Nutrition Division, International Food Policy Research Institute, Washington, DC.

Hall, Peter A., and David Soskice, eds. (2001). *Varieties of Capitalism: The Institutional Foundations of Comparative Advantage.* Oxford: Oxford University Press.

Handa, Sudhanshu, and Benjamin Davis. (2006). "The Experience of Conditional Cash Transfers in Latin America and the Caribbean." *Development Policy Review*, 24 (5): 513–36.

Hannum, Emily, and Claudia Buchmann. (2005). "Global Educational Expansion and Socio-economic Development: An Assessment of Findings from the Social Sciences." *World Development*, 33 (3): 333–54.

Harriss-White, Barbara. (2007). "Destitution in India and Peru." In Frances Stewart, Ruhi Saith, and Barbara Harriss-White, eds., *Defining Poverty in the Developing World*, pp. 198–216. New York: Palgrave Macmillan.

Himmelstein, David, Elizabeth Warren, Deborah Thorne, and Steffie Woolhandler. (2005). "Illness and Injury as Contributors to Bankruptcy." *Health Affairs*, February 2.

Hirway, Indira. (2000). "Dynamics of Development in Gujarat: Some Issues." *Economic and Political Weekly*, August 26: 3106–20.

Hout, Michael. (2006). "Economic Change and Social Mobility." In Göran Therborn, ed., *Inequalities of the World: New Theoretical Frameworks, Multiple Empirical Approaches*, pp. 119–35. London: Verso.

—— Thomas DiPrete. (2006). "What Have We Learned: RC28's Contribution to Knowledge about Social Stratification." *Research in Social Stratification and Mobility*, 24: 1–20.

Hulme, David, and Andrew Shepherd. (2003). "Conceptualizing Chronic Poverty." *World Development*, 31 (3): 403–24.

Iliffe, J. (1987). *The African Poor: A History.* Cambridge: Cambridge University Press.

ILO (International Labor Office). (2002a). *Decent Work and the Informal Economy.* Geneva: ILO. Available at <www.ilo.org/public/english/standards/relm/ilc/ilc90/pdf/rep-vi.pdf>.

—— (2002b). *Women and Men in the Informal Economy: A Statistical Picture.* Geneva: Employment Sector, ILO.

Iyer, Aditi, Gita Sen, and Asha George. (2007). "The Dynamics of Gender and Class in Access to Health Care: Evidence from Rural Karnataka, India." *International Journal of Health Services*, 37 (3): 537–54.

Jacoby, H., and F. Skoufias. (1997). "Risk, Financial Markets, and Human Capital in a Developing Country." *Review of Economic Studies*, 64 (3): 311–36.

Jalan, Jyotsna, and Martin Ravallion. (1998). "Geographic Poverty Traps? A Micro Model of Consumption Growth in Rural China." Available at <http://www.gdnet.org/pdf/580_Jalan.pdf>.

—— (2000). "Is Transient Poverty Different? Evidence for Rural China." *Journal of Development Studies*, 36 (6): 82–99.

Jantti, Markus, Bernt Bratsberg, Knut Roed, et al. (2005). "American Exceptionalism in a New Light: A Comparison of Intergenerational Earnings Mobility in the Nordic

Countries, the United Kingdom, and the United States." Available at <papers.ssrn. com/sol3/papers.cfm?abstract_id=878675>.

Jayne, T. S., T. Yamano, M. Weber, et al. (2003). "Smallholder Income and Land Distribution in Africa: Implications for Poverty Reduction Strategies." *Food Policy*, 28: 253–73.

Jeffrey, Craig, Patricia Jeffery, and Roger Jeffery. (2008). *Degrees without Freedom: Education, Masculinities, and Unemployment in North India*. Stanford: Stanford University Press.

Jencks, Christopher, and Laura Tach. (2005). "Would Equal Opportunity Mean More Mobility?" KSG Working Paper No. RWP05-037, Kennedy School of Government, Harvard University, Cambridge, MA. Available at <papers.ssrn.com/sol3/papers. cfm?abstract_id=779507>.

Jodha, Narpat S. (1988). "Poverty Debate in India: A Minority View." *Economic and Political Weekly*, Bombay, November: 2421–8.

Johnson, Deb. (2002). "Insights on Poverty." *Development in Practice*, 12 (2): 127–37.

Kabeer, Naila. (2005). "Gender Equality and Women's Empowerment: A Critical Analysis of the Third Millennium Development Goal." *Gender and Development*, 13 (1): 13–24.

Kakwani, Nanak, and Hyun H. Son. (2006). "New Global Poverty Counts." Working Paper No. 29, International Poverty Center, United Nations Development Programme. Available at <www.undp.org/povertycentre/pub/IPCWorkingPaper29.pdf>.

Kanbur, Ravi. (2001). "Economic Policy, Distribution and Poverty: The Nature of Disagreements." *World Development*, 29 (6): 1083–94.

——ed. (2003). *Q-Squared: Combining Qualitative and Quantitative Methods in Poverty Appraisal*. Delhi: Permanent Black.

——Lyn Squire. (1999). "The Evolution of Thinking About Poverty: Exploring the Interactions." Available at <www.worldbank.org/prem/poverty/wdrpoverty/evolut. htm>.

Kangas, Olli, and Joakim Palme. (2005). "Coming Late—Catching Up: The Formation of a 'Nordic Model.'" In Olli Kangas and Joakim Palme, eds., *Social Policy and Economic Development in the Nordic Countries*, pp. 17–59. New York: Palgrave Macmillan.

Kappel, R., J. Lay, and S. Steiner. (2005). "Uganda: No more Pro-poor Growth?" *Development Policy Review*, 23 (1): 27–53.

Karshenas, Massoud. (2003). "Global Poverty: National Account Based versus Survey Based Estimates." *Development and Change*, 34 (4): 683–712.

Kasza, Gregory, J. (2006). *One World of Welfare: Japan in Comparative Perspective*. Ithaca, NY: Cornell University Press.

Kenjiro, Y. (2005). "Why Illness Causes More Serious Economic Damage than Crop Failure in Rural Cambodia." *Development and Change* 36(4): 759–83.

Khan, Azizur Rahman, and Carl Riskin. (2001). *Inequality and Poverty in China in the Age of Globalization*. Oxford: Oxford University Press.

Klitgaard, Robert. (1997). "Unanticipated Consequences in Anti-Poverty Programs." *World Development*, 25 (12): 1963–72.

Kochar, Anjini. (1995). "Expanding Household Vulnerability to Idiosyncratic Income Shocks." *AEA Papers and Proceedings*, 85 (92): 159–64.

Kohli, Atul. (2004). *State-directed Development: Political Power and Industrialization in the Global Periphery*. Cambridge: Cambridge University Press.

Kozel, Valerie, and Barbara Parker. (2007). "Poverty and Vulnerability in Zambia: Perspectives on Policy Challenges." Paper presented at Q-Squared in Policy: A Conference on the Use of Qualitative and Quantitative Methods of Poverty Analysis in Decision-making. Hanoi, July 7–8.

Kremer, M., N. Chaudhury, F. Rogers, K. Muralidharan, and J. Hammer. (2004). "Teacher Absence in India: A Snapshot." *Journal of the European Economic Association*, 3 (2–3): 658–67.

Krishna, Anirudh. (2002). *Active Social Capital: Tracing the Roots of Development and Democracy*. New York: Columbia University Press.

——(2003). "Falling into Poverty: The Other Side of Poverty Reduction." *Economic and Political Weekly*, Bombay, India, February 8.

——(2004). "Escaping Poverty and Becoming Poor: Who Gains, Who Loses, and Why? People's Assessments of Stability and Change in 35 North Indian Villages." *World Development*, 32 (1): 121–36.

——(2006). "Pathways Out of and Into Poverty in 36 Villages of Andhra Pradesh, India." *World Development*, 34 (2): 271–88.

——(2007a). "For Reducing Poverty Faster: Target Reasons before People." *World Development*, 35 (11): 1947–60.

——(2007b). "Poverty and Health: Defeating Poverty by Reducing Its Creation." *Development*, 50th Anniversary Special Issue, 50 (2): 63–9.

——(2007c). "The Conundrum of Services: Why Services are Crucial for Making Service Provision Better." In Shantayanan Devarajan and Ingrid Widlund, eds., *The Politics of Service Delivery in Democracies: Better Access for the Poor*, pp. 11–24. Stockholm: Ministry of Foreign Affairs, Government of Sweden.

——(2007d). "Escaping Poverty and Becoming Poor in Three States of India, with Additional Evidence from Kenya, Uganda, and Peru." In Deepa Narayan and Patti Petesch, eds., *Moving Out of Poverty: Cross-Disciplinary Perspectives on Mobility*, pp. 165–98. Washington, DC: World Bank; and New York: Palgrave Macmillan.

——(2007e). *The Dynamics of Poverty: Why Don't 'The Poor' Act Collectively?* 2020 Focus Brief on the World's Poor and Hungry People. Washington, DC: IFPRI. Available at <http://www.ifpri.org/sites/default/files/publications/beijingbrief_krishna.pdf>.

—— (2007f). "The Stages-of-progress Methodology and Results from Five Countries." In Caroline Moser, ed., *Reducing Global Poverty: The Case for Asset Accumulation*, pp. 62–79. Washington, DC: Brookings Institution.

—— (2007g). "Why Don't 'the Poor' Have a Louder Voice When they are Many?" Paper presented at 2020 Seminar Series: Action for the World's Poorest and Hungry, International Food Policy Research Institute, Washington DC. Available at <http://www.ifpri.org/event/why-dont-poor-have-louder-voice-when-they-are-many>.

—— (2009). "Why Don't 'the Poor' Make Common Cause? The Importance of Subgroups." *Journal of Development Studies*, 45 (6): 1–19.

—— Vijay Brihmadesam. (2006). "What Does it Take to Become a Software Engineer? Educated Parents, Information Networks, and Upward Mobility in India." *Economic and Political Weekly*, Bombay, India, July 29.

—— Jesse Lecy. (2008). "The Balance of All Things: Explaining Household Poverty Dynamics in 50 Villages of Gujarat, India." *International Journal of Multiple Research Methods*, 2 (2): 160–75.

—— Jan Nederveen Pieterse. (2008). "Hierarchical Integration: The Dollar Economy and the Rupee Economy." *Development and Change*, 39 (2): 219–37.

—— Norman Uphoff, and Milton Esman. (1997). *Reasons for Hope: Instructive Experiences in Rural Development*. West Hartford, CT: Kumarian Press.

—— Patricia Kristjanson, Maren Radeny, and Wilson Nindo. (2004). "Escaping Poverty and Becoming Poor in Twenty Kenyan Villages." *Journal of Human Development*, 5 (2): 211–26.

—— Mahesh Kapila, Mahendra Porwal, and Veerpal Singh. (2005). "Why Growth is Not Enough: Household Poverty Dynamics in Northeast Gujarat, India." *Journal of Development Studies*, 41 (7): 1163–92.

—— Christina Gibson-Davis, Liz Clasen, Milissa Markiewicz, and Nicolas Perez. (2006). "Escaping Poverty and Becoming Poor in Thirteen Communities in Rural North Carolina." Working Paper, Sanford Institute of Public Policy, Duke University. Available at <www.pubpol.duke.edu/krishna>.

—— —— Judith Kuan, et al. (2006). "Fixing the Hole in the Bucket: Household Poverty Dynamics in Forty Communities of the Peruvian Andes." *Development and Change*, 37 (5): 997–1021.

—— Daniel Lumonya, Milissa Markiewicz, et al. (2006). "Escaping Poverty and Becoming Poor in 36 Villages of Central and Western Uganda." *Journal of Development Studies*, 42 (2): 346–70.

Kristjanson, Patricia, Anirudh Krishna, Maren Radeny, et al. (2007). "Poverty Dynamics and the Role of Livestock in the Peruvian Andes." *Agricultural Systems*, 94: 294–308.

—— Nelson Mango, Anirudh Krishna, Maren Radeny, and Nancy Johnson. (2009). "Understanding Poverty Dynamics in Kenya." *Journal of International Development*. In press.

Kundu, Amitabh. (2000). "Globalizing Gujarat: Urbanization, Employment and Poverty." *Economic and Political Weekly*, August 26: 3172–81.

Kwon, Soonwon, ed. (1998). "National Profile of Poverty." *Combating Poverty: The Korean Experience*, pp. 29–60. Seoul: United Nations Development Programme.

Labonte, Ronald, and Ted Schrecker. (2007). "Globalization and Social Determinants of Health." Part 1: *Globalization and Health*, 3 (5): 1–10; Part 2, *Globalization and Health*, 3 (6): 1–17; Part 3, *Globalization and Health*, 3 (7): 1–15.

Laderchi, C., R. Saith, and F. Stewart. (2003). "Does it Matter that We Don't Agree on the Definition of Poverty? A Comparison of Four Approaches." Queen Elizabeth House (QEH) Working Paper Series 107, QEH, Oxford, UK.

Landes, David S. (1999). *The Wealth and Poverty of Nations*. New York: Norton.

Lanjouw, Jean Olson. (1998). "Demystifying Poverty Lines." Available at <www.undp.org/poverty/publications/pov_red/Demystifying_Poverty_Lines.pdf>.

Lanjouw, Peter, and Nicholas Stern. (1991). "Poverty in Palanpur." *World Bank Economic Review*, 5 (1): 23–55.

Lawson, David. (2004). "Uganda: The Influence of Health on Chronic and Transitory Poverty." CPRC Working Paper 41, Chronic Poverty Research Centre, Manchester, UK. Available at <www.chronicpoverty.org>.

Lecomte, Bernard, and Anirudh Krishna. (1997). "Six-S: Building upon Traditional Social Organizations in Francophone West Africa." In Anirudh Krishna, Norman Uphoff, and Milton Esman, eds., *Reasons for Hope: Instructive Experiences in Rural Development*, pp. 75–90. West Hartford, CT: Kumarian Press.

Leonard, David. (1991). *African Successes: Four Public Managers of Kenyan Rural Development*. Berkeley: University of California Press.

Lipton, Michael. (1997). "Editorial: Poverty—Are There Holes in the Consensus?" *World Development*, 25 (7): 1003–7.

—— Martin Ravallion. (1995). "Poverty and Policy." In J. Behrman and T. N. Srinivasan, eds., *Handbook of Development Economics, Vol. III*, pp. 2551–657. Amsterdam: Elsevier Science.

Litvack, Jennie, Junaid Ahmad, and Richard Bird. (1998). *Rethinking Decentralization in Developing Countries*. Washington, DC: World Bank.

Lok-Desallien, Renata. (1999). "Review of Poverty Concepts and Indicators." Available at <www.undp.org/poverty/publications/pov_red/Review_of_Concepts.pdf>.

Lwanga-Ntale, Charles, and Kimberley McClean. (2003). "The Face of Chronic Poverty in Uganda as seen by the Poor Themselves." CPRC Working Paper, Chronic Poverty Research Centre, Manchester, UK.

Macinko, James, Leiyu Shi, and Barbara Starfield. (2004). "Wage Inequality, the Health System, and Infant Mortality in Wealthy Industrialized Countries, 1970–1996." *Social Science and Medicine*, (58): 279–92.

Macleod, Jay. (1995). *Ain't No Makin' It: Aspirations and Attainment in a Low-income Neighborhood*. Boulder, CO: Westview Press.

Manor, James. (1999). *The Political Economy of Democratic Decentralization*. Washington, DC: World Bank.

Matin, Imran, and Shantana R. Halder. (2002). "Combining Targeting Methodologies for the Better Targeting of the Extreme Poor: Some Preliminary Findings from BRAC's CFPR/TUP Programme." CRPR/TUP Working Paper 1, Research and Evaluation Division, Dhaka: BRAC.

Mayer, Susan E. (1997). *What Money Can't Buy: Family Incomes and Children's Life Chances*. Cambridge, MA: Harvard University Press.

Mazumdar, Bhashkar. (2005). "Fortunate Sons: New Estimates of Intergenerational Mobility in the United States using Social Security Earnings Data." *Review of Economics and Statistics*, 87 (2): 235–55.

McGee, Rosemary. (2004). "Constructing Poverty Trends in Uganda: A Multidisciplinary Perspective." *Development and Change*, 35 (3): 499–523.

McIntyre, Diane, Michael Thiede, Goran Dahlgren, and Margaret Whitehead. (2006). "What are the Economic Consequences for Households of Illness and of Paying for Health Care in Low- and Middle-income Country Contexts?" *Social Science and Medicine*, 62: 858–65.

McKernan, S., and C. Ratcliffe. (2002). "Transition Events in the Dynamics of Poverty." Washington, DC: Urban Institute. Available at <www.urban.org>.

Mehta, Aasha Kapur, and Amita Shah. (2003). "Chronic Poverty in India: Incidence, Causes and Policies." *World Development*, 31 (3): 491–511.

Mellor, J. W. (1999). "Pro-poor Growth: The Relation between Growth in Agriculture and Poverty Reduction." Report prepared for USAID, Washington, DC.

Milanovic, Branko. (2005). *Worlds Apart: Measuring International and Global Inequality*. Princeton: Princeton University Press.

Milly, Deborah, J. (1999). *Poverty, Equality, and Growth: The Politics of Economic Need in Postwar Japan*. Cambridge, MA: Harvard University Press.

Molyneux, Maxine and Shahra Razavi. (2005). "Beijing plus Ten: An Ambivalent Record on Gender Justice." *Development and Change*, 36 (6): 983–1010.

Moore, Mick, Madhulika Choudhary, and Neelam Singh. (1998). "How Can *We* Know What *They* Want? Understanding Local Perceptions of Poverty and Ill-being in Asia." IDS (Institute of Development Studies) Working Paper 80, IDS, Brighton, UK.

Morduch, Jonathan. (2000). "Sibling Rivalry in Africa." *American Economic Review*, 90 (2): 405–9.

——(2005). "Consumption Smoothing Across Space: Testing Theories of Risk-Sharing in the ICRISAT Study Region of South India." In Stefan Dercon, ed., *Insurance against Poverty*, pp. 38–58. Oxford: Oxford University Press.

——(2006). "Micro-insurance: The Next Revolution?" In Abhijit Banerjee, Roland Benabou, and Dilip Mookherjee, eds., *Understanding Poverty*, pp. 337–56. Oxford: Oxford University Press.

Morgan, Stephen L. (2006). "Past Themes and Future Prospects for Research on Social and Economic Mobility." In Stephen L. Morgan, David B. Grusky, and Gary S. Fields, eds., *Mobility and Inequality*, pp. 3–22. Stanford, CA: Stanford University Press.

Moser, Caroline. (1998). "The Asset-vulnerability Framework: Reassessing Urban Poverty Reduction Strategies." *World Development*, 26 (1): 1–19.

——Andrew Felton. (2007). "Intergenerational Asset Accumulation and Poverty Reduction in Guayaquil, Ecuador, 1978–2004." In Caroline Moser, ed., *Reducing Global Poverty: The Case for Asset Accumulation*, pp. 15–50. Washington, DC: Brookings Institution.

Muller, Edward N. (1988). "Democracy, Economic Development, and Income Inequality." *American Sociological Review* 53: 50–68.

Munshi, Kaivan, and Mark Rosenzweig. (2005). "Traditional Institutions Meet the Modern World: Caste, Gender and Schooling Choice in a Globalizing Economy." Available at <www.econ.brown.edu/fac/Kaivan_Munshi/bombay12.pdf>.

Narayan, D., R. Chambers, M. Shah, and P. Petesh. (2000). *Voices of the Poor: Crying Out for Change*. New York: Oxford University Press.

——Patel, R., K. Schafft, A. Rademacher, and S. Koch-Schulte. (2000). *Voices of the Poor: Can Anyone Hear Us?* New York: Oxford University Press.

——Pritchett, L., and S. Kapoor. (2009). *Moving Out of Poverty Volume 2: Success from the Bottom Up*. New York: Palgrave Macmillan.

Naschold, Felix, and Christopher Barrett. (2007). "Do Short-term Observed Income Changes Overstate Structural Economic Mobility?" Working Paper, Cornell University. Available at <aem.cornell.edu/faculty_sites/cbb2/Papers/Mobility%20_Naschold%20&%20Barrett_%20Dec%202007.pdf>.

Newman, Katherine S. (1988). *Falling from Grace: Downward Mobility in the Age of Affluence*. Berkeley: University of California Press.

Noponen, Helzi. (1991). "The Dynamics of Work and Survival for the Urban Poor: A Gender Analysis of Panel Data from Madras." *Development and Change*, 22: 233–60.

North, Douglass C. (1990). *Institutions, Institutional Change, and Economic Performance*. New York: Cambridge University Press.

Obama, Barack. (2006). *The Audacity of Hope: Thoughts on Reclaiming the American Dream*. New York: Random House.

O'Connor, Alice. (2001). *Poverty Knowledge: Social Science, Social Policy, and the Poor in 20th Century US History*. Princeton: Princeton University Press.

OECD. (2001). "When Money is Tight: Poverty Dynamics in OECD Countries." Available at <www.oecd.org/dataoecd/29/55/2079296.pdf>.

Oldenburg, Veena T. (2002). *Dowry Murder: The Imperial Origins of a Cultural Crime*. New York: Oxford University Press.

Olson, Mancur. (2000). *Power and Prosperity: Outgrowing Communist and Capitalist Dictatorships*. New York: Basic Books.

Ostrom, Elinor. (1996). "Crossing the Great Divide: Coproduction, Synergy, and Development." *World Development*, 24 (6): 1073–87.

—— (2001). "Vulnerability and Polycentric Governance Systems." *IHDP (International Human Dimensions Programme on Global Environmental Change) Newsletter UPDATE*, 3(1): 3–4.

—— Larry Schroeder, and Susan Wynne. (1993). *Institutional Incentives and Sustainable Development: Infrastructure Policies in Perspective*. Boulder, CO: Westview Press.

Palmer-Jones, Richard, and Kunal Sen. (2001). "On India's Poverty Puzzles and the Statistics of Poverty." *Economic and Political Weekly*, January 20: 211–17.

Paxson, Christina, and Norbert Schady. (2005). "Cognitive Development among Young Children in Ecuador: The Roles of Wealth, Health and Parenting." World Bank Policy Research Working Paper Series 3605, World Bank, Washington, DC.

Pei, Minxin. (2006). "The Dark Side of China's Rise." *Foreign Policy*, March/April: 32–40.

Pender, J., P. Jagger, E. Nkonya, and D. Sserunkuuma. (2004). "Development Pathways and Land Management in Uganda." *World Development*, 32 (5): 767–92.

Perlman, Janice. (2007). "Elusive Pathways Out of Poverty: Intra- and Intergenerational Mobility in the Favelas of Rio de Janeiro." In Deepa Narayan and Patti Petesch, eds., *Moving Out of Poverty: Cross-Disciplinary Perspectives*, pp. 227–72. New York: Palgrave Macmillan.

Prahalad, C. K. (2005). *The Fortune at the Bottom of the Pyramid: Eradicating Poverty through Profits*. Singapore: Pearson Education, Inc.

Preker, Alexander S., Guy Carrin, David Dror, et al. (2002). "Effectiveness of Community Health Financing in Meeting the Cost of Illness." *Bulletin of the World Health Organization*, 80 (2): 143–50.

Pritchett, Lant, and Michael Woolcock. (2004). "Solutions When the Solution Is the Problem: Arraying the Disarray in Development." *World Development*, 32 (5): 191–212.

Pryer, J., S. Rogers, and A. Rahman (2003). "Work, Disabling Illness, and Coping Strategies in Dhaka Slums, Bangladesh." Paper presented at the International Conference on Staying Poor: Chronic Poverty and Devleopment Policy, Manchester, April 7–9, 2003. Available at <http://idpm.man.ac.uk/cprc/Conference/conferencepapers/Pryer%20Jane%20Workdisab28.02.03.pdf>.

Quisumbing, Agnes R. (2006). "Investments, Bequests, and Public Policy: Intergenerational Transfers and the Escape from Poverty." CPRC Working Paper. Available at <www.chronicpoverty.org/pdfs/2006ConceptsConferencePapers/Quisumbing-CPRC2006-Draft.pdf>.

Quisumbing, Agnes R. (2007). "Poverty Transitions, Shocks, and Consumption in Rural Bangladesh: Preliminary Results from a Longitudinal Household Survey." CPRC Working Paper 105. Chronic Poverty Research Centre, Manchester, UK.

Rajasekhar, D. (2008). "Social Security for Unorganized Workers in India: Status and Issues." *India Economy Review*, V: 125–31.

Ranis, Gustav, and Frances Stewart. (2001). "Growth and Human Development: Comparative Latin American Experiences." *The Developing Economies*, 39 (4): 333–65.

Ravallion, Martin. (2001). "Growth, Inequality and Poverty: Looking Beyond Averages." *World Development*, 29 (1): 1803–15.

——(2007). "Economic Growth and Poverty Reduction: Do Poor Countries Need to Worry about Inequality?" *2020 Focus Brief on the World's Poor and Hungry People*. Washington, DC: IFPRI.

——Shaohua Chen. (2004). "China's (Uneven) Progress Against Poverty." World Bank Policy Research Working Paper 3408, World Bank, Washington, DC.

——Gaurav Datt. (1996). "How Important to India's Poor is the Sectoral Composition of Economic Growth?" *World Bank Economic Review*, 10 (1).

Ravnborg, H. M., J. Boesen, and A. Sorensen. (2004). "Gendered District Poverty Profiles and Poverty Monitoring: Kabarole, Masaka, Pallisa, Rakai and Tororo Districts, Uganda." DIIS Working Paper 2004: 1, Danish Institute for International Studies, Copenhagen.

Ray, Debraj. (2006). "Aspirations, Poverty, and Economic Change." In Abhijit Banerjee, Roland Benabou, and Dilip Mookherjee, eds., *Understanding Poverty*, pp. 409–21. Oxford: Oxford University Press.

Reddy, Sanjay G. (2008). "The New Global Poverty Estimates—Digging Deeper into a Hole." Available at <http://www.undp-povertycentre.org/pub/IPCOnePager65.pdf>.

——Camelia Minoiu. (2007). "Has World Poverty *Really* Fallen?" *Review of Income and Wealth*, 53 (3): 484–502.

——Thomas W. Pogge. (2002). "How *Not* To Count the Poor." Available at <www.socialanalysis.org>.

Reid, T. R. (2009). *The Healing of America: A Global Quest for Better, Cheaper, and Fairer Health Care*. New York: Penguin Press.

Robinson, Marguerite S. (2001). *The Microfinance Revolution*. New York: Open Society Institute.

Rodgers, Harrell R., Jr. (2000). *American Poverty in a New Era of Reform*. Armonk, NY: M. E. Sharpe.

Rodrik, Dani. (2000). "Institutions for High-Quality Growth: What They Are and How to Acquire Them." *Studies in Comparative International Development*, (35) 3: 3–31.

——(2002). "Growth and Poverty Reduction: What are the Real Questions?" *Finance and Development*, 37 (4).

——(2007). *One Economics, Many Recipes: Globalization, Institutions, and Economic Growth*. Princeton: Princeton University Press.

——Francisco Rodríguez. (2001). "Trade Policy and Economic Growth: A Skeptic's Guide to the Cross-national Evidence." In Ben Bernanke and Kenneth S. Rogoff, eds., *Macroeconomics Annual 2000*. Cambridge, MA: MIT Press for NBER.

Roemer, John E. (1998). *Equality of Opportunity*. Cambridge, MA: Harvard University Press.

——(2000). "Equality of Opportunity." In Kenneth Arrow, Samuel Bowles, and Steven Durlauf, eds., *Meritocracy and Economic Inequality*, pp. 17–32. Princeton: Princeton University Press.

——(2004). "Equal Opportunity and Intergenerational Mobility: Going Beyond Intergenerational Income Transition Matrices." In Miles Corak, ed., *Generational Income Mobility in North America and Europe*, pp. 48–57. Cambridge: Cambridge University Press.

Rondinelli, Dennis A., James S. McCullough, and Ronald W. Johnson. (1989). "Analyzing Decentralization Policies in Developing Countries: a Political-economy Framework." *Development and Change*, (20): 57–87.

Root, Hilton, L. (2006). *Capital and Collusion: The Political Logic of Global Economic Development*. Princeton: Princeton University Press.

Rothschild, Michael, and Joseph Stiglitz. (1976). "Equilibrium in Competitive Insurance Markets: An Essay on the Economics of Imperfect Information." *Quarterly Journal of Economics*, 90 (4): 629–49.

Rueschemeyer, Dietrich, Evelyne Huber Stephens, and John D. Stephens. (1992). *Capitalist Development and Democracy*. Cambridge: Cambridge University Press.

Russell, Steven. (2004). "The Economic Burden of Illness for Households in Developing Countries: A Review of Studies Focusing on Malaria, Tuberculosis, and Human Immunodeficiency Virus/Acquired Immunodeficiency Syndrome." *American Journal of Tropical Medicine and Hygiene*, 71 (Suppl. 2): 147–55.

Sachs, Jeffrey, D. (2005). *The End of Poverty: Economic Possibilities for Our Times*. New York: Penguin Press.

Sahlins, Marshall. (1972). *Stone Age Economics*. Chicago: Aldine-Atherton.

Sahn, David E., and David C. Stifel. (2003). "Progress Toward the Millennium Development Goals in Africa." *World Development*, 31 (1): 23–52.

Saith, Aswani. (2005). "Poverty Lines versus the Poor: Method versus Meaning." *Economic and Political Weekly*, October 22.

Salmen, Lawrence. (1987). *Listen to the People: Participant-Observer Evaluation of Development Projects*. New York: Oxford University Press.

Salonen, Tapio. (2001). "Sweden: Between Model and Reality." In Pete Alcock and Gary Craig, eds., *International Social Policy*, pp. 143–60. New York: Palgrave.

Samoff, Joel. (1990). "Decentralization: The Politics of Interventionism." *Development and Change*, 21: 513–30.

Sandbrook, Richard, Marc Edelman, Patrick Heller, and Judith Teichman. (2007). *Social Democracy in the Global Periphery: Origins, Challenges, Prospects.* Cambridge: Cambridge University Press.

Sawhill, Isabel V. (1988). "Poverty in the US: Why Is It So Persistent?" *Journal of Economic Literature*, 26: 1073–119.

Schelzig, Karen. (2001). "Escaping Poverty: Behind the Numbers." *Public Administration and Development*, 21: 259–69.

Schönwälder, Gerd. (1997). "New Democratic Spaces at the Grassroots? Popular Participation in Latin American Local Governments." *Development and Change*, 28: 753–70.

Schubert, Bernd, and Rachel Slater. (2006). "Social Cash Transfers in Low-income African Countries: Conditional or Unconditional?" *Development Policy Review*, 24 (5): 571–8.

Scott, Christopher. (2000). "Mixed Fortunes: A Study of Poverty Mobility Among Small Farm Households in Chile, 1968–86." *Journal of Development Studies*, 36 (6): 155–80.

—— Julie A. Litchfield. (1994). "Inequality, Mobility and the Determinants of Income among the Rural Poor in Chile, 1968–1986." Development Economics Research Programme Discussion Paper 53, STICERD, London School of Economics, London.

Scott, James, C. (1999). *Seeing Like a State: How Certain Schemes to Improve the Human Condition Have Failed.* New Haven: Yale University Press.

Scruggs, L., and J. P. Allan. (2006). "The Material Consequences of Welfare States: Benefit Generosity and Absolute Poverty in 16 OECD Countries." *Comparative Political Studies*, 39 (97): 880–904.

Sen, Abhijit, and Himanshu. (2004). "Poverty and Inequality in India—I and II," *Economic and Political Weekly*, September 18: 4247–63; and September 25: 4361–75.

Sen, Amartya. (1981). *Poverty and Famines: An Essay on Entitlement and Deprivation.* Oxford: Clarendon Press.

—— (1984). *Resources, Values and Development.* Oxford: Blackwell.

—— (1999). *Development as Freedom.* New York: Random House.

—— (2002). "Globalization, Inequality and Global Protest." *Development*, 45 (2): 11–16.

Sen, Binayak. (2003). "Drivers of Escape and Descent: Changing Household Fortunes in Rural Bangladesh." *World Development*, 31 (3): 513–34.

Sen, G., A. Iyer, and A. George. (2002). "Structural Reforms and Health Equity: A Comparison of NSS Surveys, 1986–87 and 1995–96." *Economic and Political Weekly*, Mumbai, April 6.

Sewell, William H., Jr. (1992). "A Theory of Structure: Duality, Agency, and Transformation." *American Journal of Sociology*, 98 (1): 1–29.

Shavit, Yossi, and H. P. Blossfeld. (1993). *Persistent Inequality.* Boulder, CO: Westview Press.

Sherraden, Michael. (1991). *Assets and the Poor: A New American Welfare Policy.* Armonk, NY: M. E. Sharpe.

——(2001). "Assets and the Poor: Implications for Individual Accounts and Social Security." Invited Testimony to the President's Commission on Social Security. Washington, DC, October 18. Available at <www.csss.gov/meetings/Sherraden_Testimony.pdf>.

Shourie, Arun. (2006). *Falling Over Backwards.* New Delhi: Rupa Publications.

Sinha, Saurabh, and Michael Lipton. (1999). "Damaging Fluctuations, Risk and Poverty: An Overview." Background paper for the World Development Report 2000/2001. Poverty Research Unit, University of Sussex. Available at <www1.world-bank.org/prem/poverty/wdrpoverty/background/sinhaliptn.pdf>.

Smeeding, Timothy, M. (2005). "Public Policy, Economic Inequality, and Poverty: The United States in Comparative Perspective." *Social Science Quarterly*, 86 (Suppl.): 955–83.

Smith, B. C. (1985). *Decentralization.* London: George Allen & Unwin Pulishers.

Smoke, Paul, and Blane D. Lewis. (1996). "Fiscal Decentralization in Indonesia: A New Approach to an Old Idea." *World Development*, 24 (8): 1281–99.

Solon, Gary. M. (2002). "Cross-country Differences in Intergenerational Earnings Mobility." *Journal of Economic Perspectives*, 16(3): 59–66.

Srinivasan, T. N. (2004). "The Unsatisfactory State of Global Poverty Estimation." Available at <www.undp-povertycentre.org/newsletters/infocus4sep04eng.pdf>.

Stevens, Ann Huff. (1999). "Climbing Out of Poverty, Falling Back In: Measuring the Persistence of Poverty Over Multiple Spells." *Journal of Human Resources*, 34 (3): 557–88.

Stewart, Frances, Caterina R. Laderchi, and Ruhi Saith. (2007). "Introduction: Four Approaches to Defining and Measuring Poverty." In Frances Stewart, Ruhi Saith, and Barbara Harriss-White, eds., *Defining Poverty in the Developing World*, pp. 1–35. New York: Palgrave Macmillan.

Stiglitz, Joseph E. (2000). "The Contributions of the Economics of Information to Twentieth Century Economics." *Quarterly Journal of Economics*, 115 (4): 1441–78.

——(2001). "Information and the Change in the Paradigm in Economics," *Nobel Prize Lecture.* Available at <nobelprize.org/nobel_prizes/economics/laureates/2001/stiglitz-lecture.pdf>.

——(2002). *Globalization and its Discontents.* New York: Norton.

Strauss, J., and Thomas, D. (1998). "Health, Nutrition and Economic Development." *Journal of Economic Literature*, 36: 766–817.

Tendler, Judith. (1997). *Good Government in the Tropics.* Baltimore: The Johns Hopkins University Press.

Therkildsen, Öle. (2000). "Contextual Issues in Decentralization of Primary Education in Tanzania." *International Journal of Educational Development*, 20: 407–21.

Timmer, Peter C. (1997). "How Well do the Poor Connect to the Growth Process?" CAER Discussion Paper No. 178, Harvard Institute for International Development, Cambridge, MA.

Townsend, R. (1995). "Consumption Insurance: An Evaluation of Risk-bearing Systems in Low-income Economies." *Journal of Economic Perspectives*, 9: 83–102.

Toye, John. (1999). "Nationalising the Anti-poverty Agenda." *IDS Bulletin*, 30 (2): 6–12.

Trzcinski, Eileen, and Susan Randolph. (1991). "Human Capital Investments and Relative Earnings Mobility: The Role of Education, Training, Migration, and Job Search." *Economic Development and Cultural Change*, 40 (1): 153–69.

UNDP (United Nations Development Programme). (2000). *Overcoming Human Poverty*. New York: UNDP.

——(2005). *Human Development Report, 2005*. New York: UNDP.

United Nations. (2005). *The Inequality Predicament: Report on the World Social Situation, 2005*. New York: United Nations, Department of Social and Economic Affairs. Available at <www.ilo.org/public/english/region/ampro/cinterfor/news/inf_05.pdf>.

Uphoff, Norman, Milton Esman, and Anirudh Krishna. (1998). *Reasons for Success: Learning from Instructive Experiences in Rural Development*. West Hartford, CT: Kumarian Press.

USAID (United States Agency for International Development). (2000). "Decentralization and Democratic Local Governance Programming Handbook." Washington, DC: USAID, Center for Democracy and Governance.

Vaidyanathan, A. (2001). "Poverty and Development Policy." *Economic and Political Weekly*, Mumbai, May 26.

Valdivia, M., and J. Escobal. (2004). "Hacia Una Estrategia de Desarrollo para la Sierra Rural." Available at <www.grade.org.pe>.

Van der Gaag, Jacques. (2007). "Health Care for the World's Poorest: Is Voluntary (Private) Health Insurance an Option?" *2020 Focus Brief on the World's Poor and Hungry People*. Washington, DC: IFPRI.

Van Schendel, W. (1981). *Peasant Mobility: The Odds of Life in Rural Bangladesh*. Assen, Netherlands: Van Gorcum.

Visaria, Pravin. (1999). "Poverty in India during 1994–98." Working Paper, Institute of Economic Growth, Delhi.

Wade, Robert H. (2002). "Globalization, Poverty and Income Distribution: Does the Liberal Argument Hold?" Working Paper No. 02-33, Development Studies Institute, London School of Economics and Political Science, London.

——(2004). "Is Globalization Reducing Poverty and Inequality?" *World Development*, 32 (4): 567–89.

Wadley, Susan. (1994). *Struggling with Destiny in Karimpur, 1925–1984*. Berkeley and London: University of California Press.

Walker, T., and Ryan, J. (1990). *Village and Household Economies in India's Semi-arid Tropics*. Baltimore: Johns Hopkins University Press.

Wang, Hong, Yanfeng Ge, and Sen Gong. (2007). "Regulating Medical Services in China." Report co-published by the Milbank Memorial Fund and the Department of Social Development, Development Research Center (DRC), the State Council of P.R. China. Available at <www.milbank.org/reports/0704china/0704china.html>.

Weiner, Myron. (1990). *The Child and the State in India: Child Labor and Education Policy in Comparative Perspective*. Princeton: Princeton University Press.

Whalley, J., and X. Yue. (2006). "Rural Income Volatility and Inequality in China." National Bureau of Economic Research Working Paper 12779.

Whang, In-Joung. (1981). *Management of Rural Change in Korea*. Seoul: Seoul National University Press.

Whitehead, A. (2000). "Continuities and Discontinuities in Political Constructions of the Working Man in Sub-Saharan Africa: The 'Lazy Man' in African Agriculture." *European Journal of Development Research*, 12 (2): 23–52.

Whitehead, Margaret, Goran Dahlgren, and Timothy Evans. (2001). "Equity and Health Sector Reforms: Can Low-income Countries Escape the Medical Poverty Trap?" *The Lancet*, September 8: 833–6.

Wiggins, Steve. (2000). "Interpreting Change from the 1970s to the 1990s in African Agriculture through Village Studies." *World Development*, 28 (4): 631–62.

World Bank. (2006). *World Development Report, 2006: Equity and Development*. Washington, DC: World Bank.

——(2008). *World Development Report, 2008: Agriculture for Development*. Washington, DC: World Bank.

Xiaojian, Fan. (2007). "China's Poverty Alleviation and Development: Review and Outlook." Keynote Speech at Conference on Taking Action for the World's Poor and Hungry People by the Deputy Chief, Chinese State Council Leading Group of Poverty Alleviation and Development, Beijing, October 17.

Xu, Ke, David B. Evans, Kei Kawabata, et al. (2003). "Household Catastrophic Health Expenditure: A Multi-country Analysis." *The Lancet*, July 12: 111–17.

Yates, Jenny, Ros Cooper, and Jeremy Holland. (2006). "Social Protection and Health: Experiences in Uganda." *Development Policy Review*, 24 (3): 339–56.

Yunus, Muhammad. (1997). "The Grameen Bank Story: Rural Credit in Bangladesh." In Anirudh Krishna, Norman Uphoff, and Milton Esman, eds., *Reasons for Hope: Instructive Experiences in Rural Development*, pp. 9–24. West Hartford, CT: Kumarian Press.

Zhao, Zhongwei. (2006). "Income Inequality, Unequal Health Care Access, and Mortality in China." *Population and Development Review*, 32 (3): 461–83.

INDEX

Abed, H. M. 142
Aboud, A. 184
Acemoglu, D. 178, 190
Adato, M. 185
Addison, T. 180
Adelman, I. 193
Africa 56–7, 101, 134
agriculture 84, 160
 high growth rates 187
 and poverty reduction 97, 103–4, 116–18
 see also land
Ahluwalia, M. S. 180
Ahuja, V. 191
aid budgets 108
Akerlof, G. A. 190
alcohol 18, 75, 85–6
Aldaz-Carroll, E. 188
Alderman, H. 188
Aliber, M. 182
Allan, J. P. 192
Andhra Pradesh 33, 59
 Bhojathanda 55–6
 case studies 136–8
 debt 82–3
 East Godavari 105, 117
 highest positions 133
 ill-health 76
 industrial growth 102
 irrigation 84
 Khamman 105
 Nalgonda 55, 104, 117
 poverty flows 53
 social and customary expenses 80
 Sultanpurthanda 55–6
Appadurai, A. 138, 179, 187, 190
Appleton, S. 182
Arap Moi, D. 189–90
Asfaw, A. 184, 193
Asgary, A. 193
Asia 56–7, 101

aspirations 135–6, 142, 151
asset:
 acquisition 36
 assets and poverty:82, 167
 ownership 82, 170–1
Attewell, P. 189
Attwood, D. W. 179, 182
Australia 157

Babajob.com 141
Bad habits
 See alcohol, drug addiction, laziness
Bagchi, B. 189
Bane, M. J. 69, 180, 182, 183
Banerjee, A. 194
Bangalore 141
 software engineers 20, 125, 126–32, 160
Bangladesh 14, 134
 apparel industry 118–19
 BRAC 89, 143
 burial societies 160
 Grameen Bank 93, 152–3
 health insurance 89
Bärninghausen, T. 193
Barr, A. 190
Barrett, C. B. 180, 182, 183, 184, 185, 187, 194
Barrientos, A. 186
Baulch, B. 178, 180, 182, 183, 194
Bearak, B. 187
Behrman, J. 184, 188, 189
Benabou, R. 188
Berner, E. 190
Berry, A. 190
Bezuneh, M. 184
Bhattamishra, R. 185
Bhide, S. 186, 188
Bian, Y. 188, 190
Bigsten, A. 190
Bird, R. M. 192
Birdsall, N. 188

Birkelund, G. F. 188
Blagsvedt, S. 141, 191
Blair, H. 192
Blossfeld, H. P. 188
Boix, C. 190
Bollen, K. 190
Booth, J. A. 190
Botswana 93, 160
Bourdieu, P. 188
Bowles, S. 182, 188
Brady, D. 192
Breen, R. 188
Breman, J. 168, 184, 194
Brihmadesam, V. 189
Buchmann, C. 188

capabilities 36, 149
capacity, individual's 22
capital stocks 98
careers:
    aspirations 135–6, 142, 151
    information 22–3, 24, 125–6, 129,
        138–9, 151
Carter, M. R. 179, 182, 194
Case, A. 184
Castaneda, T. 188
Castells, M. 98, 186
Chambers, R. 179, 184, 191, 192, 194
Chang, H.-J. 179, 192
Chaudhuri, S. 190, 193
Chaudhury, N. 184
Chayanov, A. V. 179
Cheema, G. S. 192
Chen, M. A. 186
Chen, S. 187
child labor 101
child mortality 88
China 162
    agriculture 116
    health services 87, 89, 90, 158–9
    increased inequality 23, 134
    industrialization 103
Chitra 34
Christiaensen, L. 178, 184, 188
Chuma, J. M. 184
Cisneros, H. 34
civil servants 190–1
Clark, D. A. 190
Clark, G. 194
co-operatives 93
Coady, D. M. 191
Cohen, J. M. 192
Collier, P. 24, 178, 179, 182

Collins, D. 184, 186
Colombia 158, 159
communications 22
communities:
    changing composition 175–6
    characteristics 105
    highest positions in 132–40
    new 174
    organization 107
    representative group within 35–6
    types of 33
conditional cash transfer
        programs 90–1
Cook, C. 189
Corak, M. 188
Corcoran, M. 182
Costa Rica 158
credit 98
Crook, R. 192
Cuba 158
Currie, J. 188

Danzinger, S. 188
Dardanoni, V. 188
Das, J. 185
Dasgupta, S. 187
data 8
    longitudinal 150
    recall 169, 171
    see also methodology
Datt, G. 179, 187
Davis, B. 185
Davis, M. 118, 187
Davis, P. 180
    De Soto, H. 101, 186
De Waal, A. 184
Deaton, A. 178, 179, 184
debt:
    bondage 75, 82–3
    high-interest 71, 78, 82–3, 157
    and ill-health 82
    repayment 37
Deininger, K. 184, 186, 188
Denmark 158
Deolaliker, A. 184
Dercon, S. 180, 182, 185, 194
Devereaux, S. 182
Diamond, J. 178
Dichter, T. 191
Dilip, T. R. 184
DiMaggio, P. 188
DiPrete, T. 188
Disha 34

diversification 72, 104, 134
　of crops 97, 103
　of income sources 99, 103
divorce 75
Djurfeldt, G. 194
Dollar, D. 192
Dreze, J. 191
Dror, D. M. 193
drug addiction 75
drunkenness [see alcohol]
　Duflo, E. 194
Duggal, R. 184
Duncan, G. J. 182
Durlauf, S. N. 191

earthquake 97, 109–11
Easterly, W. 138, 147, 190, 191
economic growth 1, 154–6
economic and social backgrounds 127
Eder, J. 180
education 22, 61, 81, 96, 98, 105–6
　of parents 128–9
　primary school 36, 37
　quality of 142, 161
　and social mobility 124
　see also literacy
Egypt 57
Ekman, B. 185
Elbers, C. 178
elite domination 175
Ellis, F. 178, 186
Ellwood, D. 69, 180, 182, 183
employment exchanges 139, 142
Ensor, T. 184
Erikson, R. 188
Escobal, J. 186
Esping-Andersen, G. 188
Estudillo, J. 189
Ethiopia 77, 93, 160
ethnographic studies 180
European Community Household Panel 63
Evans, P. 179, 192
event histories 42–3
events:
　balance of 16–19, 24
　location-specific 84–5
　ordinary and momentous 15, 109–11
　positive 75
　region-specific 75
　see also ordinary events

Fabricant, S. 184, 185, 193
family size 80–1

Farmer, P. 90, 184, 185
Felton, A. 180, 188
Findlay, R. 193
Flat world 98, 186
food 36, 37
France 157
Franco, S. 194
French, H. W. 193
Friedman, T. L. 186, 189
funeral expenses 18, 71, 75, 78, 84, 157

Gaiha, R. 179, 182, 183
Gan, L. 193
Gangl, M. 188
Ganzeboom, H. 188
Garg, A. 189, 193
Gelbach, J. 191
Germany 157
Gibson-Davis, C. 181
Gintis, H. 188
Giridhardas, A. 191
Glewwe, P. 182
Goldthorpe, J. H. 188
government assistance 107–9
Graham, C. 188
Grawe, N. D. 188
Griffin, K. 188
Grootaert, C. 182
Gujarat 59, 168
　agriculture 104
　case studies 6–7
　debt bondage 82
　divorce 75
　earthquake 97, 109–11
　formal jobs 102
　health care costs 87–8
　ill-health 76
　social and customary expenses 80
　Vadodara 33, 51, 117
Gupta, I. 193

Hacker, J. 62, 178, 182, 185
Haddad, L. 194
Haiti 77
Halder, S. R. 183
Hall, G. 182
Hall, P. A. 192
Handa, S. 185
Hannum, E. 188
Harriss-White, B. 182
health care:
　consumer protection 159
　costs 71, 73, 75–8, 87

health care (*cont.*)
   a key factor 17–18, 22, 24, 155, 156–60
   need for improvement 161
   quality control 159
   schemes 88–9, 94
   see also ill-health
health poverty trap 73, 86–91
help from relatives 72
Himanshu 179, 194
Himmelstein, D. 185
Hirway, I. 186
Hoddinott, J. 178, 180, 182, 185
Honduras 88
Hong Kong 162
household head:
   age 61, 81, 106
   education 61
   gender 82, 94, 105, 106
households:
   characteristics 75, 80–2
   composition 41
   definition 181
   interviews 43–4
   size 106, 113
   unit of analysis 41–2
housing 38
Hout, M. 188
Hulme, D. 182, 186
human agency 17

Ickowitz, A. 188
idleness 18, 75, 85–6, 148
Iliffe, J. 184
ill-health 17, 71, 73, 75–8, 112
   and debt 82
   types of 86–7, 184
   see also health care
incentives 138
income, stable polarization 134
income sources, diversification 99, 103
India 70, 147, 157, 172, 175
   agriculture 103, 116
   castes 50
   Dungarpur 92
   economic growth 1, 155
   education 105
   health care costs 87–8, 89, 158
   industrialization 103
   inequality 23
   Karnataka 132, 135
   Mumbai 118
   national emergency 42
   New Delhi 118

poverty descent 59
poverty flows 55–6
poverty statistics 26
Shanti Bhavan 143
social mobility 125
southern 14
Tamil Nadu 168
time periods 165
   see also Andhra Pradesh; Bangalore;
     Gujarat; Rajasthan
Indonesia 89
industrial growth 102–3
industrialized countries 62
inequality 122–4
   increasing 23, 98, 134
   of opportunity 138
informal sector 160
   formal sector 97, 99, 102–3, 119
   glass ceiling 118–19
   urban 97, 99–102
information 98, 105, 106
   on careers 22–3, 24, 125–6, 129, 138–9, 151
   gaps 130
information institutions 126, 131–2,
     140–3, 161
infrastructure 22, 105
Insurance 18, 77, 82, 84, 88–91, 94, 95, 119,
     141, 158, 159, 162, 185, 193
International Livestock Research Institute 34
investment 96, 97, 140–3
IQ 124
irrigation 56, 84
insurance
Iyer, A. 194

Jackman, R. 190
Jacoby, H. 184
Jalan, J. 182, 183, 194
Jantti, M. 188
Japan 88, 155–6, 158
Jayne, T. S. 178
Jeffrey, C. 186
Jencks, C. 188
jobs:
   formal 97, 99, 102–3
   losses 84
   private sector 113
Jodha, N. 179, 194
Johnson, D. 193
Jonsson, J. O. 188

Kabeer, N. 194
Kafuko, A. 34

Kakwani, N. 194
Kanbur, R. 156, 178, 181, 182, 192, 194
Kangas, O. 193
Kappel, R. 182
Karan, A. K. 193
Karshenas, M. 194
Kasza, G. J. 192
Kenjiro, Y. 179, 184
Kenya 1, 33, 60, 114, 147, 169
  case studies 52
  debt 83
  demise of President Kenyatta 42
  ill-health 76
  informal sector 101, 103
  International Livestock Research
    Institute 34
  jobs 99
  Juakali 101
  Kisumu 73
  landholdings 117
  livestock 104
  Mombasa 62, 103
  Nairobi 38, 62, 103
  poverty flows 55
  social and customary expenses 78, 157
  vulnerability 63, 65
  Western 38, 52, 55, 59, 76
Khan, A. R. 186, 187
Klitgaard, R. 187
Kochar, A. 184
Kohli, A. 179
Kozel, V. 183
Kraay, A. 192
Kremer, M. 191
Krishna, A. 178, 179, 180, 181, 182, 183, 184,
  186, 187, 189, 192, 194
Krishnan, P. 194
Kristjanson, P. 34, 180, 183, 187, 194
Kuan, J. 34
Kulkarni, V. 182
Kundu, A. 186
Kwon, S. 191

Labonte, R. 178, 185
LabourNet 141
Laderchi, C. 194
land 75, 113, 160
  landholdings 59, 117, 173
  see also agriculture
Landes, D. S. 178
Lanjouw, J. O. 193, 194
Latin America 101, 134
Lavin, D. F. 189

Lawson, D. 183
laziness 18, 75, 85–6, 148
Lecomte, B. 192
Lecy, J. 183, 187
Leonard, D. 190
Lewis, B. D. 192
Lipton, M. 183, 186, 191, 192, 194
Litchfield, J. A. 188
literacy 20
  see also *education*
Litvack, J. 192
Livelihoods 14, 38, 65, 87, 97, 99, 101,
  104, 117
livestock 97, 104
Lok-Desallien, R. 193
Lumonya, D. 34, 183, 187
Lwanga-Ntale, C. 183

McClean, K. 183
McCulloch, N. 183, 194
McGee, R. 183, 194
Macinko, J. 192
McIntyre, D. 184
McKernan, S. 178, 182, 183
Macleod, J. 191
McPeak, J. G. 183
macro-micro links 9–14, 163
Madagascar 77
Malaysia 89, 158
Mango, N. 34
Manor, J. 192
marriage expenses 18, 75, 80, 113, 157
Matin, I. 183
May, J. 182, 194
Mayer, S. E. 188
Mazumdar, B. 188
MDC 34
Mehta, A. K. 182, 186, 188
Mellor, J. W. 187
methodology 5–6
  disputes over 165
  international comparisons 165
  retrospective studies 31, 167
  sample sizes 57
  stratified random sampling 65
  time periods 30–1, 41–2, 57, 59–61,
    165, 171
  see also data; panel data studies;
    Stages-of-Progress
micro credit operations 93
micro poverty trap 9, 14, 24, 61, 65
migration 167–8, 175
Milanovic, B. 179

Milly, D. J. 192
MindTree 127
Minoiu, C. 194
Mitra, A. 193
Moldova 77
Molyneux, M. 194
Moore, M. 191
Morduch, J. 179, 185, 189
Morgan, S. L. 188
Moser, C. 180, 185, 188
Mugumya, F. 34
Muller, E. N. 190
Munshi, K. 186
Museveni, Y. 190

Narayan, D. 179, 181, 182, 183,
    184, 187
Naschold, F. 194
Nehru, J. 149, 191
Nepal 134
Newman, K. S. 182
NGO assistance 107–9
Noponen, H. 184
North, D. 179
North America 56–7
North Carolina 2, 33, 37, 147, 155, 174–5
    chronic poverty 60–1
    debt 83
    divorce 75
    Duke University 34–5
    formal jobs 99
    ill-health 73, 77
    information 105
    job losses 84
    poverty flows 54, 62
    two poverty lines 39
    vulnerability 63, 64

Obama, B. 193
occupational structure 134
O'Connor, A. 191
Okidi, J. 184, 186, 188
Oldenburg, V. T. 184
Olson, M. 179
opportunity 20, 23, 138, 150
    see also information
ordinary events 14–16, 23, 61, 109–11, 147
    chains of 70–4, 97, 148
    and economic status 110–11
    negative 16, 70–4, 97
    positive 16, 70, 97
    see also events
Ostrom, E. 192

Pakistan 88
Palme, J. 193
Palmer-Jones, R. 179
panel data studies 29–31
Parker, B. 183
Patel, R. 179
Paxson, C. 188
Pei, M. 193
Perlman, J. 180, 188
Peru 2, 33, 80, 132, 147
    Cachachi 61
    Cajamarca 104, 117, 133
    case studies 61, 103–4
    chronic poverty 60–1
    CONDESAN-CIP 34
    crop diversification 103–4
    debt 83
    funeral expenses 84, 157
    highest positions 133
    ill-health 76
    informal sector 101
    poverty descent 66
    poverty flows 54
    Puno 103–4, 107, 133
    social mobility 125
    vulnerability 63, 64
Peterson, S. B. 192
pharmaceutical drugs 90
Philips 127
Pieterse, J. N. 186
pilot studies 11–13, 18, 31, 32–3, 36–7, 85
    Pogge, T. W. 192, 193
policies:
    and balance of events 16
    centralized or decentralized 152–3
    and changing circumstances 111–14
    decentralized 85
    for poverty escape 27
    poverty prevention 27, 70, 73, 94–5
    poverty reduction 149
    targeting people 151
    targeting reasons 152
poor:
    definitions 29
    identification of 29
    near-poor 118–19
poverty:
    changing understandings of 176
    chronic and transitory 59–61, 68
    collective description 36–41
    creation of 3–4, 66–8
    definitions 6
    dynamics 21–2

and economic growth 154–6
escape: quality of 19–23, 24, 97, 114–19,
    120; reasons for 96–121; routes
    from 48–9
functional understandings 32–3
measures of 164, 166–7
prevention 66–8, 145–6
reduction 9
rural communities 115
status categories 42
stock 6, 8, 26, 50
structural and stochastic 167
poverty descent 3, 6, 8–9, 50
micro-level reasons 29
reasons for 74–5, 148
size of 58–9
poverty flows 8, 26–47, 148
extent of 53–5
geographical disaggregation 55–6
nature of 53–7
poverty lines 39
World Bank 22
poverty monitoring stations 114, 120,
    153–4, 192
poverty traps:
health 73, 86–91
macro 14, 24
micro 9, 14, 24, 61, 65
Prahalad, C. K. 191
Preker, A. S. 185
preventive medicine 90
Pritchett, L. 191
prosperity 38–9
protection from negative events 95, 150
Pryer, J. 184
public policy *see* policies

Quisumbing, A. R. 180, 188
Q2 methods 44, 181

Radeny, M. 34
radio programs 142
rainfall failure 71
Rajasekhar, D. 186
Rajasthan 59, 167, 171, 172
case studies 12–13, 71, 78
community organization 107
debt 78
diversification 104
highest positions 133
ill-health 73, 76
    social and customary expenses 80, 92
Ramanathan, R. 189

Randolph, S. 188
Ranis, G. 190
Ratcliffe, C. 178, 182, 183
Ravallion, M. 10, 178, 179, 182, 183, 186, 187,
    190, 191, 192, 193, 194
Ravnborg, H. M. 194
Ray, D. 179, 190
Razavi, S. 194
Reddy, S. G. 192, 193, 194
Reid, T. R. 193
Rhoney, T. 175
risk 8, 16, 18, 59, 61, 65, 69, 82, 87, 88, 91,
    93–5, 146, 160, 183, 185
Riskin, C. 186, 187
Robinson, J. A. 190
Robinson, M. S. 184
Rodgers, H. R., Jr. 182
Rodríguez, F. 192
Rodrik, D. 179, 192
Roemer, J. F. 188, 189
role models 142–3
Rondinelli, D. A. 192
Root, H. L. 192
Rosenzweig, M. 186
Rothschild, M. 190
Rueschmeyer, D. 190
Russell, S. 184
Ryan, J. 180, 182

Sachs, J. 108, 156, 187, 192
safety nets 95, 150
Sahlins, M. 194
Sahn, D. E. 192
Saith, A. 179
Saith, R. 194
Salmen, L. 179
Salonen, T. 192
Samoff, J. 192
San, P. B. 184
Sandbrook, R. 192
Sasken 127
Sawhill, I. V. 180, 182
Schady, N. 188
Schelzig, K. 193
Schönwälder, G. 192
Schrecker, T. 178, 185
Schubert, B. 185
Scott, C. 182, 188
Scruggs, L. 192
self-advancement 20, 23
Self-Employed Women's Association
    (SEWA) 34, 109
self-help groups 93

Seligson, M. A. 190
Sen, Abhijit 179, 194
Sen, Amartya 22, 149, 161, 179,
    180, 191
Sen, B. 179, 183, 193
Sen, G. 185
Sen, K. 179
Senegal 77
Seva Mandir 34
Sewell, W. H., Jr. 179
Shah, A. 182
Sharp, K. 182
Shavit, Y. 188
Shepherd, A. 182
Sherraden, M. 194
Shourie, A. 191
Sierra Leone 77
Sinha, S. 183, 194
Sisson, M. 194
Skoufias, F. 184
Slater, R. 185
Smeeding, T. M. 188
Smith, B. C. 192
Smoke, P. 192
social capital 107
social and customary expenses 78–80, 160
    difficulty of changing 91–3
    funerals 18, 71, 75, 78, 84, 157
    marriages 18, 75, 80, 113, 157
social mobility 125, 140, 149, 161
    studies of 123–4
software engineers 20, 125, 126–32, 160
Solon, G. M. 188
Son, H. H. 194
Soskice, D. 192
South Africa 57, 58, 78
South America 56–7
South Korea 88, 140
    Samuel Undong program 162
Squire, L. 194
Sri Lanka 89, 134, 160
    Death Donation Societies 93
Srinivasan, T. N. 165, 192, 194
Stages-of-Progress 19, 28–47, 56, 59, 63, 74,
    109, 151, 166–77
    adaptations of xii, 46, 181
    advantages of method 45–6
    explained 35–45
    local interviewers 174
    methodology development 28–32
    poverty measures 166–7
    retrospective design 167
    risks and remedies 174

triangulation 175
    verification 169, 170
Stephens, E. H. 190
Stephens, J. D. 190
Stevens, A. H. 182
Stewart, F. 190
Stifel, D. C. 192
Stiglitz, J. E. 190
stigmatization 175
Strauss, J. 184
Subbarao, K. 184
Sweden 88, 139, 140, 157, 158
Szekely, M. 188

Tach, L. 188
    talent pool 23, 123, 149
talent transfer 120
Tanzania 93
Tendler, J. 192
Thailand 89, 158
Therkildsen, O. 192
Thomas, D. 184
Timmer, P. C. 187
Townsend, R. 179
Toye, J. 67, 183
transportation 22, 106, 161
Treiman, D. 188
Trzcinski, E. 188

Uganda 1, 33, 80, 103, 132, 147
    agricultural land 84, 117, 157
    case studies 2, 60, 71–2, 115
    Central Region 53, 64, 71–2, 113, 170
    debt 83
    Eastern Region 84
    education 105
    growth 64
    highest positions 133
    ill-health 76
    informal sector 101
    Makerere University 34
    poverty flows 53, 112–13
    social mobility 125, 133
    vulnerability 63–4
    Western Region 53, 64, 84, 113, 170
Ultee, W. 188
unemployment, educated youth 189–90
United Kingdom 123
United Nations, Human Development Index
    (HDI) 164
United States 69, 88, 123, 156
    career information 130
    increasing vulnerability 62

Panel Study of Income Dynamics
    (PSID) 63
  see also North Carolina
Uphoff, N. 185, 187

Vaidyanathan, A. 179
Vaillancourt, F. 192
Valdivia, M. 186
Van der Gaag, J. 193
Van Schendel, W. 179
Vietnam 77, 82, 88
Visaria, P. 179, 194
von Braun, J. 184, 193
vulnerability 62, 63–6, 73, 84, 118, 157

Wade, R. H. 179, 192, 194
Wadley, S. 180
Waldvogel, J. 188
Walker, T. 180, 182
Wang, H. 185

water, salinity 56
Weiss, I. 185
well-being 21, 31, 33, 164, 167, 169, 190
Wellisz, R. 193
Whang, I.-J. 191, 193
Whitehead, A. 184
Whitehead, M. 185, 193
Wiggins, S. 178
Woolcock, M. 191
World Bank: dollar-a-day index 164
    World Development Report 2008 116

Xiaojian, F. 187, 193
Xu, K. 184

Yates, J. 183
Yunus, M. 152–3, 192

Zambia 66
Zhao, Z. 178, 185, 193